Splendid Failure

Splendid Failure

Hart Crane
and the Making of *The Bridge*

Edward Brunner

University of Illinois Press

Urbana and Chicago

Publication of this work was supported in part by
a grant from the Andrew W. Mellon Foundation.

© 1985 by the Board of Trustees of the University of Illinois
Manufactured in the United States of America

This book is printed on acid-free paper.

Library of Congress Cataloging in Publication Data

Brunner, Edward, 1946-
   Splendid failure.

   Bibliography: p.
   Includes index.
   1. Crane, Hart, 1899–1932. Bridge.   I. Title.
PS3505.R272B7318   1984   811'.52   84-2690
ISBN 0-252-01094-9 (alk. paper)

In memory
Merle Brown

Contents

Acknowledgments

I want to thank Brom Weber for his kindness and for granting permission to quote from *The Letters of Hart Crane* (University of California Press, 1952); unless otherwise noted, all quotations from Crane's letters are from this collection, and they are identified in the text by date rather than page number. All quotations from Crane's poetry are from *The Complete Poems and Selected Letters and Prose of Hart Crane* (Liveright, 1966), edited by Brom Weber. Copyright 1933, (c) 1958, 1966 by Liveright Publishing Corporation. Quotations from the work are used by permission of Liveright Publishing Corporation. Portions of Chapters 7, 8, and 9 appeared in a different form in the *Iowa Review*, and I am grateful to the University of Iowa for permission to reprint. For the most part, I have only dealt with manuscripts and revisions that are already available in various critical studies. The curators of the Rare Book Room at the University of Pennsylvania (Philadelphia) Library and the Special Collections of the Joseph Regenstein Library at the University of Chicago helpfully provided me with copies of manuscripts. Marc Simon answered a difficult question in some detail, and John S. Mayfield supplied background information for a manuscript in his possession.

Much of the writing for this study was originally drafted when I was employed as an operator and dispatcher for the Illinois Division of the now-defunct Chicago, Rock Island & Pacific Railroad. The density and obscurity of Crane's poetry had its equal in the intricacy of daily dispatching maneuvers, and it seemed to me that the two disciplines mutually enforced each other; but I see now that on the railroad I had the immense benefit of working with a number of talented individuals whose skill and intelligence made a difficult job seem easy. Without the aid and encouragement of Jerry Marsengill, Larry Mongan, Dennis Stowe, Tony Knight, and Kenny Shumate, I would not have learned as much as I did about operating under complex conditions. I look back on those days with fondness. Life away from home was made enjoyable largely through the grace and humor and wit of friends in Princeton and Bureau Junction and Peoria, Illinois: John Durick, William and Martha DuPree, and Stu Eidson.

Several friends have supported this project over a lengthy period: Tracy Moore, Jon Silkin, Robert and Kaye Ober, Nancy Connor, Bob Tauber, and Carolyn Brown. I owe the greatest thanks to Nancy Maull and Stephen Holmes, who intervened at a crucial moment and virtually created the situation under which this book finally took shape. But at all stages of the writing, Jane Cogie remained the reader with the clearest insight into what should be done, anticipating objections and offering solutions at every turn.

It is customary in acknowledgments, after thanking one's friends, then to disallow them from having had any influence on ideas ineptly or inadequately developed in one's book. Not only do I want to continue this tradition but take it one step further by bearing full responsibility for such typographical errors as appear in the finished volume. The entire manuscript was transferred through a word processor to disks from which the University of Illinois Press had this final version produced. The task could not have been accomplished without the scrupulous care of Pat Hollahan of the University of Illinois Press and without the encouragement of Tom Slockett, Johnson County Auditor, and it would not have been possible at all without the extensive aid of Lee Rehnquist, of the University of Iowa Hospitals; any errors that appear in this final product should be ascribed not to them or to the programs they helped develop but solely to the incompetence of its typist.

I have had the good fortune to study with two teachers whose view- though both insisted on the greatness of his poetry. In seminars, in correspondence, in conversation, Sherman Paul has been an unfailingly generous guide to Crane's work in particular and to American poetry in general. As I wrote, I had in mind standards of scholarship I learned from him, and the manuscript has benefited greatly from his close and careful reading. My earlier debt is to Merle Brown, who urged his students to find their own approaches, especially if they were at variance with his own, and to think them through, no matter how far they led in unexpected directions. This study of Hart Crane is different from the one he would have written, and I wish he were able to see this outcome of his care and understanding.

Splendid Failure

1
Modern Beauty

Because Hart Crane's poetry is so complex and so original, it is often a temptation to pull back from its elaborate entanglement and decide that the very whirl of the surface interplay of words is itself the point of the poem. Early reviewers of his work were particularly eager to regard it as written in an all but private language, the product of his conversion to some remote brand of mysticism.[1] The reason, they explained, that his language was so dense, so obscure, was that as a mystic he habitually saw into a dimensional realm separate from that of ordinary experience. Therefore, any reader not tuned in to an identical wavelength found most of the writing inscrutable.

Crane was dismayed by such suppositions. After reading the first extended treatment of his work—a 1926 essay in which Gorham Munson heedlessly confessed: "What he is, is a 'mystic' on the loose and I, it seems, shall have to do my best to keep up with him"[2]—he went to considerable lengths to correct what he strongly felt to be an exaggeration and oversimplification of his aims, following up a personal encounter with a lengthy letter. He might have responded with equal fervor to Waldo Frank's well-meant characterization of him (in Frank's Introduction to the posthumously published *Collected Poems* of 1933) as a man who lived "Exacerbated in a constant swing between ecstasy and exhaustion." For Frank is repeating Munson's idea that Crane tends "in his writing to oscillate between a description of his personal wretchedness of life and the moments of supernal beauty he experiences."[3] And finally, he might have reacted in a similar way to the first full-length study which argued his claim as a major poet, R. W. B. Lewis's critical work of 1967. Lewis adopts an overall view of his poetry which is in harmony with the conclusions of Munson and Frank. He argues that Crane's purpose from 1921 until his death in 1932 remained essentially unchanging, though his skill in attaining it varied from poem to poem: as a visionary, he sought to redeem the ugliness of the actual world. When the poet looks upon the actual world lovingly, its empty trash cans are transformed into grails of exceptional radiance. Because of the slant of Crane's visionary mind, certain passages in the poems are bound to seem opaque and obscure; they are, Lewis maintains, just as likely to be examples of magnificent rhetorical flourishing in which, impossibly, unimaginably, the impossible and the unimaginable are imaged as possible. We are meant to be overwhelmed, dazzled, awed, Lewis states, by these dizzying transformations. The surface of the poem is not always meant to be pierced; indeed, it can be enjoyed for itself, savored as an intense experience.[4]

The great disadvantage of this approach is that it perpetuates the belief that Crane's writing is, to a large extent, deliberately beyond the mark: a rush of images, a flow of phrases, all in a surging rhythm designed to compel our enthusiasm, to rouse us from torpor. To consider the poems in this way is, however, to deny the very spirit in which the best of them were written; it mistakes the genuine excitement in the writing for a more accessible and conventional thrill, as though Crane were of interest primarily because he deployed his energy to stir up sluggish emotions. The genuine excitement of the poems is, instead, that of the poet continually surpassing himself, generating his poem out of his increasing awareness, realizing that what he had thought to be conclusive has lingering within it further implications which need carrying forward, which call out to be identified and explored. In the entire body of his work, there are very few casual turns: virtually every passage, however obscure it appears in early readings, becomes with familiarity a specific move made in clear relation to a previous understanding.

But Crane's first extended sequence, "For the Marriage of Faustus and Helen" (1922−23), is undeniably the work of a very young man, a young man who clearly resembles the poet described by Munson, Frank, and Lewis. "Faustus and Helen," as a whole, is an uneven, erratic, volatile performance, more defiant than poised, more assertive than assured. Its failings can be enumerated easily enough: its diction is often outrageous, its rhythms are frequently ponderous and amateurish, its images are jostling their neighbors for attention, and its very structure is somewhat pompous and occasionally misdirected. All in all, it is a poem more precocious than polished.

Yet it cannot easily be dismissed as a failure. If it is unpolished, it also has its own beguiling energy; if it is defiant, it also resists its own strident tone. And in regard to Crane's previous poetry, it represents an important breakthrough, the sheer energy of which carries the poetry a considerable part of its distance. In it, the poet crowds his way forward into the center of his poem; he no longer plays, as he had in his earlier verse, the role of the outcast or the exile. He stands up for a passion in which he believes, yet he avoids turning the poem into an occasion for a manifesto. Though it gives him the opportunity to announce, somewhat defiantly, that this poet intends to pursue erotic love no matter what its cost, the poem is equally prompted by Crane's uneasy sense that the beauty he would pursue is scorned by others. This in turn leads him to an awareness of the pressures within his culture that, impinging upon him, cramp his style and distort his vision.

Just how clearly the poem is a radical departure from his earlier verse can be seen in "Porphyro in Akron," written three years earlier in 1920, published in 1921, but excised from the manuscript of his first volume.[5] In that poem, he argues that the current role of the poet has dwindled into that of a helpless spectator. Akron is a stand-in for America, America in a state of Prohibition for which the Eighteenth Amendment is a perfect emblem. The essence of the problem is summed up in the concluding lines: "In this town, poetry's a / Bedroom occupation." That is, beauty—the timeless subject and eternal goal of poetry—is regarded these days as a private matter, to be enjoyed in privacy if at all. And worse yet, such standards of beauty as feebly exist have been handed down reverently as though heirlooms from a dim past, encouraging all the more the notion that beauty is in no way a living element in the present.

In the third and final section of "Porphyro," the speaker is, appropriately enough, isolated and reading these lines by Keats:

> "Full on the casement shown the wintery moon,
> And threw warm gules on Madelaine's fair breast,
> As down she knelt for heaven's grace and boon . . ."

This is an image of virginal beauty that, though once vital and pure (or vital because pure), has now grown oppressive. Today, such a standard of beauty encourages seclusion. In the poet's troubled mind, beauty is associated with "The only rose on the bush / In the front yard." Beauty comes down to a matter of memory, and while the "only rose" remains, Madelaine-like, pure and virginal, by being so pristine it is all too likely to fade away, to remain unpicked, languishing apart. Pure beauty has become beauty rarefied, beauty in amber.

That Crane is critical, not appreciative, of rarefied beauty is evident enough in sections I and II of the three-part "Porphyro." Genuine beauty may still be found but only in the most unlikely places. For example, the gusto of "some Sunday fiddlers, / Roumanian business men" who "Played ragtime and dances before the door" is offered without qualification as a spontaneous good. Even this, however, is threatened; Akron, like America, is a melting pot:

> The dark-skinned Greeks grin at each other
> In the streets and alleys.
> The Greek grins and fights with the Swede,—
> And the fjords and the Aegean are remembered.

It is increasingly difficult to maintain ties to the Old Country. As the immigrants are assimilated to modern culture, the firm connections are also being reduced to a memory. Just as "Akron, 'high place,'" loses its echo of the original Greek as it is submerged within "A bunch of smoke-ridden hills / Among rolling Ohio hills," so the majority of immigrants eagerly aspire to cast off their heritage. They "'will be Americans,' / Using the latest icebox and buying Fords."

But there are the distinct few for whom Crane reserves his praise, distinctive because they resist assimilation. Yet their very resistance also clouds what the poet sees as his future: they are above the poet's dilemma simply because they plan to return to Europe. For them, America is only a stepping-stone, a means of enjoying their European heritage all the more fully, until they have the money saved to return home. They possess a beauty that is earthy and generous and homely:

> And his wife, like a mountain, coming in
> With four tiny black-eyed girls around her
> Twinkling like little Christmas trees.

These immigrants are attractive because they are so temporarily in exile from their heritage; they have a home to which they expect to return. Crane, by contrast, is out of place; he is Porphyro in Akron, the romantic hero in twentieth-century industrialized America. And he is painfully aware of the way these admirable immigrants appear, to other Americans, as alien and suspect, out-of-bounds.[6] They sit down to a table of "raisin-jack and wine," they make loud music on Sunday, and their businessmen play ragtime. Under the oppressive air of industrialized America, those things which should be innocent and spontaneous and joyful are regarded with distrust and suspicion. Conspicuously, Crane and his friend, "the gentlemen," are the only native-born in the speakeasy.

Throughout "Porphyro," Crane plays neatly on the theme of exile. The immigrants, who seem to be in exile, have a vital heritage to which they can always return. It is the poet, as an American, who is truly in exile; his heritage, the poet's heritage of beauty, is neglected, fading, a matter of dim memory, a "bedroom occupation." Modest as it is, the poem holds up a number of concerns for close inspection. There is a question of whether beauty—and by extension, poetry—can exist under industrialism, or in a modern culture. Equally uncertain is what the role of the poet should be, for if energy and gusto are regarded with suspicion, then the poet has only the option of the delicate lyric, the afterscent of the "only rose on the bush." And finally, there is the lingering doubt that what may prove most memorable in the poet's experience, at least in this poem, are events in which he cannot participate except as spectator: the Europeans, with their energy, have mastered the art of living anywhere, even in Akron. The American poet, who seems to have everything (he's one of "the gentlemen"), has nothing.

"Faustus and Helen" is an effort to address the questions that "Porphyro in Akron" raised. But it is not, in "Faustus and Helen," that Crane has discovered a heritage that had been hitherto unnoticed: he has decided (perhaps in a bold embrace of his American heritage) to invent one for himself. If the traditional standards of beauty are dusty, overlaid with amber, perhaps it is because they are truly outmoded and no longer apply. Turning away from traditional beauty to seek a modern beauty, Crane must reinvent himself—see with new eyes, write with a new language. If modern beauty is to exist, it will exist in a thoroughly new form—not the circumspect, wry ironic style of "Porphyro," but an explosive, dynamic, urgent style as fresh and bold and discordant as jazz. "Let us invent an idiom," he wrote in a May 16, 1922, letter to Allen Tate, "for the proper transposition of jazz into words! Something clean, sparkling, elusive!" This long poem was intended from its start to be a tumultuous break, a demonstrative shift away from the hesitant passivity that had made him, in his previous poetry, write from the perspective of the black man (in the 1921 poem "Black Tambourine") trapped underground halfway between the nobility of his African heritage and the stifled self-expression of his silenced tambourine, or from the viewpoint of a shipwrecked and silent observer (in the 1921 "Poster") who knows that "The bottom of the sea is cruel" but who cannot imagine a way of conveying his knowledge to the "brilliant kids" who "frisk on the shore," or from the vantage point of the clown (in "Chaplinesque," also of 1921) who can only mock the pretensions of authority and win momentary applause for a fleeting, graceful gesture.

Yet in "Faustus and Helen" Crane never fully escapes the burden of his exile, and it is just his inability to escape that provides the work with a large measure of its interest. What remains fascinating in this otherwise awkward, uneven work is Crane's keen sense of the pressures working against him. On the one hand, his lines seethe with energy, pressing forward in any number of directions, almost simultaneously, surging around even each other; and on the other hand, his lines are cramped, distorted, impacted, never quite moving with ease and grace. The overall impression of the poem is, in fact, at odds with its own ambition. Ostensibly, Crane is celebrating unfettered sensuality, the spontaneity and abandon of erotic love. But what is striking in the poem is neither sensual nor spontaneous: it is the complexity the poet demonstrates as he works within and against and beyond the constraints of a Puritan-dominated business-oriented culture which would dismiss as fearsome all overt expressions of passion.

As befits her contradictory role as a beauty who is also modern, Crane regards his Helen in a double way. On the one hand, she is a representative figure, an emblem of the passion which lives on eternally, carried from generation to generation, a type of ideal love; on the other hand, she is not the pure love represented by Madelaine, but a stolen love, and she is something of an outlaw or a harlot. She is both light lady and dark lady, and sometimes these opposites blend together remarkably well, while at other times they mingle only as accompanied by deep anxieties. But by the close of his poem, Crane has argued his case well enough for us to understand why such an uneasy alliance of opposites could coexist, however awkwardly, at this time and in this culture.

1

Helen first appeared to Crane, unnamed and unidentified, in a poem given the working title "The Springs of Guilty Song" (eventually to become part II of "Faustus and Helen").[7] As a flapper dancing to modern jazz, she possessed a reputation that was doubtful at best: in the early 1920s jazz dancing was widely decried as a national scandal, the subject of concerned editorials and syndicated newspaper columns, a convenient example of the deplorably lax morality of modern youth. Just as one took an attitude toward narcotics, and marijuana in particular, in the 1960s, so one took in the 1920s an attitude toward jazz and jazz dancing in particular. The position adopted insistently divided one generation from another. As marijuana was to be avoided not so much for its immediate effects as for where it seemed inevitably to lead, so jazz dancing was to be eschewed for the temptations toward further moral degradation that it seemed so clearly to encourage. There is no doubt that Crane's subject matter was, by the standards of his own time, outrageous and provocative. Such boldness was a measure of his own new confidence in himself, his willingness to declare that while the poet in America may be an outcast, he is one precisely because of his commitment to passion and sensuality and joy.

In this initial poem, written before the long poem had been conceived, Crane's emphasis falls not on Helen or even on the flapper but on jazz dancing. It is a poem in praise of youth, acknowledging—or, more accurately, flouting—the generation gap. Jazz dancing, which might be all too easily condemned as rigidly mechanical or decadently disordered, is presented as an affair of much complexity and agility. The dance is a "cultivated storm," an intricately managed response to what may appear to be confusing and chaotic. And both "The Springs of Guilty Song" and jazz dancing itself share a form that provides a challenge to all who participate. The reader must be as prepared as the jazz dancer to be involved in an event that has all the potential to be no more than sheer confusion and to turn it into an opportunity for a display of deft exuberance. If one has that capacity to adapt, and to "Greet naively—yet intrepidly / New soothings, new amazements," then one can respond to surprise with surprise:

> And you may fall downstairs with me
> With perfect grace and equanimity.
> Or, plaintively scud past shores
> Where, by strange harmonic laws
> All relatives, serene and cool
> Sit rocked in patent armchairs.

The lines are, to be sure, more than a little awkward and clumsy, but they are also straining to assert a definite proposal: the discord of one generation is the harmony of another. Values are relative, and the foundation of the elders may be rocked by that which is, to the young, not a "fall downstairs" but a gesture of "perfect grace and equanimity." In 1923, seldom in American poetry had seduction been defended so wittily and playfully.

The delight of "The Springs of Guilty Song" is supposed to lie in the deftness of Crane's own play as poet, plucking grace from vulgarity, turning his poem this way, then that. Crane is not as adept at this as he would like, but despite the clumsiness of his steps, an impression emerges of moving dizzily between two generations, one of which resists all forms of conflict and withdraws to view the dancing with a condemnatory eye, emphasizing its evident chaos, and the other of which relishes conflict and hazard and embraces them exuberantly. One of the better examples of this flurrying, fleeting brush between generations is:

> A thousand light shrugs balance us
> Through snarling hails of melody.
> White shadows slip across the floor
> Splayed like cards from a loose hand;
> Rhythmic ellipses lead into canters
> Until somewhere a rooster banters.

The older generation hears the "snarling hails of melody" as though it were merely aggressive; to that generation, the "light shrugs" of the dancers are a mark of the fateful indifference of modern youth, heedless and thoughtless. To the younger generation, however, the adversity of a "snarling" melody is easily accepted, to be shrugged off in a "thousand light shrugs" that strike a balance against the anger in the music. In this passage, Crane enjoys some success pivoting on words with contradictory meanings: "Hails," for example, may represent to the older generation the onslaught of a threatening storm, but to the younger generation they are a greeting. Twin meanings of the word "loose" are spun around a few lines later. What the older generation judges as chaotic, full of errors, like cards inadvertently displayed (they believe in holding their cards close to their chest), is to the younger generation a form of calculated, flirtatious exposure (in which they carefully expose just enough of their own hand to make their meaning evident). "Slip," too, holds its contradictory force, both an error and a graceful slide. And finally, the ballroom with its braying animal noises may seem, on the one hand, to be reduced to a barnyard of roosters and hens; but the crowing rooster, on the other hand, is a clear symbol of potency. (On a more literal level, Crane is also evoking the realistic animal cries which could be duplicated on "new" instruments like the saxophone and which were novelty effects central to some dance bands at this time.)[8]

To pull a glimpse of a different kind of order out of apparent chaos, to turn deftly and perceive that what could be censured (and censored) for its dishevelment is, from another angle, an intricate balancing act—this is an impressive enterprise. Through the turns he makes, viewing an identical episode from two opposing facets and bringing his double vision into its own focus, Crane himself participates in a form of jazz dancing in his own writing. At the very least, he rather remarkably defines the standards for his own unique writing in the way he finds what is valuable in his off-limit subject. To pluck grace from vulgarity, to find vitality in frenzy, requires an agility and a flexibility that the dancers hold in high esteem.

2

"The Springs of Guilty Song" takes the measure of the restrictive, repressive attitudes leveled at the younger generation at the same time as it hopes to deflate those attitudes, reinterpreting them from a wholly different perspective. The forces of free play intend to swirl brightly around the forces of oppression. And as the poem proceeds, Crane grows more confident. By the close of "Springs," actions that could have been condemned outright are rendered so as to be acceptable. If one fear of jazz dancing is that it can be a form for seduction, in the last stanza Crane shows that fear is founded, but he presents this knowledge so blithely that it should be difficult to be offended.

If "The Springs of Guilty Song" (or "Faustus and Helen II") is a relatively successful work, the same cannot be said for "Faustus and Helen I." Apologists for this poem have claimed that the virtue of its uncertain rhetoric is that it invites the reader to participate by filling in its suggestive gaps.[9] But Crane himself remains thoroughly undecided as to whether his Helen is a sensual or a spiritual woman. Apart from the opening dozen lines, the poem was written after completing "The Springs of Guilty Song," and it is all too likely that, in "Springs," Crane felt he had stepped over the mark and needed now to back off, downplaying the sensuality that he had elsewhere affirmed. The best that can be said of his poem is that he may have intended to evoke a sensual woman by approaching her with the same regard he would have shown for a spiritual woman; sensuality would then be accorded the same reverence and

respect usually reserved for spirituality. But whether Crane is deliberately attempting such a blend, or simply registering his own uncertainties by viewing Helen as spiritual, then sensual, then spiritual again, is
impossible to determine.

Sensuality and spirituality are mixed confusingly in the poem, that
much is certain. In one moment, the woman Crane imagines is pictured
as a demure, cool snow maiden—

>   None better knows
>   The white wafer cheek of love, or offers words
>   Lightly as moonlight on the eaves meets snow.

But a moment later, she is thoroughly sensual:

>   Reflective conversion of all things
>   At your deep blush, when ecstasies thread
>   The limbs and belly, when rainbows spread
>   Impinging on the throat and sides.

It is possible that such shifts were intended to dramatize a deepening
relationship. The lines which view Helen as a snow maiden are spoken
by Crane before he imagines she could acknowledge his interest; when
she recognizes him, responding with a "deep blush," this is a moment of
"reflective conversion" when their involvement moves to a more intimate
level. The problem with such an interpretation, however, is that Crane is
not dismayed at the prospect of Helen as a snow maiden. His movement
away from that portrayal, then, hardly seems an advance.

Perhaps the only way to understand the effect Helen has upon Crane is
by granting that she is not an actual woman but a secret dream. As the
poet addresses her, he releases the repressions he feels even as he rehearses the conflicts such a person would create if indeed she did appear. She would not be pure and virginal but a knowledgeable woman,
and if she turned away, it would not be to rebuff him out of her shyness
but because she knew too much:

>   But if I lift my arms it is to bend
>   To you who turned away once, Helen, knowing
>   The press of troubled hands, too alternate
>   With steel and soil to hold you endlessly.

This figure is both the ancient Helen, whose difficult role as the source of
a major war between rival cultures caused so much destruction, and the
modern Helen, whose familiarity with other relationships makes her

wary of establishing a new liaison. Out of his own sensitivity to the way passion is frowned upon and judged as an excess and condemned as destructive, Crane then pledges to be free of such narrowness:

> I meet you, therefore, in that eventual flame
> You found in final chains, no captive then—
> Beyond their million brittle, bloodshot eyes;
> White, through white cities passed on to assume
> That world which comes to each of us alone.

Perhaps Crane is stating that, by meeting her on her own terms, the terms of sensual devotion, he affirms the "final chains" of bodily loving, and simultaneously denies the importance of the "million brittle, bloodshot eyes" of the multitudes who look on passion only to condemn it. To be linked to Helen is to move sensually through "white cities," cities like bodies, whose heat of passion is purifying, onward to that interior aloneness, that expansive "world which comes to each of us alone."

The continual guesswork involved in winnowing out just what Crane is trying to evoke suggests that there is another aspect of the poem apart from its celebration of sensual spirituality or spiritual sensuality. Its rhetoric is not simply designed to be ravishing and melodious, nor is it only that there is an analytic impulse additionally at work, fostering an understanding of why spontaneous passion should be so difficult to attain. The poem is also circumspect, and its dense and obscure language is in part erected as a protective shield. This aspect, however, is less distressing than it might first seem because it points to the sense in which Helen is a secret dream, a dream struggling to emerge into the open. As a secret dream, what is most interesting about Helen is that she cannot be whatever Crane desires. He is continually aware of her background, and he cannot simply embrace her but must always be reminded that he is on the verge of the disreputable. She trails with her not clouds of glory but approbation, the "million brittle, bloodshot eyes" that watch judgmentally. Instead of providing him with the opportunity to roam through unexplored territory with inviting vistas, she involves him in a test of his own earnestness. In this culture, to be in love sensually, bodily, passionately, exacts a definite price.

Though Crane develops that point most exhaustively in his third poem, he also draws upon it to connect the opening lines of this first poem, in which the modern city appears as a place of formidable restraint and oppressive rigidity, with the last half-dozen stanzas of the first

poem, in which he pledges his love with a passion that he knows not just
as a glory but also as a burden. Pledges of love are valid only if they
require certain sacrifices. In contrast to the playful, wanton atmosphere
of "The Springs of Guilty Song," "Faustus and Helen I" is almost earnest
and sober, with its obscure or excessive language functioning as a mark
of discretion.

In the opening lines, the city permits only the shallow customs necessary for conducting business and making money. If money is the staff of
life, then living is a matter of sharing a useless common wafer, "The
baked and labeled dough / Divided by accepted multitudes." There are,
in the midst of all this, cheap flirtations:

> Across the memoranda, baseball scores,
> The stenographic smiles and stock quotations
> Smutty wings flash out equivocations.

But there is no room for any open, public expression of genuine devotion. "Equivocations" is just one more check on passion. And at the
close of the day everyone crowds into the streets only to disappear in
separate directions, dissolving back into their individual private lives:

> Numbers, rebuffed by asphalt, crowd
> The margins of the day, accent the curbs,
> Convoying divers dawns on every corner
> To druggist, barber and tobacconist,
> Until the graduate opacities of evening
> Take them away as suddenly to somewhere
> Virginal perhaps, less fragmentary, cool.

> *There is the world dimensional for*
> *those untwisted by the love of things*
> *irreconcilable . . .*

Here is the major turn of the poem, the crucial decision taken by Crane.
Instead of joining the multitudes who melt away into their solitary private lives, Crane as poet clings to that twilight instant in which the suddenly emptied city blocks seem populated by shadowy memories of the
crowds. In the twilight city, deserted but populated with shadows—a
city suffused now with the feelings that had been repressed throughout
the routine workday—Crane hears the whispered words that release the
furtive longings of the entire city. His principal task will be to follow up

this nighttime world of longings, a nighttime world of secret dreams that the daytime world believes it must keep in check.

What is the precise meaning of the italicized lines, the whisper that is both within the poet as he stands among the shadows and within the city? It cannot be that Crane urges himself toward a world of spiritualized ideals, a world that forbids flappers, that lies as far as possible from the inner core of the modern city. Quite the opposite, Crane invites himself to turn back to the twilight city, to discover it as a world of dimensions rather than of "stacked partitions." Instead of rejecting as unthinkable *"things / irreconcilable"* he must embrace them; he must search for love though he knows full well the challenge of such a quest. But only in this way can he hope to be truly untwisted, distinct from that daytime business culture which twists feelings by suppressing them. Instead of escaping the city by evoking a spiritualized Helen, he is bent back toward the city, and the Helen he envisions is not only an expression of the secret dreams of the city but a challenge to his own persistence. The city clamps a lid on all sensual expression by restricting all activity to the routine; but when the poet breaks away from that simplified existence, he does not enter a sensual realm so much as a realm that is profoundly uncertain and difficult and threatening.

3

The concluding poem is, in some respects, the most unsettling of all, though Crane climaxes it with a lofty peroration which offers to lead us away from troubling thoughts. He had some difficulty in conceiving this third part to his poem (and at one point abandoned all work on it and offered the first two parts to journals, once as individual poems, then as a group of related works). By the time he began writing it, he had left behind the playful spirit of "Springs." In fact, he had—with an impulsive ambition that would be characteristic of his career—expanded his whole scope monumentally.

He now entertains the daring suggestion that, while the recent Great War may indeed have been tragic, to those involved in it, it was also an elating spectacle, dynamic, exhilarating, and sensual. (Crane was not in the war.) The passage that introduces this notion begins with a description of the airplanes of war, and Edmund Wilson, for one, objected to the curious use of the word "corymbulous" to describe a group of warplanes in formation. He took it as an example of Crane's willfully eccentric diction, a disruptive word apparently introduced for no definite reason.[10] Crane met his objection—as he would later meet similar objections by Harriet Monroe in her inquiry into "At Melville's Tomb"—by petulantly defending his work in the simplest possible terms rather than attempting to justify it in all its intricacy. "It's as plain as day that I'm talking about war and aeroplanes in the passage," he complained to Yvor Winters in a letter of May 29, 1927. But in truth the lines are not at all obvious:

> We even,
> Who drove speediest destruction,
> In corymbulous formation of mechanics,—
> Who hurried the hill breezes, spouting malice
> Plangent over meadows, and looked down
> On rifts of torn and empty houses
> Like old women with teeth unjubilant
> That waited faintly, briefly and in vain . . .

With "corymbulous" Crane associates the aerial formation of warplanes with a flower and its petals. The connection is not particularly dextrous until one takes it as a cue that these engines of destruction can also be appreciated for their attractive formations. The tug of the two discordant viewpoints—that the planes are murdering persons yet they have a pleasing shape to the eye—is precisely the clash emphasized as the passage continues:

> We know, eternal gunman, our flesh remembers
> The tensile boughs, the nimble blue plateaus,
> The mounted, yielding cities of the air!
>
> That saddled sky that shook down vertical
> Repeated play of fire—no hypogeum
> Of wave or rock was good against one hour.

Crane boldly strives to hold together both the horror of war and what he considers to be the elation of warfare. Though he does not shrink from recognizing that war has its dire effects, he stoutly refuses to allow any guilt to enter the poem. The pilots may look with regret "On rifts of torn and empty houses" but they also know the thrill of hurrying the hill breezes. What "our flesh remembers" is not just the destruction but also the elation of flying as masters of the air: "The tensile boughs, the nimble blue plateaus, / The mounted, yielding cities of the air!" With "mounted" and "yielding," the passage verges toward the explicitly sexual, while "tensile" and "nimble" convey qualities akin to those of the jazz dancers.

Crane's reason for including the Great War is not, it would seem, to draw some obscure parallel with the Fall of Troy. He must have hoped to convince readers that it would be an error simply to try to blank out that war. To try to ignore it would be to risk perpetuating its violence as a dim suppressed feeling that poisons the air. Let the pilots admit that in their warfare they discovered a longing of their own for freedom and flight. The passage, then, is directed against the conventional piety that deplores warfare as unrelievedly repugnant, a cause only for guilt, retribution, and dismay. Destruction—Crane may also be suggesting—is not always as destructive as it appears to be: it may carry within it seeds of creativity, new angles of vision. And here Crane may be obeying the injunction with which he introduces the warplane sequence: "Let us unbind our throats of fear and pity." There is no catharsis more potent than that which uncovers a comedy within a tragedy.

That injunction also recalls the Eliot not of *The Waste Land* (which had been published only a month before) but of "Prufrock." Echoes of "Prufrock"—a poem deeply absorbed with the problems of repression— are most apparent in the opening to section III and provide a clue to an otherwise cryptic phrase in the poem, that which identifies the figure of Helen as a "religious gunman" and an "eternal gunman." This new identity is puzzling, associated as closely as it is with death. It is plausible, though, that Helen, a shady personage, a woman of the night who must withdraw before the onset of day, a secret dream that appears only furtively, carries with her the potential for genuine destruction: guilt, for example, after the excess of evening. Crane may have determined that it is better to face his loss boldly than shrink from it in fear. Helen's disappearance, for example, should only be a spur to make one yearn for her reappearance. Death and loss, then, are forms of destruction that can be turned into particular challenges; out of experiencing them, one gains an even sharper sense of what he values.

Prufrock, of course, folds up under the pressure of even the hint of a challenge; Eliot encourages us, in the following lines, to regard the "eternal Footman" as not only an emblem of tedious rounds of visits but also as an appropriately dull image of death:

> I have seen the moment of my greatness flicker,
> And I have seen the eternal Footman hold my coat, and snicker,
> And in short, I was afraid.

Eliot's passage also suggests that Prufrock is waking up to a new world of degraded values in which the servants feel free to scorn their masters, a world in which sure signs of order are being eradicated. Crane, of course, is bent on disrupting conventional attitudes, and he inclines to the opposite view: death is a goad to life. The "eternal gunman" who appears to be merely án agent of destruction is, from another angle, man in flight, most creatively soaring on the breeze. Death sharpens, not dulls, perception, somewhat as the repressive forces in the culture cannot destroy a Helen but actually serve to make her eventual emergence all the more inevitable.

Just that pressure exerts itself most forcibly in the final stanzas as Crane reiterates, in several different phrasings, the persistence of passion:

> The lavish heart shall always have to leaven
> And spread with bells and voices and atone
> The abating shadows of our conscript dust.

Feeling ourselves as "dust," but dust conscripted together and all sensing our inevitable death, we should feel spurred to seize the moment, to embrace a lavishness that atones for our "abating shadows." One must be prepared to spend himself, to rise above despair by taking those actions fraught with risk, courting even self-destruction; the alternative is to live out one's day in a "meager penance" of frustration:

> Laugh out the meager penance of their days
> Who dare not share with us the breath released,
> The substance drilled and spent beyond repair
> For golden, or the shadow of gold hair.

Life is such, Crane concludes, that one always has to adopt the stance of "The lavish heart"; only as one creatively adds to his own existence will he elevate himself beyond the routine, the ordinary. If one can break from his daily routine to pursue the secret dreams he has activated, he will discover, Crane confidently promises, that "The imagination spans beyond despair." The way is fraught with risk, but the alternative is the dusty death of the routine existence.

Only a very young man—perhaps only a very desperate young man—

could have offered so confident a conclusion. At the time, Crane was desperate: trapped in the relatively provincial air of Cleveland, Ohio, working in a dead-end job, far from sympathetic literary friends, borne down by the burdens of his unconventional sexual proclivities. On the strength of "Faustus and Helen" (and with the added impetus of his new project, tentatively titled *The Bridge*), he was to uproot himself from Cleveland and return to New York City. At the very least, then, the poem lifted Crane out of his doldrums; he followed his own advice at the end of the poem and launched himself in a bold and daring manner, trusting his imagination to sustain him.

The process through which the poem unfolds, not in its published form but in the order of its composition—gradually growing more ambitious—may have spurred Crane into action, leading him out of the provinces and back to the city; but it also reveals a problem he would contend with again and again in his career. At first, in "Springs," he stays with a subject that is close to him—jazz dancing, the pleasures of intoxication, the generation gap. With part I, however, he begins to expand his original point and, waxing rhapsodic, drifts toward confusion. With part III, he tries to recover his lost poise; but he invokes for aid not the spirit of Helen so much as the spirit of Topical Controversy. By introducing the Great War, he hopes to win attention for himself automatically, stamping his work with the imprimatur of the timely. From one perspective, his flexibility appears as a strength: he is pushing himself, growing into a situation that he recognizes is developing in elaborate new ways. From another perspective, though, he is forcing his development, too hurriedly leaving behind what he knows intimately and actually betraying his originality by depending upon subjects, such as the Great War, that confer authority by virtue of their own importance. By the time he is ready to begin *The Bridge* in 1923, he is even more willing to appeal to the important or the timely instead of his own originality and intuitions.

Yet the poem, despite its awkwardness, despite its tendency to verge toward gigantic themes, displays a genuine intelligence. It is never simply indulgent, and when its language grows dense and convoluted, it does so usually because the multiple effects for which he is striving have eluded his grasp. "Your poem reeks with brains," Harriet Monroe would say to him of a later composition, "—it is thought out, worked out, sweated out. And the beauty which it seems entitled to is tortured and lost."[11] That charge is relevant to much in "Faustus and Helen." It is ambitious, it is plotted, it is provocative when Crane might have preferred it to be commanding and confident and bold. He might have wished that his Helen was a dazzling creation, a magnificently resounding example of the passion that the culture around him would deny. But the best parts of the poem convey a different Helen, one who is agile, flexible, alert, experienced, inclined to appreciate the double viewpoint, sensitive to details that others might overlook.

2

Alternatives to Eliot

In "Faustus and Helen" Crane as poet, acting as critic of his culture, avidly accepted the chance to stir up a culture grown complacent and vapid and cautious. However, in letters of 1923 as well as in a later essay, "General Aims & Theories," Crane as critic, commenting on his own poetry, insisted that Crane as poet was not a troublemaker but a synthesizer, a mediator, unifying what had been hitherto disparate. To some extent, of course, "Faustus and Helen" does bring together the two conflicting generations, but primarily to stress the enormous gap between them. Yet in his letters and his essay, Crane claims that he had accomplished what *The Waste Land*, for instance, could not: "Faustus and Helen," he maintains, was an integration of the past with the present, the ancient with the modern.

In "General Aims & Theories" he states, accurately enough, that his particular conception of beauty, instead of leading him into an interior private world, actually kept him in touch with the "seething, confused cosmos of today": "The name of Helen . . . has become an all-too-easily employed crutch for evocation whenever a poet has felt a stitch in his side. The real evocation of this (to me) very real and absolute conception of beauty seemed to consist in a reconstruction in these modern terms of the basic emotional attitude toward Beauty that the Greeks had. And in so doing I found I was really building a bridge between so-called classic experience and many divergent realities of our seething, confused cosmos of today."[1] But he also implies that this bridging was accomplished without strain. Later in the same essay he refers to his poem as "a kind of grafting process," as though the intertwining had been undertaken in a spirit of clinical neutrality. "The importance of this scaffolding," he writes, referring to the dual presence of the ancient and modern, "may easily be exaggerated, but it gave me a series of correspondences between two widely separated worlds on which to sound some major themes of human speculation—love, beauty, death, renascence."

Throughout this essay, he downplays what is most striking in his own poem: the explosive effect of the Greek "emotional attitude toward Beauty" once it is sought within the orderly American business culture. Though in his letters of 1923 he characterized his poem as "a bit of Dionysian splendor" and remarked that his poem was "Dionysian in its attitude," in his essay he never elaborates on the disruptive impact of Dionysus in the Age of Prohibition.[2] Indeed, the meeting of the two cultures as he recalls it happened both casually and inevitably: "So I found 'Helen' sitting in a street car; the Dionysian revels of her court and her seduction were transferred to a Metropolitan rooftop garden with a jazz orchestra; and the *katharsis* of the fall of Troy I saw approximated in the recent World War." According to this recollection, the ancient could easily be viewed as implicit in the modern: Helen is on a trolley, Bacchanalian rites are jazz riffs, one major war is just like another.

The "General Aims & Theories" essay was probably written for Eugene O'Neill when O'Neill considered contributing a foreword to Crane's first volume.[3] Crane's simplifications could have been a result of trying to explain his work in a manner that was straightforward and uncontroversial. But his letters of 1923, written just after completing his first long poem, are composed in a similar spirit, minimizing conflict and emphasizing harmony. In a letter to Louis Untermeyer—who had recently characterized *The Waste Land* in a review as a "misleading document" that ignored "the greatest of . . . emotional needs, the need to believe in something"[4]—Crane eagerly proposed "Faustus and Helen" as a noteworthy alternative. Submitting his unpublished manuscript to Untermeyer, he offered this guidance: "Practically all the current images used have their counter equivalents 'of ancient days,' yet at the same time they retain their current colour in the fusion process. This mystical fusion of beauty is my religion. Simply, then, I regard my poem as a kind of bridge that is, to my way of thinking, a more creative and stimulating thing than the settled formula of Mr Eliot, superior craftsman that he is."[5] And in a letter to Waldo Frank dated February 7, 1923, he offered a virtually identical interpretation and added a further description of his two main characters; once again, his emphasis falls on unity: "Almost every symbol of current significance is matched by a correlative, suggested or actually stated, 'of ancient days.' Helen, the symbol of this abstract sense of beauty, Faustus the symbol of myself, the poetic or imaginative man of all times." One might have expected him to assign the ancient role to Helen, the modern role to Faustus, with the woman representing the sensual spirit, the man representing the scientific, exploratory spirit. Instead, he downplays any conflict by presenting the two as identical to each other. The "abstract sense of beauty" is, after all, what "the poetic or imaginative man of all times" sees whenever he looks.

Crane clings to his interpretation, in short, with a marked tenacity—a tenacity stubborn enough to raise the question as to just where such a unity of ancient and modern can be found. The answer, however, is not to look in "Faustus and Helen" but in a new poem whose title appears in the letters and essays almost as frequently as the name of Helen: "I regard my poem as a kind of bridge, . . ." "I found I was really building a bridge."

1

In November 1922, when *The Waste Land* appeared in *The Dial*, "Faustus and Helen" was incomplete; part III had still to be written. But it is unlikely that Crane had time to mull over *The Waste Land* sufficiently to respond to it in his part III (written in January 1923). In part III, the Eliot who is on Crane's mind is the Eliot of "Prufrock," not *The Waste Land*.[6]

But if Eliot's new poem had little effect on the way "Faustus and Helen" was written, it had a significant effect on the way Crane's poem was received. Certain elements in Crane's poem that might have otherwise kept to the background became, after the publication of Eliot's poem, thrust into the foreground; and material that had once been crucial to Crane's poem would simply fade away, lost to the sight of eyes suddenly retrained to look for new things. The rather casual scaffolding, for example, which drew a submerged and unemphatic parallel between the Great War and the fall of Troy would now edge its way into prominence; after *The Waste Land*, any comparison between past and present would attract attention. Before Eliot's poem, the seduction at the close of part II would appear to be, in contrast to the flamboyant jazz dancing, gentle and discreet; but in contrast to the typist's seduction in *The Waste Land*, Crane's version would seem positively buoyant.

The appearance of Eliot's poem changed the ground rules for contemporary poetry. It is no exaggeration to say that, so overshadowing was the presence of *The Waste Land* even in 1923, that "Faustus and Helen" was impossible to see except in relation to it. This was a great burst of luck for Crane, since the reception of "Faustus and Helen" marked a turning point in his youthful career. It is one reason why Crane's ungainly poem, appearing at such a propitious time—almost as a prophetic retort to Eliot—could garner praise and command attention.[7] But Crane's latest project was intended to turn the tables and overshadow *The Waste Land*. "Faustus and Helen" had been, among other things, an indirect reply to the Eliot of "Prufrock"; through the winter, spring, and summer of 1923, Crane lavished his attention on a new work entitled *The Bridge*, a forthright reply to the Eliot of *The Waste Land*.[8] When he explains "Faustus and Helen" to his friends in 1923, the poem on his mind is *The Bridge*, especially its "Finale," the only lasting result of his months of writing and revision.

Though the "Finale" to *The Bridge* began as an offshoot of "Faustus and Helen," the differences between the two poems are more striking than any similarities. As "Faustus and Helen" progressed, Crane had grown increasingly ambitious and extended the scope of his poem into the public realm, including even the Great War. *The Bridge,* however, was planned from the start as a truly public poem, both ambitious and prudent, a work which would display the poet as a responsible, thoughtful (if inspired) individual—not a wild man mocking his elders but an elder himself. In "Faustus and Helen" Crane is a love poet who turns into a cultural critic because the culture is incapable of accepting his form of love; in the "Finale" Crane is a civic poet who refuses to be critical and who praises his culture (and the modern city) as though it could be loved. The sources for admiration in each of the poems are quite distinct. Helen must be summoned, imagined as the multitudes melt into shadows at the close of day; she appears as the hidden inner life of the city, crying out for release. The Bridge is in the open, a part of the firmament, existing for all to see; if Helen is a manifestation of a suppressed inner life, the Bridge is a public object, an equivalent to the whole of the city. Helen, as the representative of Beauty, is deeply disruptive, shimmying with flappers and high-steppers to the strains of a jazz orchestra. The Bridge is august and commanding, with an air of remote dignity, as it towers over the city. There is nothing elusive about the Bridge. While Helen must slip away at the first sign of dawn, with the poet pledging to seek her out if he can summon the courage, the Bridge lasts and lasts into the sunlight. It is a steadfast, enduring treasure; no alarming reversals are anticipated from it. Finally, Helen is clearly a feminine presence, though the attributes inspiring passion are generalized enough so that she can represent all passion; the Bridge is an object of ambiguous status, neither masculine nor feminine but uniting the two.

In sum, Helen is an unpredictable beauty; her presence makes things appear in a new light. Without her by his side, would the poet have dreamed that warfare had its positive attributes? But in the stiff regimen of the present culture, the novelty she encourages is regarded with suspicion. As a result, modern beauty takes the measure of present culture and finds it wanting: a culture not supple enough to bear surprising new insights is not a true civilization. A true civilization would have the capacity to welcome such novelty. The radical assertion of "Faustus and Helen" is that unless individuals are free to participate in new forms of self-expression, the culture is liable to become a hollow structure for the orderly conduct of profit and loss, work and sleep.

By contrast, the Bridge makes no such provocation. An asset to modern culture, it is a "booster." Viewed from a distance, viewed from the lofty heights of the Bridge, the city is gilded with an alluring radiance. From such a vast distance, in fact, the eternal and the contemporary appear as one. If a person only abandons his personality to the Bridge—if he disavows his inner turmoil, his secret dreams, and simply looks outward along with this magnificent structure, identifying wholly with its dignified presence of power and authority—he will be renewed.

In a July 1923 version of the "Finale," the Bridge is praiseworthy because it unites the contemporary and the eternal. It knits up the fractures that Eliot trades upon:

> Expansive center, purest moment and electron
> That guards like eyes that must look always down
> In reconcilement of our chains and ecstasy
> That crashes manifoldly on us as we hear
> The looms, the wheels, the whistles in concord
> Tethered and welded as the hills of dawn
> Whose feet are shuttles, silvery with speed
> To tread and weave our answering world—
> Recreate and resonantly risen in this dome.[9]

Crane presents the Bridge as an "Expansive center" that, even though it is above us and larger than us (it "must look always down"), yet reconciles "our chains and ecstasy." How? Crane hopes to achieve the recon-

ciliation by fusing together details of the urban landscape with the traditional beauty of a sunrise. The first rays of dawn are "shuttles, silvery
with speed"—"silvery" associating the pale colorations of dawn with the
blur of machinery in motion, "shuttles" envisioning the rays of sunlight
as bands in a cosmic loom. The ancient or eternal beauty of a dawn is at
one with contemporary machinery, the shuttle-mechanism or the wheels
and whistles "in concord." In this poem, it is not enough for modern
culture to possess its own distinctive beauty which has, up to this moment, perhaps gone unappreciated or even reviled (for instance, the apparent discordancy of jazz); in the "Finale," the beauty of the modern
city is no less than the equal of eternal beauty: a machine is a sunrise.

Crane's intentions with regard to Eliot must now be clear. The fact that
the Bridge exists, to be recognized by anyone with the inner resources to
look outward and upward—to be seen, that is, by anyone who is not
morbidly immersed in his own private problems—is intended as a poetic
proof that Eliot's impersonal poem is, as Untermeyer had remarked, "a
misleading document." From the perspective of "Finale," *The Waste
Land* is not a "document" at all but an extremely personal poem, and
Eliot stands nakedly exposed at its center, the source of the vision of
despair in the poem. The problems displayed in *The Waste Land* are not
the problems of the culture but the problems of the narrator. Crane, turning outward with the Bridge, finds himself easily able to see any number
of uplifting examples of the unity of the past and the present. There is no
gap between ancient and modern, Crane insinuates, if one looks from the
proper perspective, if one knows how to use his eyes.

2

Aggressively confronting Eliot, Crane is determined to be positive. In
a letter of January 20, 1923, he records his dismay at Eliot's ascendancy:
"I find that I have derived considerable stimulation from *Secession*.
Without it there would be only the vague hope that the steady pessimism
which pervades *The Dial* since Eliot and others have announced that
happiness and beauty dwell only in memory—might sometimes lift.
I cry for a positive attitude!" By March 2, however, he has launched into
the first versions of the "Finale" and his temperament is measurably improved. "Potentially I feel myself quite fit to become a suitable *Pindar*
for the dawn of the machine age, so called," he writes to Gorham Munson. "I have lost the last shreds of philosophical pessimism during the

last few months. O yes, the 'background of life'—and all that is still there, but that is only three-dimensional. It is to the pulse of a greater dynamism that my work must revolve. Something terribly fierce and gentle." The Bridge, of course, represents that "greater dynamism."

Because of such remarks as "the 'background of life' . . . is only three-dimensional," Crane has been identified as a follower of the mystic P. D. Ouspensky, a system-builder in vogue among New York intellectuals in the early 1920s.[10] But there were influences other than Ouspensky acting on Crane at this point in his life. Ouspensky was dear to him because he asserted a belief that the exceptional individual, the poet, could perceive a fourth-dimensional realm within the other three; a poet was as superior to all mankind, Ouspensky maintained, as a man was to a dog. This disdainful comparison would have been important to Crane, searching for confidence in his own powers. It would have encouraged him to believe in the poet as more than just an outcast with special insights that had been provided, to some extent, by the perspective of his or her exile (as in "Faustus and Helen"); instead, as Ouspensky suggested, the poet is actually the spokesperson for the community, superior to the multitudes, a figure of authority who actually holds the answer that everyone, whether knowingly or not, is searching for. The poet is the seer with the power to invigorate one and all.

Pleasing as this idea must have been to Crane, a more important factor in guiding him in the direction of the civic verse of The Bridge was his revived interest in the writings of Waldo Frank. Crane's friend Gorham Munson, an enthusiastic supporter of Ouspensky and, in 1923, Crane's one strong contact with the New York literary community, had urged him to read Frank's Our America on its publication in 1919. But Crane's initial reaction, as Robert L. Perry points out,[11] was negative. His own interest at the time centered on Sherwood Anderson, and he preferred Anderson's more modest aims. "I am glad to see so much justice done to Sherwood Anderson," he wrote Munson on December 13, 1919, referring to Frank's study, "but this extreme national consciousness bothers me. I cannot make myself think that these men like Dreiser, Anderson, Frost, etc. could have gone so far creatively had they read this book in their early days. After all, has not their success been achieved more through natural unconsciousness combined with great sensitiveness than with a mind so thoroughly logical or propagandistic (is the word right?) as Frank's?"

Crane's attitude toward Frank was changed in part by a study Munson had just completed and which Crane read twice, once in July 1922, when beginning the first section of "Faustus and Helen," and again in January 1923, when beginning the "Finale." Munson's analysis of Frank is very nearly a commentary on the poetry of "Faustus and Helen." In *Our America*, according to Munson, Frank had argued that the industrial culture of America had served to bury the true genius of the country, genius exemplified by the person of Walt Whitman, advocate of a mystical consciousness, anti-Puritan, anti-pragmatic. Crane, at this time, was disturbed by his own lack of a vital heritage (as indicated by "Porphyro in Akron"), and the example of Whitman would appeal to him for several reasons.

If Munson's study was an important impetus to "Faustus and Helen," it was even more important to "Finale." There, Crane takes the advice that Munson had, in his study, addressed to Frank. As Robert Perry has pointed out, Munson disagreed with Frank over one major issue, Frank's attitude toward the machine. "Frank had taken a stand against the machine," Perry writes, "and had seen it, in Munson's words, as 'a mere appendage of the human body.' . . . Frank saw mirrored in the merciless impersonality of the machine the ruthless practicality of the Puritan." But, Perry continues, Munson argued that Frank was limiting himself unnecessarily. "The role of art is to adjust man to his environment. . . . It was absolutely necessary that the artist 'bring the machine into the scope of the human spirit.'"[12] Munson believed that Frank's previous studies, for all their intelligent evaluations of the limits of the present culture, failed to acknowledge how vitally alive that culture might perhaps be. This request for a shift in attitude, addressed by Munson to Frank, is taken up expeditiously by Crane, specifically in his movement from "Faustus and Helen" to "Finale."

Munson's study of Frank had a significant impact on Crane's poetry in 1923. His study held out the promise of an American heritage, and it provided support within that heritage for the role of the visionary seer. It insisted that the seer performed an important task by countering the inevitable drift of a technological society. It provided the poet with a vastly expanded subject, challenging him to accommodate the machine to modern culture. It asked the poet to set aside the facile task of criticizing modern culture and take up the burdensome chore of defending it. And of course it provided a ringing alternative to Eliot and to the "deep and dirgeful *Dial*" that, Crane believed, had been declaring "the fruits of civilization are entirely harvested."[13]

Knowing Crane's probable intentions does not make the "Finale" into a better poem, but it does go far in explaining much of its oddity. Crane writes it as a seer, using a celebratory language, but equally important is his refusal to restrict himself only to a celebratory language. He also draws upon a vocabulary that is "modern" in that it utilizes scientific and technical terms. Out of this continual effort to forge a unity out of diversity, his overall goal is to be uplifting, to inspire confidence; we must abandon our individuality and be "in vision bound" to the Bridge:

> O whitest instruments, in pain addressed
> And so applied in beams of driven fire,
> In ordered sheaves remission gathered up
> And multiplied with steps to such a sum
> That scatheless, we assume and predicate
> The tempered axis of the world in joined
> Sidereal phalanx to that tolling star
> That fills us and renews us as a sun!
>
> To be, Great Bridge, in vision bound of thee,
> So widely belted, straight and banner-wound
> Multi-colored, river-harbored and upbourne
> Through the bright drench and fabric of our veins,—
> With white escarpments swinging into light,
> Sustained in tears the cities are endowed
> And justified, conclaimant with the fields
> Revolving through their harvest in sweet torment.

It is not just that the words point to an act of self-sacrifice and transubstantiation, in "gathered up" and "assume and predicate" and "vision bound of thee." The procession of words also draws the reader along as one line melts magically into another, as all sense of scale is confounded by a rapid and constant shifting of perspective. The words are chosen for their lofty dignity, and the vocabulary is that of the professional whose mastery should be beyond question: "instruments," "axis," "phalanx," "escarpments." This diction of technology is coupled with a supporting set of images taken from the world of nature: "driven fire," "tolling star / That . . . renews us as a sun," "river-harbored," "fields / Revolving through their harvest." In short, the individual is to be absorbed in this dazzling flow, surrounded by words that, even as they come toward him in a thoroughly unexpected fashion, nonetheless convey a secure sense of importance and dignity and authority. The poem is

intended to provoke and resolve anxiety at the same time. It recalls all
the intricate panoply of a modern, technological, professional, scientific, urban culture at the same time as it closely relates itself to occur-
rences as solid and substantial as stars and sun, the course of a river,
and fields of ripened grain.

Crane's intentions are evident; whether he succeeds is a different
question. Despite the serious ambitions discernible in the "Finale," it is
also one of the few poems in which Crane's occasional employment as an
advertising copywriter noticeably intrudes. At times, the poem is remi-
niscent of an elegant football fight song: "To be, Great Bridge, in vision
bound of thee, / So widely belted, straight and banner-wound." These
stanzas were never submitted for publication; they were shared only with
friends, and in 1926 revised thoroughly and, in addition, placed in a
particular context that limited them quite stringently. The dead-end
quality of this verse must have become apparent. For all its virtue, the
poem is perilously close to being a set piece and no convincing reply to
Eliot at all. Each detail of the "contemporary" could be transformed
rhetorically into a detail of the "eternal" and each scientific or technical-
sounding phrase could run parallel with a natural image; but the inge-
niousness of such an enterprise had to gall. These lines only conveyed a
superficial, exotic glitter, a wash of words novel enough but not enduring.

Yet the fascination of the "Finale" was that, at least in 1923, it permitted Crane to fulfill so many roles simultaneously. Here was an energetic, optimistic work, woven out of a textured rhetoric like nothing in
The Waste Land. It dealt with modern materials and it stepped boldly
into the machine age. As the work of a seer, it placed Crane in the company of other poets such as Whitman who formed a unique American
tradition. And rather than expose the limitations of modern culture, it
sought to present that culture in an ideal light; it answered Munson's request of Frank and therefore proved to be prophetic. Since the "Finale"
was capable of playing all these parts, it is not surprising that it should
have engaged Crane's attention for so long.

3

The essential problem such a poem as "Finale" poses, once it has entered a poet's career, is: what can possibly follow after it? What is there
left to write? In 1923 there is only the one true poem, that apostrophe to
the Great Bridge in which one abandons his small personality to join up

with a powerful force, a "pulse of greater dynamism." True to this feeling, the poetry Crane completes immediately after "Finale" is poetry
about the poet's inability to write poetry, poetry that underscores the
sanctity of the poetry of the Great Bridge.

It has been taken for granted that the only surviving portions of Crane's
efforts to begin *The Bridge* are his numerous versions of "Finale" and
four lines once projected as the opening stanza. [14] But a few of the short
poems written after "Finale" evince such strong connections to Crane's
original idea of his epic that they are best considered as extensions of it.
For example, "Possessions" (written in the fall of 1923) relates so clearly
to "Finale" that it is heedless of Crane to characterize it, as he did, as
one of those "smaller poems that crop out from time to time very naturally" when work on his long poem had been temporarily thwarted. [15]

"Possessions" is written in a mode counter to that of "Finale"; it is the
anti-poetry for which "Finale" is the poetry. If "Finale" is sweeping, radiant, glorious, "Possessions" is mean, contorted, and bleak:

> O undirected as the sky
> That through its black foam has no eyes
> For this fixed stone of lust . . .

Life in the modern city bristles with unbearable torments; the inhabitants are unable to find any release for their passions except in the form
of lust. Consider, in the opening lines, how the words "Witness now this
trust!" slowly turn ironic as Crane embellishes on the only sort of meeting the city encourages, and "trust" will begin to sound like "tryst." The
opening lines, which at first may be taken as a joyous pronouncement,
ultimately wither into sardonic contempt.

The only escape from the ugliness gathering throughout the poem occurs at the very last, and then it appears gratuitously, as if from nowhere:

> The pure possession, the inclusive cloud
> Whose heart is fire shall come,—the white wind rase
> All but bright stones wherein our smiling plays!

This unanticipated instant of release rings hollowly, bafflingly unearned,
a wish from the sky, unless one considers the Bridge as an offstage presence, awaiting the speaker's turn toward it. The Bridge is that new unity,
that innocence and freedom, which suddenly appears once one has
abandoned his personality to its pure flow of dynamic energy.

At first glance, the notion that the Bridge is a presence in "Posses-sions" seems highly speculative; Crane never overtly refers to it. But a good deal that is in the poem might prepare for a sudden turn to the Bridge. The city-dweller, Crane states, simply by living in the city, is always losing his individuality. He is reduced to a "blind sum," "Record of rage and partial appetites"; when he totals up his daily frustrations, it only emphasizes his anonymity. The source of this despair, Crane be-lieves, is self-induced: it is brought on by the fact that the city-dweller has "partial appetites"—"partial" in a double sense, both "preferential" and "incomplete." He is possessed because he believes in having pos-sessions, in needing to be assertive, to arrange a tryst, to total up his advantages. Instead of being open and inclusive toward one and all, he is self-centered and partial toward himself.

The only way to be unpossessed is, as the last lines affirm (in a suit-ably blissful innocence), to let go, to give over. Instead of trying to "take up the stone," let the white wind play over it. Become a "bright stone" that is brilliantly anonymous, a glittering ingredient, part of a larger whole. By dramatizing life in the city as a series of ugly self-assertions that only leave the city-dweller more immersed in his anonymity, Crane is precipitating a crisis the next step of which is to abandon all person-ality by becoming one with the Bridge. The sudden, gratuitous shift of the last stanza is unexplainable, but it is what happens when one suddenly has had enough and just lets go. The anti-poetry of "Posses-sions" creates the need for the pure poetry of dynamism like that of the "Finale."[16]

At least in "Possessions" the "white cloud" at the end emerges from a sense of oppression so burdensome that it seems bound to give way to some sort of relief; and the poem faithfully conveys the zigzag distortions of city life. "Recitative" (written in the fall and winter of 1923 and re-vised perhaps in early 1925) is, however, straightforwardly magical. It might, in fact, have served as a proem to the 1923 *Bridge* since its pur-pose is to invite the reader to abandon himself to the poet (who in turn, in the revised version, then abandons himself to the wind). In the opening lines, it remains unclear whether the poet is addressing himself in a mir-ror or speaking to the reader who is imagined to be a double of the poet. This ambiguity may be precisely what Crane hoped to present. In our present fallen state (which the poem would lead us out of) we are regret-tably "Janus-faced," two when we should be one, divided when we should be identical. That division should be overcome: the poet speaking to himself in a mirror should be addressing an audience composed of everyone. And if we "Inquire this much-exacting fragment smile, / Its drums and darkest blowing leaves ignore,"—if we take note of what is fragmentary and defer our inclination to suppress any sympathy—then through that interest and that deferral we blend in sympathy with another and discover the "one crucial sign."

In the original version, which appeared in the spring 1924 number of the *Little Review*, Crane then proceeded directly to the final stanza. In his revised version, he provides an additional three stanzas which draw the poet and reader together to share the challenges of a forbidding cityscape. These added stanzas continue in the same mode as the previous three in that an act of will is required which, once exercised, lofts us above the need for an act of will. If we "Look steadily," then "darkness, like an ape's face, falls away / And gradually white buildings answer day." If poet and reader agree to unite, the dark night passes to a new dawn (and to a new evolution in mankind). Poet and reader together, though encircled by "the same nameless gulf," are protected by the charm of their willed union. Merged together, they move safely through the treacherous, tempting splendors of the city. Ultimately, "The bridge swings over salvage, beyond wharves; / A wind abides the ensign of your will." If you give your will to the wind, then the wind follows your will; the need for will is, in effect, obviated.

If one has been lured this far into the poem, then it is possible that the final stanza would evoke the sound of "All hours clapped dense into a single stride." Crane phrases his climactic stanza as a question—"Have you not heard . . . ?"—not because he is himself unsure or uncertain, but because the form of a question is designed to catapult the reader back to recall the experience of the poem. As one wonders indeed just what he has heard, Crane intervenes to ask pardon for presenting but an "echo of these things." An echo, yes, may have been heard, especially if one is straining hard to recount the course of the poem. At the very least, by being asked to recall that sound, the reader may discover a longing for it. "Recitative" is supposed to lure the reader deep into the world of the poem, creating a craving for certain qualities the poet promises tantalizingly. And those qualities—soaring aloft to overcome dividedness or merging with a larger will—are to be found more explicitly in "Finale."[17]

Though these poems are an advance over the earnest enthusiasm of "Finale," they do not as yet represent Crane as he will become. The notions out of which the poems develop are grand and vague and diffuse,

and, more often than not, the language in which they are written strains
stiffly to encompass diversity. In late 1923, Crane was introduced to the
work of Samuel Greenberg, a writer whose eccentric and unformed verse
bears comparison with Crane's at this stage in his development. If Crane
had not already been growing aware of the awkwardness in his postures
of enthusiasm, studying Greenberg's verse would have provided an occasion for such an awareness. As L. S. Dembo has pointed out, when
Crane rewrote segments of several Greenberg poems to form "Emblems
of Conduct" (in early 1924), he consistently altered Greenberg's celebratory statements into ironic commentaries. Greenberg's artist sketching "valley groves" becomes Crane's wanderer sketching "uneven valley
graves." Greenberg's lines "For bowls and cups found historians / Sacred
adorations" became Crane's "Bowls and cups fill historians with adorations,—/ Dull lips commemorating spiritual gates." Greenberg's artist is
borne triumphantly aloft in recognition of his ability; Crane's wanderer
never receives recognition.[18]

"Emblems of Conduct" is a poem of disillusionment; as such, it may
have been intended as a wry homage to Greenberg, whose own work
earned him no recognition in his lifetime and who died at twenty-three.
But it is just as likely that the poem displays Crane's growing disenchant-
ment with defending the role of the disciple; exposed by the poem is the
way a vital idea, once taken up and institutionalized, becomes an empty
idea. Though the parable of the poem is murky, it seems to place the
wanderer and the apostle at odds with each other. The wanderer (the artist) is actually dissociated from the apostle: the wanderer only happens
to be nearby, sketching "uneven valley graves," at the time the apostle is
giving "Alms to the meek." As the apostle distributes his alms, a volcano
erupts magnificently in a sheer explosion of energy: "For joy rides in stu-
pendous coverings / Luring the living into spiritual gates." But this explosion is as unrelated to the apostle's deeds as the apostle's deeds are to
the wanderer's sketching. However, the people do not perceive that: they
prefer to identify the apostle with the explosion. In truth, it is the wanderer who has more in common with the volcano. The apostle, after all,
had been occupied in the orderly task of dispensing alms, while the wanderer had been sketching the uneven graves; the wanderer seems the one
closer to nature. "Aureate rocks" recalls "laureate," and the volcanic
outpouring of sulphur hardly fits with the gentle gestures of the apostle.

Ultimately, the apostle becomes an institution:

> Orators follow the universe
> And radio the complete laws to the people.
> The apostle conveys thought through discipline.
> Bowls and cups fill historians with adorations,—
> Dull lips commemorating spiritual gates.

We have come a long way from the initial explosion. That life-force is absent from these orators who "radio the complete laws" and the apostle who "conveys thought through discipline" and from historians who worship dead artifacts. When the wanderer reenters the poem in the final stanza, he is still at a tangent to the apostle. He chose the peninsula as a "spot of rest" because the cloud formations resemble marble; they form a living, organic tomb as they seem to "support the sea." For a different reason, "A chosen hero" (presumably the apostle) is also borne to the same spot, because his "vision" originated at this site. But the volcano is long dormant: "By that time summer and smoke were past." Of course the vitality of nature is still in evidence (as, the artist knows, it always will be), but it is ignored by the people, who may be anticipating some recurrent sign. Their expectation would be a form of blindness. They see that "Dolphins still played, arching the horizons, / But only to build memories of spiritual gates." They are not alert, as the wanderer-artist is, to the true spiritual gates that surround them everywhere.

It would be too simple to say that "Emblems of Conduct" reflects Crane's disillusionment with programs, cure-alls, and credos, whether practiced by Ouspensky or his followers; surely he was also meditating on the neglect Greenberg had suffered, a neglect real enough to Crane to cause him to take a position rather different from what one might have expected from his previous verse. As a pastiche of Greenberg's verse, the poem is an epitaph for him—a dark commentary on the obscurity of the artist who dies unrecognized while the apostle appears to flourish. The poem is an early indication of Crane's growing dissatisfaction with his own role as a civic poet; it is a prelude to a period of upheaval and change in his own life. By early 1924, when the poem was stitched together, Crane had taken one extended vacation from New York City (even quitting his job to do so), he had experienced some of the infighting among members of opposing literary circles (reporting to friends that Stieglitz and Frank had quarreled with one another), and he had made new companions closer to him in age and temperament—rambunctious personalities: Eugene O'Neill, E. E. Cummings, Slater Brown, less committed to systematic thinking than his older mentors Gorham Munson and Waldo Frank (though Frank would remain a close friend for several more years). He was preparing himself to begin a new poetry which was not organized to declare his firm allegiance to a creed but which would free him to explore the sensations that were his own.

3
Voyages

The history of *Voyages* is almost as tangled as the history of *The Bridge* but with this difference: Crane completes *Voyages* successfully, even strengthening it with his late additions. His final version is a coherent sequence which effectively unites a group of poems written at widely separated intervals in his career. To arrive at that coherent sequence, Crane had to make a number of decisions that required some extensive reevaluation of his own aims. Expanding the group of individual poems into an effectively connected suite pressed him in genuinely new directions. To follow this sequence as it expands is to witness his shift away from the role of the seer intent upon animating all that he contacts toward a more vulnerable yet substantial role as the poet pressed to evaluate the significance of his own actions. As M. D. Uroff describes the poem: "The self-congratulatory statements of 'For the Marriage of Faustus and Helen' give way to self-inquiry, a careful and tentative probing of the depth of the poet's sensation."[1]

But *Voyages* is even more than a portrayal of "the depth of the poet's sensation." Though the sequence is intended to convey the elation and excitement (as well as the bitterness and betrayal) of a specific love affair, it also sets forth Crane's understanding of what composes the basis for genuine loving. In the course of shaping *Voyages* out of a scattered group of drafts, fragments, and previous poetry into a coherent but diverse sequence of related poems, he recognizes that there is a law to loving. And by the end of his sequence he is not simply a shattered man who had been at the heights and who has now plunged to the depths: he is a poet who understands how and why he has come to this point, and his final poem is suffused with a bittersweet awareness of the truth of loving.

The essence of loving, he realizes, is that it is never possessive. One must respect the wishes of his lover in order for love to exist at all; it is

35

an act of sharing in which one's own personality is mingled with that of
the other person. And if one moves toward another possessively, that
is the death of loving. To hold another person with love is to let go of
one's own needs, desires, longings, and replace them with an awareness
of the other person. That awareness of the other—even when it reveals
that one's lover wishes to break the relationship—is more valuable than
anything one wants for oneself.

To anyone familiar with Crane's family background (especially the unwavering demands for loyalty placed upon him by his mother) it will
come as no surprise that Crane's central discovery is that genuine love
never can be, never should be, possessive. Not only, then, is *Voyages* a
poem in which Crane undergoes a major advance in his own writing,
using his language to explain and evaluate and defend his actions (instead of writing in a fiery language that swirls the reader in clouds of
rhetoric), but it is also a poem which touches on Crane as an individual
in a more intimate way than anything he had previously written. He succeeds in communicating the sensation of a specific love affair, his relationship in the spring of 1924 with a mariner, and the poem is, on one
level, a letter to his lover, recalling their past, their moments of joy, in
seafaring imagery appropriate to a mariner. But he also writes a poem
which allows him to discover his attitude toward love in general; *Voyages*
is not simply a record of this particular erotic experience but a realization
of the value of love as it emerges from this specific affair. And finally, his
insistence on the belief that love must never be possessive turns the sequence into an indirect address to his family, to his mother especially. To
his mother, reading the poem is instructive; it might cause her to recognize the destructive nature of the demands she makes upon him.

1

As a sequence of poems involving love and the sea, *Voyages* originated in the summer and fall of 1924. In a November 16, 1924, letter to
his mother, Crane announced: "My work is becoming known for its formal perfection and hard glowing polish, but most of these qualities, I'm
afraid, are due to a great deal of labor and patience on my part. Besides
working on parts of my *Bridge*, I'm also engaged in writing a series of six
sea poems called 'Voyages' (they are also love poems), and one of these
you will soon see published in *1924*." By November 1924, Crane had
most of the material for *Voyages* assembled, though as yet in no particu-

lar order. In the first days of his love affair in April, he had written a poem entitled "Sonnet," a small portion of which would eventually appear in "Voyages III." In June he mailed Jean Toomer an early version of "Voyages IV." (This was the poem scheduled to appear in *1924*.) In late September he had started to labor over versions of another poem which would soon become "Voyages II." And he had on hand two other poems, both written on different occasions and with different circumstances in mind, that would ultimately form the beginning and the conclusion of his final sequence: "Poster" (composed in 1921 and revised to appear in a 1923 issue of *Secession*) and "Belle Isle" (composed in February 1923 when he was leaving close friends in Cleveland and returning to New York City for an extended stay).[2]

How did Crane originally begin his extended sequence? "Voyages IV," the first of the "series of six sea poems" to be completed, is representative of Crane's early ambitions for *Voyages*. It is recognizably in the mode of Crane's "visionary" poetry; the lines, for example, run on and on endlessly, shifting from one realm of experience to another, the diction drawing on a range of various specialties, much as in "Finale." Exclamatory, ecstatic, expansive, it is a relatively simple poem written in a most complex language. It is an erotic work in which Crane strives to portray the passions of loving with a candor he had not dared previously. Though its imagery is dense and convoluted, a reader opening to page 119 of *1924* and reading "Voyages" (the title under which it appeared) for the first time could make his way through the work by following the noticeable changes in rhythm in each of the four stanzas. In the first stanza, the poet steps forward with increasing assertiveness, ranging in ever more expansive circles that ultimately flow into

> No stream of greater love advancing now
> Than, singing, this mortality alone
> Through clay aflow immortally to you.

The second stanza, as Sherman Paul says, "conveys a sense of sensual riot, presents a confusion of senses as an image of ecstasy."[3] Here the rhythms duplicate the experience of "Madly meeting logically," and with a reference to the "chancel port and portion of our June" it is as though a wedding is in celebration. The third stanza, by contrast, is a moment of deepening calm. Despite the sundering that must occur after the pitch of intensity in the second stanza, the two lovers are more intimate with each other than before. Though this passage is difficult to follow, the

dominant feeling is that of assurance; a pact has been made, "In signature of the incarnate word," and though the poet's lover looks away from
the poet toward offshore islands, the poet accepts this because of the
"mingling / Mutual blood" between them. In the final two lines—"In this
expectant, still exclaim / Receive the secret oar and petals of all love"—
the poet offers, and the lover presumably accepts, a pledge of continuing
love. This calm concluding statement suggests the solidarity of this love
affair.

As it stands in 1924, as an individual poem, "Voyages IV" is an uneasy blend of the public and the private. Publicly, the poem orchestrates
a flow of increasing passion and traces it beyond consummation into a
moment of enduring harmony and deepening love. Here is an affair
which is both erotic and loving; the poem asserts that love can not only
endure beyond its most intense physical expression but it can actually
deepen afterward. Privately, the poem dwells on personal moments in
Crane's specific affair, elements that are never quite assimilated into the
poem. For example, there are quirky references to the act of writing—
"signature of the incarnate word" and "Bright staves of flowers and
quills"—that imply that the writing of the poem is somehow swept into
the experience of making love. There is imagery drawn from the sea
("Whose counted smile . . . I know as spectrum of the sea") which also
seems out of place, never specifically defined in relation to either poet or
lover. Finally, there is a surreptitious imagery appearing in the several
references to sexual matters; the concluding image of the "secret oar and
petals" is, as R. W. B. Lewis notes, an image of the male genital, "the
symbolism being adjusted to the seafaring nature of the departing lover."[4]

"Voyages IV" displays the essential problem Crane needed to overcome in order to begin his sequence. He wanted to remain true to the
actual love affair with his mariner, to draw on specific details from it,
while at the same time he hoped to generalize his affair into an overall
view of the experience of love. The erotic does not exhaust love but actually deepens and sustains it. With respect to this crucial theme, the earlier poem "Sonnet" clearly stands outside the sequence, probably because Crane did not yet know his lover well enough to discover that this
affair was different from all others. There is no interest shown in associating loving with seafaring, and there is only a single brief reference to
"your breath which overcomes all tides."[5] The poem displays none of the
tension between erotic love and spiritual love implicit in "Voyages IV,"
and the work tends to ramble garrulously, not clearly shaped or formed in

any way. "Voyages IV" gathers impetus from Crane's awe at realizing that this love deepens after intercourse; "Sonnet" is a self-consciously shy and teasing work, in which a denial of love ultimately leads to a confession of love. It resembles the eclectic speech found in Samuel Greenberg's sonnets (which are also sonnets only by virtue of being fourteen lines long) that Crane had been reading at this time.

Much has been made of the extent to which Greenberg's verse influenced Crane; one point that has not been properly emphasized, however, is that in several of his poems Greenberg experimented with marine imagery to convey the presence of deep, vital forces. In "Life," a verse by Greenberg from which Crane borrowed one phrase ("vanished lily grove") that appeared in several early drafts of "Voyages II," there is this example: "O pure ebbing strain—shadows permanent / Must vanquish in its tide—of lust through times content." The tone, the convoluted syntax, the shifting, suspended metaphors, even the oxymoron of "shadows permanent" are all typical of Crane's dense writing in early drafts of *Voyages*. In another poem entitled "Love," Greenberg opens with reference to the sea:

> Ah ye mighty caves of the sea, there pushed onward
> In windful waves, of volumes flow
> Through rhines—there Bacchus, Venus in lust cherished
> Its swell of perfect ease, repeated awe.[6]

Since Crane displayed no predilection for sea imagery prior to 1924 (when he wanted to convey a sense of powerful forces, he referred to the wind or he spoke of a dazzle of light as in the close of "Possessions"), it is likely that Greenberg's marine imagery, which associated waves and water with passion, invited him to attempt the same.

Whether the source of the sea imagery was Greenberg's verse or his lover's vocation as a sailor, or, as is most likely, a combination of the two, Crane began in his drafts of late September to introduce seafaring into his sequence. At first, however, it appeared as a background element only. In the fall of 1924, *Voyages* was primarily a maze of erotic images, more audaciously sexual than anything Crane had previously attempted. The governing idea seemed to be that lovers, if immersed in a sea, are sensually laved by the waters that surround them. Herbert Leibowitz, in his discussion of *Voyages*, quotes an early draft:

> The emulating tides that stroke
> Our sides and clothe by pawing coves

> The swarty superscriptions of a perfect lust,
> Timeless as your leading, towering falling hair—

and comments: "In this stanza, unlike the last draft, the sea is relegated to a secondary role; its motions emulate the lovers' embraces, putting the seal, as it were, on their 'perfect lust.' In candidly using the word lust instead of love and praising it as timeless, Crane creates a problem of belief: the reader is likely to hold back assent to this extravagant substitution of terms."[7] Leibowitz points out a major difficulty: Crane wants to speak of a "perfect lust." He wants to convey the eroticism of his affair (and in a language that is suitably intense, that evokes the very air of heightened passion), at the same time as he insists that such eroticism is sublimely pure, "perfect" and "Timeless." That was the way he spoke of this affair from the start. In an April 21, 1924, letter to Waldo Frank he wrote: "I know now that there is such a thing as indestructability. In the deepest sense, where flesh became transformed through intensity of response to counter-response, where sex was beaten out, where a purity of joy was reached that included tears." This affair had a special quality, though that quality was one that Crane had prepared himself to recognize: it resembles what he had projected imaginatively in "Faustus and Helen"—a fusion of the spiritual and the sensual, a contradictory combination that had become awesomely real to Crane.

To abandon that extraordinary fusion would have been to abandon the poem, and it was surely out of a loyalty to that elusive blend of opposites that Crane drove himself to revise so thoroughly each successive draft of "Voyages II." Here is a further attempt:

> Bells ringing off San Salvador
> To see you smiling scrolls of silver, ivory sentences
> brimming confession, O prodigal,
> in which your tongue slips mine—
> the perfect diapason dancing left
> wherein minstrel mansions shine.[8]

He has not yet succeeded. His tactic amounts to edging slowly toward an erotic moment, letting the moment suddenly appear, only to turn immediately away. The "you" of the poem smiles "scrolls of silver, ivory sentences" (and "scrolls" lends an air of antique respectability to sentences of "silver" and "ivory," traditional symbols of high worth), but these sentences turn into "brimming confessions" and then the erotic is suddenly upon us with "your tongue slips mine"; after this, Crane swerves away to talk of a "perfect diapason," and we are left in a "minstrel mansion," quite remote from anything sensual. This method, disastrously enough, only draws attention to the moments when Crane's tongue slips, as it were. Instead of creating a texture in which the sensual and the spiritual are inseparably woven, he points up a drama in which spicy details emerge from a cloud of rhetoric.

Crane moves closer to resolving his problem when he adopts a different attitude toward the sea. In an important revision, he strikes out the word "Imaginary" in

> Take this sea, then. Imaginary hands
> enlist us by what sceptres roving wide

and replaces it with the word "Foreboding."[9] The sea is now a feminine personality, a seductive presence:

> And though
> in terror of her sessions she enlists us
> to her body endlessly, subscribe. She
> is our bed.[10]

Here is a new attitude indeed. Though the sea is fearful, lovers are drawn to it; this absolves the lovers of much responsibility for their actions. They cannot help themselves. They draw back in terror but are drawn in "endlessly." This new vision of the sea notes the sense in which love is a powerful, even demonic, force and, for the first time, some of the awesome strength of the sea begins to appear in the poem.

With this sense of the sea as both frightening and seductive, Crane is on the verge of breaking through to the center of "Voyages II." The final turn he must make is to present the sea as an imperious tyrant that would ordinarily disdain the mere mortals that voyage within its enormous expanse. But in this case, the sea is charmed by the poet who so thoroughly displays all the signs of being deeply in love. With this new version of the sea, Crane has admitted into his poem his own fears that his love may be judged adversely by outsiders, but he has also maintained that his fears are without basis. He invents the sea as a final judge that pronounces his love to be genuine, simply by appearing to be swayed by the lovers' actions. In the final draft, the sea is not a seductive force that draws reluctant persons into love; it is, instead, a potentially fearful tyrant delighted by the actions of the lovers.

By the time Crane comes to write the final version of "Voyages II," he

is a long way from simply celebrating the joys of erotic love. But since
the surface of the poem is itself so beguiling, such an attractive blend of
similes and metaphors, sights and sounds, commentators have been content to stop at the surface, to state that this very action of interweaving
words free of all their customary restraints is itself all that the poet
wished to display. An almost unanimous consensus exists as to the accuracy of A. Alvarez's description of the poem as "a series of checks and
balances which work upon the reader without logical paraphernalia": "It
has no clear-cut meaning. It acts as a sort of mixer: it stirs up and holds
together a number of related feelings about the sea and about love, but
does little to separate them out."[11] Quite the contrary, each instant in the
poem depends upon Crane acting toward his lover in a way that charms
the sea, and the relationship between poet, lover, and sea is intricately
distinguished. The lover, for example, hangs back, not persuaded that
loving is enough to quell the violent sea, fearful of the treachery of the
sea. The poet, always mindful of his lover's fear and hesitation, must
urge his lover to join with him to countermand the very treachery that is
feared. But the sea is already charmed because the poet's constant acts
of caring attention directed to his lover are the genuine signs of love. As
long as Crane continues to move toward his lover attentively, then the
two are woven into a caring relationship that wins approval. The love in
"Voyages II" is carefully created, sustained from moment to moment, in
the movements of the poet turning toward his lover with care.

   The work is set in motion by an important shift from the first to the
second stanza. The opening lines take off from the conclusion of "Voyages I": though "The bottom of the sea is cruel" when one is standing
alone on the shore, it becomes inviting—it offers a flirtatious "wink" and
a promise of eternity—when one is involved with another person:

> —And yet this great wink of eternity,
> Of rimless floods, unfettered leewardings,
> Samite sheeted and processioned where
> Her undinal vast belly moonward bends
> Laughing the wrapt inflections of our love.

But only if there is another person with whom to share love will the sea of
loving reveal itself as a vast expanse of endless possibility. Furthermore,
the sea is orderly only within the paradigm of a relationship: it is an expanse of "rimless floods, unfettered leewardings" and may be disorderly,
but it is "Samite sheeted and processioned" at that moment when the

tides are tugged moonward. At that moment, with the sea involved in its own relation to the moon, it is "Laughing the wrapt inflections of our love."

For the sea to be "Samite sheeted," a bed rather than a "rimless flood," a threatening chaos, one must be involved with one's lover. The second stanza, then, with its injunction to "Take this sea," is a plea from Crane to his lover to follow the example of the sea as it bends toward the moon, acknowledging the forceful swell of attraction between the two bodies:

> Take this sea, whose diapason knells
> On scrolls of silver snowy sentences
> The sceptred terror of whose sessions rends
> As her demeanors motion well or ill
> All but the pieties of lovers' hands.

Crane is quite specific here: the sea can be independent and capricious, a wrathful judge, imperiously turning into "sceptred terror" bent on destruction (much as love itself could turn into lust). Only the "pieties of lovers' hands," if joined together, protect against this possibility—just as the sea itself is composed when it acknowledges the pull of the moon. There is a wrathful sea that is fearful, and it is up to the poet's lover to act in such a way as to forestall it, even as the poet, by addressing his lover with such tender caution, has already displayed a love that has a preliminary effect. The waves can be "silver snowy sentences" that mark a cold, icy judgment, or they can be "silver snowy sentences" that are the precious, fragile exchanges of companionship.

As Crane's lover remains poised in suspension, Crane's address, which respects the doubt and hesitancy of his lover, continues to charm the sea. Within the salt of the sea (Crane argues) there is the possibility of sweet meadows, of "poinsettia meadows of her tides," but for that sweetness to come forth depends on the commitment of the lover to the poet:

> And onward, as bells off San Salvador
> Salute the crocus lustres of the stars,
> In these poinsettia meadows of her tides,—
> Adagios of islands, O my Prodigal,
> Complete the dark confessions her veins spell.

Crane's delicacy and tact in addressing his lover is most evident here. Who "Completes the dark confessions"—"Adagios of islands" or "my

Prodigal"? All the evidence points to "my Prodigal," Crane's lover, who, prodigal of the self, welcomed home to the sea, can complete the "dark confessions her veins spell" and admit the sweet to the salt. Such a direct plea, however, risks seeming coercive, and thus Crane graciously appears to speak of islands that, in their languor, their slow movements, long to give themselves to the sea, to melt from the rigidity of land to the fluidity of water. In a similar way, "bells" "Salute . . . the stars" as though the bells longed to break from their fixity and melt into the air in which they pour their sound.

The fourth stanza is the moment in which Crane presses his claim most strongly, only to hold up and check his impulse in the final stanza. It begins with the most sensual image in the poem—"Mark how her turning shoulders wind the hours"—an image in which Crane points out the timelessness of the sea as well as anxiously notes that such timelessness may be passing them by. "Mark" and "hasten" and "Hasten" all convey his urgency that his lover act at once, following the lead of "sleep, death, desire" which come together and "Close round one instant in one floating flower." But if Crane is urgently pleading for commitment here, he steps back in the next stanza and recovers his balance; it is a shift of great tenderness, acknowledging the lover's reluctance to comply with the poet's urgency. With "Bind us in time . . ." he recognizes that it is this very moment of poised suspension which is so wonderful, and his new plea is that his lover defer the decision for as long as possible so as to draw out these moments of alluring suspension to the utmost. Instead of "one instant" of fusion, the hope is for "Seasons clear" and the "awe" of forever admiring each other. "No earthly shore" is desired, for that might mark the end of this present suspension. The state Crane affirms is that of gazing widely toward paradise, a "spindrift gaze" that is a mixture of drifting luxuriantly and spinning intensely—a way of looking at another person that creates paradise.

"Voyages II" is the most intricate, as well as the loveliest, of the poems of *Voyages*. But its loveliness emerges not from its surface, however attractive it is, but from the spirit displayed as the poet speaks to his lover with tenderness and respect. The poet is the guide, making way for another in a realm that could be perilous but is rendered harmless by his knowledge and courage and care. It is the one section in the poem in which Crane's devotion to his love is most evident, and it affirms the fundamental insight of the sequence: one approaches the center of love only as he acknowledges and attends to another person who remains beyond him in freedom.

2

The excellence of "Voyages II" is that it can hold together the most delicate and subtle recognitions of the fears and hesitancies in another person at the same time as it surrounds this delicacy and subtlety with a churning, swirling, dynamic movement. By contrast, neither "Voyages III" nor "Voyages IV" is so complex. With "Voyages III," for example, Crane returns to the eroticism that he had been careful to minimize in "Voyages II." With the sea in "Voyages II" charmed by the poet's actions, placing its imprimatur on the lovers and pronouncing their love as genuine, Crane is now free in "Voyages III" to be more overtly sensual than before. In "Voyages III" the poet and his lover enact what had been the promise of "Voyages II."

In the first eight lines, poet and lover are immersed in the sea, and the emphasis is on their intimacy. Previously Crane had asked his lover to "Mark" how the "turning shoulders" of the sea "wind the hours"—now he is in the midst of those waves and can say: "ribboned water lanes I wind." The "pieties of lovers' hands" now grow demonstratively active as "this hour / The sea lifts, also, reliquary hands." These opening lines are gentle, a washing, laving laxity, in contrast to the intricate voicings of "Voyages II." Depending on how one emphasizes the syllables in "consanguinity," the opening line—"Infinite consanguinity it bears"—may be heard as having either four or five accents, and the wavering of this first line, hovering midway between blank verse and a four-beat strong-stress rhythm, carries through the rest of the eight-line stanza. Crane's poem waxes and wanes as it wishes, with lines that shift back and forth from four accents to five accents (lines 4 and 8). Runover lines prevail, inviting a tendency to wander from one line to the next:

> Infinite consanguinity it bears—
> This tendered theme of you that light
> Retrieves from sea plains where the sky
> Resigns a breast that every wave enthrones;
> While ribboned water lanes I wind
> Are laved and scattered with no stroke
> Wide from your side, whereto this hour
> The sea lifts, also, reliquary hands.

Poet, lover, and sea blend together. The "tendered theme" the lover now
offers the poet is the theme of the seamless wholeness of light playing on
water and water reflecting on light—an image which evokes absolute
oneness. It is reinforced by being duplicated immediately, as "the sky /
Resigns a breast that every wave enthrones": no sooner does a wave
reach up into the air than the sky draws back to make way for the wave.
And the poet, swimming in this fluid element, luxuriates in the sense
that each wave he causes touches the lover, till there is "no stroke /
wide" from his side that does not reach the lover.

But even this is not enough. Once an identity has been established
among lover, poet, and sea—so that they are all one body—then Crane
can move below the surface of the sea and explore the body of his lover:

> And so, admitted through black swollen gates
> That must arrest all distance otherwise,—
> Past whirling pillars and lithe pediments,
> Light wrestling there incessantly with light,
> Star kissing star through wave on wave unto
> Your body rocking!

The dark depths of the sea, those fearful "black swollen gates," are radi-
antly filled with light—a light that emanates from "wrestling," from
"Star kissing star." Though sensual, these actions are purified by the
presence of light, and the poem shifts to a firm iambic pentameter with
few runover lines. Because of the new assurance in the rhythm, the poet
appears purposeful and convinced of his rightness. At this most sensual
moment, then, we are not shocked but awed.

If the second stanza dissolves space (drawing poet, lover, and sea into
a total oneness), the third dissolves time:

> and where death, if shed,
> Presumes no carnage, but this single change,—
> Upon the steep floor flung from dawn to dawn
> The silken skilled transmemberment of song.

In love, one feels immortal, as though death has been shed. And there is
no "carnage" in this death: poet and lover are interwoven, in a "trans-
memberment" where bodies and members are fused as in a song, caught
up in a reintegrated harmony. Because of this, there is a special drama in
the final line: "Permit me voyage, love, into your hands . . ." It emphasizes that though poet and lover are one, the poet still acknowledges his

lover as an individual. In a poem which bases itself almost entirely on projecting the increasing oneness of all, this last reference to the hands of the lover reveals Crane's understanding of his lover as a person even larger than the oneness in which all participate.

By contrast, "Voyages IV" now appears, interestingly enough, to be almost aggressive. What could have been overlooked or determined to be unimportant when the poem appeared by itself in the pages of *1924* now emerges in the foreground. The poem seems, especially in its first half, to be frenzied, full of urgency and strain and desperation. In a poem of twenty-five lines, Crane relies on "and" for a conjunction twelve times; and in the middle eight lines, the climax of the poem, the word appears seven times. Whether Crane intended it or not, the impression he gives is of a man straining to keep adding to his flow of thought, spinning and slipping in the process; his opening lines appear as a collection of assertive statements that lock together and lead to an undeniable conclusion:

> Whose counted smile of hours and days, suppose
> I know as spectrum of the sea and pledge
> Vastly now parting gulf on gulf of wings
> Whose circles bridge, I know (from palms to the severe
> Chilled albatross's white immutability)
> No stream of greater love advancing now
> Than, singing, this mortality alone
> Through clay aflow immortally to you.

"Voyages IV" was to be Crane's last production in his early "visionary" style, and the extent to which he matured in the few months after completing it is never more strikingly apparent. Reviewing this poem now, it seems chaotic and jumbled. The performance puts one on edge. "Counted smile" seems curiously calculated, and "Suppose / I know" unduly hesitant, and "pledge / Vastly now" stridently insistent. Another surprise is that the poet seems to be more intent on describing his own sensations than those he would share with his lover. And he is no longer primarily addressing another person; he is caught up and swept along on those towering phrases that lead him forward even as they teeter on their own excessiveness.

Approaching "Voyages IV" by way of "Voyages II" and "Voyages III" presents the poem in a new light; however, Crane is to be admired for having found an appropriate place in his sequence for a poem that truly appears to be excessive. The truth of the experience is in its excess. The sensual riot of the poem is too forceful, too extreme, as though the poet wants to sustain it at all costs. In "Madly meeting logically in this hour/ And region that is ours to wreathe again" we hear that the sound of the words "hour / And region" is virtually duplicated in the sound of the words "ours to wreathe again," as though Crane desperately longs to cling to the moment, even as the resemblance between the sounds spurs the line along faster than ever. Read in isolation, as a single poem, "Voyages IV" appeared simply to affirm, in a suitably complex language, that love deepened after physical consummation; read with the other poems still sounding in our ears, we hear a note of assertion and aggression and even a sense of desperation escaping from the lines. The sequence as a whole, in fact, questions the validity of the premise which originally set the group of poems in motion: love may indeed be jeopardized by consummation, and the blend of physical love and spiritual love experienced so convincingly at one stage of the affair may become a passing moment, not a permanent feature.

3

As a poem that both consummates the act of loving and looks ahead to the dissolution of love, "Voyages IV" is a proper prelude to "Voyages V." But at one time Crane thought his sequence was complete without his final two poems. In the spring of 1925, *Voyages* appears in an early manuscript of *White Buildings* as "Voyages I-IV." As "Voyages I-IV," the poems end on an upbeat note, and the sequence is relatively straightforward: the poet accomplishes his affair successfully, moving through an introduction to loving toward a final act of consummation in which, as in the "Voyages" poem appearing in *1924*, the pledge of love is deepened. The problem with such a truncated version of *Voyages* is that it is too simple. Not only did it not reflect the actual course of the love affair, which ended by dissolving into friendship rather than enduring as companionship, but it also minimized an essential theme in the sequence— the fearful, destructive effect that possessiveness has on loving.

Possession even enters, if briefly, into the early poem that Crane adapted as "Voyages I." Originally, the poem was entitled "Poster" and Crane was less than enthusiastic about it.[12] One can understand his lack of enthusiasm. Apart from *Voyages* "Poster" seems to be a meanspirited little piece which places the poet in a position of disdain for his audience. The children who are "gaily digging and scattering" on the shore might as well be the sterile multitudes of "Faustus and Helen" for all they know of the powerful thunder and lightning of the sea. Any warnings about that sea, which the poet might offer, would of course go unheeded; these children are not appreciative of true poets. They are wrapped up in their own enterprises, not in the least concerned with the poet's involvement in tremendous, powerful forces. Thus Crane's admonition in 1921, at the end of the original version of "Poster":

> But there is a line
> You must not cross. Your hands will find beyond it
> No golden fringe to fling upon the wind.
> The bottom of the sea is cruel.

This is, in effect, a dismissal of the audience that cannot hear him, that remains self-absorbed and ignorant of the mighty forces which the poet knows so intimately. He scoffs at the notion of flinging a "golden fringe" "upon the wind," and rejects with contempt such innocence as the children brightly display. Though he rumbles menacingly, like the ocean itself, "But there is a line / You must not cross," the children give no evidence of hearing, happy as they are to frisk with their dog, delighting in a life at the edge of, not in, the sea. Perhaps Crane's lack of enthusiasm, at least back in 1921, stemmed from a recognition of the painful truth in the poem: that the poet was indeed unheralded, even ignored, by those to whom he felt he had most to offer.

However, when "Poster" is placed at the front of the sequence to become "Voyages 1," it is transformed; all the disdain in the poem vanishes and the work is suffused with a bittersweet awareness. One explanation for the change, which seems little short of miraculous since Crane only altered three lines, is that in "Voyages I" the children have a future which they lacked in "Poster": they will grow up and enter the ocean, falling in love and discovering for themselves what the poet already knows from his experience. Since "Voyages I" opens onto "Voyages II" it is now appropriate to regard the children as innocents who will someday learn the truth of what they now only hear as words. The reason they cannot hear the poet's voice, then, is not (as in "Poster") because they are facile and shallow but because they are simply too young to have experienced adult love. In this respect, the poet's warning to the children, coupled with his realization that they simply cannot hear him, reminds us that there are real differences among individuals. Some are less

adult than others. To care for the children enough to want to warn them,
yet to recognize the impossibility of doing so in any adequate way, becomes a prelude to the realization, in "Voyages II," that another person
may be fearful of love and in need of guidance.

In rewriting "Poster" for magazine publication in 1923, Crane made
only one change in the poem, yet it is significant enough to prepare the
work for *Voyages*. The ending is changed to read:

> . . . but there is a line
> You must not cross nor ever trust beyond it
> Spry cordage of your bodies to caresses
> Too lichen-faithful from too wide a breast.
> The bottom of the sea is cruel.

In "Poster" Crane had gone on in his old ironical vein, disdaining the
children's wish to "fling upon the wind" a "golden fringe." In "Voyages
I," however, he points precisely to the complexity of adult love and in a
dense and distorted syntax that presages the future of love. Earlier, the
cruelty of the sea was left unexplained; it hovered as a vague threat, part
of the poet's arsenal of special knowledge which included the thunder
and lightning of the waves. Here, the cruelty of the sea is defined as the
"Too lichen-faithful" caresses that grasp and cling, that threaten to fasten one's love possessively. In 1923, revising these lines, Crane is defini-
tive but not specific; he was probably bearing his mother in mind, since
"too wide a breast" suggests a maternal bosom that is too vast to be satisfied. In 1925 or early 1926, when he added his two final poems to the
Voyages sequence, he had greater evidence of the evil of possessiveness;
it was now a tendency that he could recognize in himself and from which
he would draw back in dismay.

"Voyages VI" is the more convoluted of the two poems; it is a revision
of "Belle Isle," an unpublished poem written in early 1923 as Crane was
preparing to leave Cleveland for New York. "Belle Isle" was apparently a
farewell to another love affair, but it is a mild and calm work in contrast
to "Voyages VI." In "VI," Crane must earn his resolution only after a
period of intense despair; in "Belle Isle" Crane simply looks back with
regret on the past, then soberly consoles himself with the thought that
at least love endures in memory. "Voyages VI" contrasts even more
strikingly with the conclusion of "Faustus and Helen." Helen is a generalized figure, a representative of passion, an idea or dream that many
persons hold though they dare not act upon it. When dawn arrives, sig-

naling the entrance of the daytime world of inhibition, Helen must return to the shadows; but Crane quickly recovers his balance by insisting that, since the spirit of Helen has been released once, it can be released again. The avatars of Helen are endless, and, though this Helen fades as all must, there will always be a Helen for those determined to seek her out.

In "Voyages VI," Crane is writing of the end of an actual love affair, thinking of one individual rather than a representative figure, and he cannot be so sanguine. There is no new Helen implicit in his future, just this one lost love, preserved in the delicate, fragile image of Belle Isle, the "white echo of the oar," the memory of love as it once had been. Specifically, Belle Isle is the name he gives to the rising sun's mirror image reflected across the water—a beautiful island that can never be inhabited, utterly insubstantial but eternally real.

The relation of sun to sea, of waves catching fire, is itself a beautiful echo of the involvement of lovers in *Voyages*. "Voyages VI" breaks into two disjunctive halves. In the first four stanzas, Crane cries out for apocalypse. When love is finished the only recourse is to view the world as destroyed. But the elements around him, the sea and sky and sun, do not heed his call—just the opposite, they continue along in their own even pace, oblivious to the poet. "Icy and bright dungeons," instead of swallowing the swimmers, keep buoying them up. After the collapse of a love affair, the world is not destroyed but goes on about its business, indifferent to the affairs of men. The shell "Steadily" "secretes its beating leagues of monotone." The harbor is about to be born into a new day as the phoenix rises again. And the poet's cry, "Let thy waves rear / More savage than the death of kings," is simply ignored; it only calls forth "Some splintered garland for the seer."

In place of the cosmic destruction called for, Crane finds that life persists without him. The promise of apocalypse melts away as the thunder and lightning storm that would match the turmoil he feels inside himself is displaced by the rising sun, the "lounged goddess" Aurora:

> Beyond siroccos harvesting
> The solstice thunders, crept away,
> Like a cliff swinging or a sail
> Flung into April's inmost day—
>
> Creation's blithe and petalled word
> To the lounged goddess when she rose

> Conceding dialogue with eyes
> That smile unsearchable repose—

The subject of the verb "crept away" is deferred until the following stanza where it becomes "Creation's blithe and petalled word" imaged in the sun at dawn. This is not the creation Crane had hoped for, with its "eyes / That smile unsearchable repose." Yet under the calm of this new presence, which is itself a hint that the passage of time may prove healing, he recaptures his love—not as it had been in all its dynamic strength, but as a memory, in the delicate image of the sun echoed by the waves:

> Still fervid covenant, Belle Isle,
> —Unfolded floating dais before
> Which rainbows twine continual hair—
> Belle Isle, white echo of the oar!
>
> The imaged word, it is, that holds
> Hushed willows anchored in its glow.
> It is the unbetrayable reply
> Whose accent no farewell can know.

To be transfixed by the "Belle Isle" that is the reflection of the sun flashing on the sea is an indication of the poet's fallen state. But that fallen state is redeemed because it is so close to the supreme state of love, that of being near to another without possessing. All the tension, it is true, has lapsed from the relationship. There is no living reply, no hint of betrayal; the lounged goddess concedes dialogue and will provide no response herself. The hollowness of memory is that in it all replies are fixed, unchanging, "unbetrayable." The whole moment, in fact, at the end of the poem is peculiarly hollow; but just because of its hollowness the poet remains true to his sense of his lover who is apart from it, in a real world of replies that can be betrayals, a real world made up of words that are exchanged, not "imaged."

The ending of "Voyages VI" is not uplifting; it is muted and sorrowful, meditative and poignant. The poet is brought up against an ultimate barrier beyond which he cannot proceed yet on which his thoughts remain, recalling a past that is too painfully complete. The willows, though beautiful, are "Hushed" and "anchored," and the word that "holds" them both embraces and fastens. And though the "unbetrayable reply"—that sign of memory dwelling upon a completed past—lingers forever, the echo we hear in the final line (with its "accent no farewell can know") is the anguished emphasis falling on "no" (and sounding again in "know").

The same reluctance to accept the end of the affair is dramatized more harrowingly in "Voyages V," the last addition to the sequence.[13] It displays the cruel aspect of loving of which Crane had been fearful from the start. Crane's lover, having decided to move on, cannot admit this decision forthrightly and thus leaves Crane dangling, free to interpret the evasiveness of his lover in other possible ways, as signs of thoughtfulness or self-absorption—till the true meaning of his lover's actions is indisputably clear. Crane, grasping the situation, keeps verging toward scorn, flashing out in anger, even as he struggles to check his bitterness, hoping still to sway his lover. It is the moment in the sequence when Crane must display how deeply his devotion lies, as he is asked to allow his lover to part from him freely. Out of this conflict emerge the stunning last lines, with their mixture of contempt and forgiveness, an extraordinary cross-rhythm of emotions that reveal anger inextricably mixed with solicitude.

For the first time in *Voyages*, there are major gaps, significant omissions, in the course of a poem. Not only do ellipses occur in lines 8 and 13, but at dramatic moments words hang precipitously between whole stanza breaks. Such pauses are included not just to convey awkwardness or the absence of any cumulative impetus but as opportunities to allow the lover to speak up, to raise a voice against this new condition and, by speaking, to alter it. The leading question addressed by Crane (and following upon the first awkward pause, in line 8) is: "What words can strangle this deaf moonlight?" Only words from the lover can break through the silence of the now-indifferent moon, the moon that draws the tides that will lead to the lover's withdrawal. When the lover offers no saving reply, no answer at all, then Crane's

> For we

> Are overtaken

—with its long, anguished pause as if waiting for the lover to intervene—is his acknowledgment that "Now no cry, no sword / Can fasten or deflect this tidal wedge." As the moon withdraws, pulling the tides in its wake, so does the lover, and a great silence, marked by the second set of ellipses, descends.

When the lover actually begins to speak at last, the moment is in-

tensely dramatic—which is why those words are strung out across the
stanza break, to convey the poet's anxious attention. But what the poet
hears as a reply:

> "There's
>
> Nothing like this in the world."

is so vapid, so inappropriate, and above all so impersonal, that it reveals
the game is up: the lover's motive for speaking is only the need to fill an
awkward silence. The additional remark, "'—And never to quite understand!'" is even more of an evasion, and it provokes a flash of anger from
Crane as he righteously flinches from his lover's demonstration of cowardice, this "piracy," this decision to be covert.

Crane, however, as a last powerful gesture of his own love, restrains
his dismay and, as his lover plainly wishes, relinquishes his hold,
speaking the words his lover would hear:

> But now
> Draw in your head, alone and too tall here.
> Your eyes already in the slant of drifting foam;
> Your breath sealed by ghosts I do not know:
> Draw in your head and sleep the long way home.

But in releasing his lover to those "ghosts" Crane does not know, he cannot quite endure his own magnanimity. He must include one last desperate sting, one last hope of shaking his lover free from the oblivion of
withdrawal. The very form of the lullaby is Crane's reprisal: his lover is a
child who requires protection. His lover has returned now to be one of
those children on the shore who cannot endure pain. It is up to Crane to
take on his old stance as the wise observer, to stop prodding for a response even as his anguish is so great he can barely check himself.
"Draw in your head," repeated at the end, underscores Crane's awareness of his lover's evasion. Here is that cruelty of love of which Crane
had been so wary. Here is manifest his own desperate desire to cling
possessively. It causes him to speak scornfully toward the one person
dearest to him, and it promotes even more anguish. Crane gives up his
love painfully, reluctantly, but with a measure of courage, unsuccessfully
masking his despair and anger in these singsong, childlike rhythms.

That Crane is capable of understanding his own actions (and those of
his lover) in such detail, with such intricacy, is a mark of how far he has

come in the course of writing *Voyages*. The early drafts of the poem and
"Voyages IV," with their ebullient emphasis on the joy of eroticism, now
seem simpleminded and naive. Even more remote, now, is his earlier
poetry in which the poet was singled out for his aura of perfection and
privileged vision. The poet, messenger of a redemptive vision, intervened in the lives of his audience to offer a saving grace; without that
intervention, his audience would remain weak, abject, craven—repressed multitudes longing for a healing wind, haunted by their secret
dreams. No doubt this belief in the weakness of the multitudes ran parallel to Crane's early attitude toward himself: he must don a fiery cloak of
inspired language, abandon his personality, take to the wind, identify
with the Bridge—otherwise he would lapse into being one more of the
many abject mortals that comprise his audience.

The change overtaking Crane in the course of *Voyages* is, then, most
extreme. At the center of the sequence is his new ability to understand
the evasions and reluctance and fears of another. He not only asks himself to forgive another, but he is liberated to the extent of revealing his
own failure, disappointment, and anger. He is no longer on display as a
civic poet but is free to explore his own desires; more important, he recognizes that his own desires may conflict with those of another person—
and that complex new idea of conflict challenges him as nothing before.
In his previous poetry he had defined himself in contrast to a nemesis, an
opposite he set out purposely to negate. Opposing Eliot, he was locked
into the role of the optimist, and to the extent that he had an identity at
all it was valid only as he demonstrated the errors, the rigidity, the weakness in others. In *Voyages* his new, strong sense of himself emerges as he
recognizes the differences between himself and another, however painful
that recognition may be. In accepting that other, Crane can begin the
large task of accepting himself.

4

Inquiry and Analysis

If Crane had succeeded in publishing the volume he had assembled for a private printer early in 1925, how would that book have seemed? Some of his finest lyrics were yet to be written. In fact, he was on the verge of an extraordinary period of creativity, beginning in the summer of 1925 and extending through the summer of 1927, in which virtually all his memorable poetry would be written. His first collection, had he published it, would have been *White Buildings* without "The Wine Menagerie," "At Melville's Tomb," and "Lachrymae Christi." *Voyages* would have appeared as a group of four poems, ending on a strong note of optimism. "Passage" and "Repose of Rivers" would await a second volume.

If the group of poems he assembled in a notebook was a guide to his intentions, this first version of *White Buildings* had its own distinctive shape. "Recitative" was the opening poem, serving as a prelude to the cityscape of "Faustus and Helen" which followed. "Possessions" acted as the transitional poem leading from "Faustus and Helen" to "Voyages I-IV." As a coda to "Voyages I-IV," Crane placed "Legend," a poem written at the time of work on *Voyages* (October 1924) which rather defiantly insists that though passionate involvement exacts a price, it is not only worth paying but necessary if one hopes to grow and mature. Next came a group of poems loosely related to various aspects of love: "Stark Major" (an early imitation of Eliot's quatrains in *Poems 1920*), "My Grandmother's Love Letters," "At Heaven Gates" (a fragment, elements of which would be worked into "Lachrymae Christi"), "Praise for an Urn," "Garden Abstract," "Belle Isle," and "Pastorale." With another new poem, "Paraphrase," also composed in October 1924, Crane modulated from a poetry of love to a poetry addressed to different versions of the artist: "Sunday Morning Apples," "Chaplinesque," and "Black Tambourine." But after this point, the assemblage grows erratic; the poetry

56

thins out into Crane's earlier verse, into imitations and parodies, even into three bizarre translations of Jules Laforgue. (And perhaps this tail-end work was never intended for a volume: after "My Grandmother's Love Letters," the poems lose their pagination, and Crane may have had plans to reshape this section and eliminate the weaker verse.) [1]

What might a reader have made of this collection? She or he would have noticed two long poems in a prominent position, both of which were unabashedly erotic (the more restrained "Porphyro in Akron" was included in the manuscript but buried in the back, in the very last pages, alongside the translations.) These long poems in turn gave way to a group of love poems and then a group of poems centering on the artist—more accurately, the popular artist in modern America, a frustrated figure offering gifts to others but rarely receiving recognition. This poet, one would conclude, was a love poet primarily, an exuberant figure, who was nonetheless aware that those who offered their love did not always find it requited. A reader pondering at greater length might conclude that this poet was also deeply concerned with problems of repression, not just in "Faustus and Helen" but in the dilemma of the artists: the black man is trapped in the cellar, and Chaplin is in trouble with the law. Finally, the reader might legitimately complain that the volume had a glaring weakness: it opened with great bold strokes, but as it continued it seemed to weaken, as the poems became shorter and simpler.

The contrast with the final version of *White Buildings*, as arranged in the spring of 1926 and published in December, is noteworthy: the progression of the poems has been reversed, and the work grows increasingly more challenging as the reader continues. Early work is still included, though by no means all, and there is much that is negligible in the first half of the book, but beyond the halfway point, the poems begin a marked increase in complexity: "Lachrymae Christi," "Passage," "The Wine Menagerie," followed by a lull in which "Recitative" and "Faustus and Helen" appear, only to recover with "At Melville's Tomb" and the six poems of *Voyages*. If the earlier manuscript promised much only to offer little after its opening, *White Buildings* begins modestly enough but concludes with undeniable strength. [2]

The change in the two collections is a mark of Crane's increasing authority: instead of placing his major poetry first, he allows the reader to approach it slowly. The emphasis on love poetry is no longer necessary, for Crane is no longer simply a poet moved by the powers of loving.

And if the progress of the poems in the final version offers increasing challenges to the reader, the poems themselves present extraordinary difficulties.

Crane's early work is difficult enough, but it is difficult for a simple reason, and once the reader has grasped the reason, much of the difficulty simply falls away. In the early poetry, what is puzzling is the excess in the poet's intense language, but that very excess, it can be discovered, is itself in line with the poet's theme, the necessity to break away from inhibiting conventions. The later poetry of *White Buildings* is genuinely difficult, inherently difficult, not to be resolved by some appeal to a general idea, because it is striving to convey simultaneously a number of overlapping ideas and contradictory movements, all of which are held in constant tension with each other. The direction in which such a poetry is moving is not easily sensed. In the early poetry, a reader could feel, almost by absorbing the overall tone, that Crane was aiming to escape from certain constrictions, and that reader might feel relatively comfortable with an intense language, however difficult it appeared to be on its surface, because the overall direction seemed in sight. The intensity was part of an intricate but harmonious effort to leap beyond strict limitations. In this new poetry, Crane is not able to offer such a general assurance; he is all indirection—allusive, suggestive, coming at matters from a number of distinctive but overlapping perspectives. Yet indirect as he is, the point to mark is that his new poetry exposes the poet himself to his own inquiry and his own analysis; that is the reason for the sudden increase in inherent difficulty, at the same time as it is the new means for resolving and understanding that difficulty. The early poetry, which charged forward with a direct momentum, employed a grandeur and a sweep that would carry the poet along with it, borne on its titanic energies. This new poetry, which shifts and hesitates and lingers, which offers multiple perspectives that expand upon the subject under concern, presses the reader to follow Crane as he is in the process of struggling to understand his own feelings. The poet is more exposed than before, no longer the giant riding the whirlwind but the individual grappling with an enormous range of conflicting emotions.

The change from "Voyages I-IV" to *Voyages* is the paradigmatic shift; one version is all intense celebration, an effort to evoke in words that sensual pleasure of physical love, while the other version is additionally concerned with understanding the nature of love, this poet's experience with it, the decisions he must make in order to accept even its dark side.

The complexities in the later poetry are not merely musical, as they frequently were in his earlier work, but actually amount to new insights. Beginning in 1925, Crane turns toward understanding, or struggling to understand, the conflicts that riddle his life instead of seeking a way up and away from them as he had earlier.

1

"Lachrymae Christi" is the crucial transitional poem between Crane's early work as a seer and his mature poetry of self-exploration. In fact, the poem was stitched together, sometime in 1925, out of two earlier, unrelated fragments, one from February 1924, the other from October 1924.[3] Though the seams joining the fragments are not particularly evident, the poem can be read in two rather different ways, one of which looks back to early work, the other of which points to the future.

In this double light, the poem is truly transitional; it is as though Crane were in the process of discovering all that he could do if he attended with care to the implications developing in his own work. There were no particular ideas to note in his early work, just a general tendency, a willingness to direct the poem in a certain way; rather precise ideas, themselves suggesting further elaborations, begin to emerge at this stage in his work. "Voyages IV," the earliest of the completed *Voyages* poems, celebrated the joys of an erotic love that had spiritual overtones, but the later additions to *Voyages* developed around Crane's realization that loving is never possessive. As he begins to define his own understanding of what it means to be in love, Crane both narrows his focus and increases his scope; he has found a theme particular to him, not simply a theme that has been sanctioned by a long tradition of other poetry, and he discovers he has more to say than he had at first realized. He even discovers the significance of work that he had written earlier but had not fully appreciated. "Lachrymae Christi" reveals Crane in a similar position: it is almost as though he depends upon his old notion of the poet as seer to guide him through this work, to sustain him and to build a base from which he then can venture out in more special and particular and distinctive directions, ultimately reaching an understanding of what it is he deeply values in the experience before him.

The old idea "Lachrymae Christi" clings to is one familiar to Crane: the poet, by virtue of his special calling, should cast his attention toward those powerful forces that are capable of acting in a regenerative fashion.

It is the opening night of spring, when the land awakens from winter's dormancy, and as the poet gradually moves in harmony with this renewal, he slowly expands his awareness to include, as running parallels, the resurrection of Christ (it is Easter) and the resurrection of Dionysus the pagan god whose rebirth the ancient world celebrated in springtime. By meditating on springtime, Crane is led through a series of variant redemptions. On this level, as an early work, the poem is relatively simple; what is confusing or intricate in the language can be referred back to the overall process of transformation. Behind this poem lies Crane's interest in combating what he perceived to be Eliot's perverse refusal to exploit the powers inherent in poetry. And it also reminds us of Crane's ambitions in his "General Aims & Theories" essay: quite deliberately, the poem sets out to fuse the ancient and the modern, to show that one can begin by thinking about moonlight on dormant factory machinery and end by participating vividly in the crucifixion-resurrection of Dionysus.

But in the process of composition, this simple idea of transformation has itself become transformed; it is no longer a poem of multiple renewals, each one running parallel to all the others: it is also a poem concerned with a search for origins, a poem that moves back, painfully and painstakingly, to uncover difficult truths. The simple poem Crane must have set out to write is eloquently synopsized in M. D. Uroff's description of the basic plot: "By associating the mill with the wool it spins and the wool with the sheep and the sheep with the sacrificial lamb and the lamb with Christ and Christ with the symbol of suffering and dying and rebirth, the poet unmangles the machine world."[4] The progess is away from the strictly secular to the densely sacred—though Crane uses the occasion to define the sacred in a way suitable to him: it involves suffering in order to be reborn, tears of joy that turn into wine, just as the crucifixion of Christ issues in the flaming, phoenixlike rebirth of Dionysus, god of celebration. "Not penitence / But song" is the motto of the poem—the simple poem—as Uroff argues it, following the lead of R. W. B. Lewis.[5]

Within the movement of this poem, however, with its accumulating momentum that acquires energy through associational leaps, there is a more disturbing, convoluted poem that involves a difficult and necessarily painful quest for origins and self-definition. From the perspective of this poem, Crane's movements appear as rather different. Instead of claiming that every old death gives rise to a new birth in a triumphant series of ongoing renewals, this poem claims that each death is a life and each life is a death. Instead of viewing his poem as a series of break-throughs, each of which is more freeing than the last, Crane views his poem as a series of additional burdens or challenges, each of which is more urgent and pressing and fearsome than the last. In this complex poem, the poet has no sooner attained one moment of poise than it is undone; he is always disrupting his last reconciliation by seeking its origin elsewhere. He is constantly moving back, further and further into territory that uncovers new, fearful challenges—which in turn also cause him to seek their origin. For example, consider his movement away from the second stanza. Instead of remaining poised in breathless admiration over the dazzle of red against white that is a bank of flowers flaring in the moonlight (as well as flecks of blood on the shanks of lambs pierced by thorns that have freshened to a point in the spring), he turns to focus on the roots which nourish the soil. This in turn leads to the worms whose tunneling aerates the earth, which brings him to the corpses that nourish the worms, onward to the ultimate corpse, the body of Christ which is the body of the world broken by tears of suffering. But those tears are empathetic and, bathing all in pity and forgiveness, become a universal wine, that in turn recalls the elemental god Dionysus, worshipped by those who knew the world is inextricably havoc and creation, disorder and reconciliation, the wine of chaos and the wine of sublimity, death and birth, fused together and inseparable.

This complex poem is dark and brooding, and it brings us to a different conclusion than the simple poem. In the simple poem, the reader contrasts the "unyielding smile" of the machinery in the first stanza with the "Unmangled target smile" on the face of Dionysus in the final stanza and concludes that the poet has transformed the inert, mechanical frames of the machinery into an organic, central, and accepting smile. The cold modern world gives way to the warm ancient one; from death to life, from inertia to activity. The complex version, rather than clearly contradicting the simple poem, develops and extends a basic notion into an understanding that is original and compelling. In the complex poem, the poet's progress is away from a hardness that resists all forms of dissolution (the moonlight dissolves "all but the windows of the mills") toward a distinct vulnerability that not only bears but actually invites destruction. The smile in the last stanza is an "Unmangled target smile" that encourages its violation (it is a target) even as it remains pure, unmangled, continually renewed. The strength of the target smile, in the complex poem, is greater than the apparent strength of the "unyielding" mill smile, be-

cause the target smile is a way of accepting destruction and pain, integrating it into life, instead of stubbornly resisting it or remaining oblivious to it. (In this respect, "Lachrymae Christi" recalls "Legend" and its
assertion that utter involvement is necessary for the highest achievement: "The only worth all granting" "is to be learned—" "But only
by the one who / Spends out himself again.") In the simple poem, the
poet simply grows more and more "dynamic," identifying himself with
stronger, more primordial forces; in the complex poem, the poet develops an understanding of why the position he is moving toward, as exemplified by Christ and ultimately Dionysus, is of great value, a meaningful
relation to life which is constantly disruptive, an attitude superior to that
stubborn, oblivious withdrawal suggested by the mills. If one is going to
live, one must be prepared to be vulnerable; every life is a death, but
every death is a life.

To follow out the development of the complex poem leads to an appreciation of the dense connections in this poem; there is no useless appa-
ratus in the work and even apparent oddities of syntax and diction are
contributing to an overall impression. For example, by shifting from a
manner of speaking in the first stanza which simply ties together one object after the next, as though a camera were roving across the scene, to
an intricately convoluted presentation in the second stanza, Crane presses
us to experience the sharp contrast between the flatness of the machinery, which is simply dead, and the multiplicity of the natural, which
is grappling with life and death, with the death of one thing becoming the
life of another and vice versa:

> Whitely, while benzine
> Rinsings from the moon
> Dissolve all but the windows of the mills
> (Inside the sure machinery
> Is still
> And curdled only where a sill
> Sluices its one unyielding smile)
>
> Immaculate venom binds
> The fox's teeth, and swart
> Thorns freshen on the year's
> First blood. From flanks unfended,
> Twanged red perfidies of spring
> Are trillion on the hill.

Grammatically speaking, "Whitely" is an adverb which modifies "binds":
the teeth of the fox are bound because the moonlight gleaming on the
teeth makes the fox too visible to be an effective predator (and hungry,
the salivating creature only polishes its teeth the more, emphasizing
their glistening, filling its mouth with a "venom" that is also "immacu-
late" because its high visibility effectively immobilizes it). But it is crucial that the adverb is suspended throughout the first stanza, because the
moonlight has no effect whatsoever on the mills. The white light works a
transformation but not on the impervious "windows of the mills" which
outshine the moon and reveal an interior of "sure machinery" which is
perfectly "still"—inert precisely because, as nonliving, it cannot respond to the changes effected by the moonlight that suddenly illuminates
what had not been before highly visible.

The parenthesis enforces the sense of a bracketed place, as does the
severe "unyielding smile" of the framing window, and the repetition of
"mills/still/sill." The moonlight has quite a different effect on the world
of the living, however, because living things must respond to changes if
they are to live. The second stanza, then, is not only swarming with
change but each change blends inseparably with another. The fox's teeth
have lost their sting because they are too bright, but what the fox's teeth
once did the "Swart thorns" now do; as the thorns flourish, they pierce
the "flanks unfended" of the lambs, but as they flourish, they also flower
on the once-bare flank of a hill. No change can be dissociated from any
other (unlike the mill interior where things are primly set apart from
each other). These are the "perfidies of spring" but they are not purposeful betrayals; they are events that occur in all their living intricacy,
without any special malice behind them. The moonlight reveals the fox
not to betray it but simply because the moon is bright, and the thorns
freshen on the blood of the lambs only because the lambs, adjusting to
the presence of the fox, brush against the thorns. It is fundamentally an
innocent world, this world of utter change, a world in which life and
death are opposite sides of an identical coin.

Crane's purpose is to adopt this innocence and internalize it. If one
can realize that the havoc in his life is not the result of retribution, that it
is not a personal force singling him out for punishment, then he can regard everything with cleansed eyes. The "nights opening / Chant pyramids" as this song of spring pyramids in increasing strength to become
an overall pattern of benign violence, with some of the predictable for-

mality of a traditionalized chant. The eyes, now anointed with innocence, find that the "perjuries," the supposed betrayals, that "Had
galvanized" the eyes now cleanse them and galvanize them into life.
"Distilling clemencies" (a first hint of the tears that will eventually accompany truly innocent seeing) now "chime / Beneath and all around."
There is "Not penitence / But song" because no one is held to be culpa-
ble; even death loses its sting, once it is recognized that the lowly worm,
the fearful worm, is inextricably involved with the flowering of the land.
The worm's tunnelings eventually create "Perpetual fountains, vines."
The bounty of the land is the result of countless deaths—if one views the
world through "Nazarene and tinder eyes": eyes that are forgiving, tender,
merciful, and above all vulnerable. To open the eyes fully, to anoint them
with innocence, to cleanse them of galvanization and galvanize them to
life, one must allow the eyes to be vulnerable. Moonlight can sting (recall the "benzine / Rinsings" of the first stanza in which the moonlight
revealed the dreadful inertia of the machinery), but its stinging can be
simultaneously cleansing and purifying; indeed, to be clean one must
be open to stinging, to be pure one must be violable.

   The gnarled parenthesis of the next stanza has been a source of confusion ever since R. P. Blackmur struggled to unravel it out of the context
of the poem.[6] What adds to the confusion, however, is that Crane temporarily shifts from imagery that centers on eyes to imagery that centers on
the tongue:

> (Let sphinxes from the ripe
> Borage of death have cleared my tongue
> Once and again; vermin and rod
> No longer bind. Some sentient cloud
> Of tears flocks through the tendoned loam.
> Betrayed stones slowly speak.)

Yet the strong pattern of the poem helps guide one through this thicket:
by looking long and hard, far past the surface, as Crane has been doing
in the previous lines, he understands the origins of things, he understands that flowers originate in corpses; and his knowledge frees him
from fearful restraints. The sphinx is an image of the impenetrable mystery at the center of creation, and if one takes up that sphinx, his tongue
is "cleared"; there are burdens that leave one freed of burdensome
guilts. (That the mute, tongueless sphinx should ultimately be an agency
for speech reinforces the pattern in the poem, where meditation on the

"ripe / Borage of death" leads to an acceptance of death which becomes a birth into new life.) The cloud of tears that "flocks through the tendoned loam" (recalling the innocence of the flock of lambs) suggests that the poet, his eyes vulnerable yet surrounded by a protective cloud of innocence—the "sentient cloud" is both feeling its way forward and protecting the eyes from harm—can move through the weight that might otherwise crush him. Indeed, the cloud seems to turn impacted earth into "tendoned loam" (with another echo of "tender" as there had been earlier in "tinder"), making it pliant, flexible, supple; what had previously been resistant and stony now begins itself to yield, affirming that as the poet adopts a willingness to be vulnerable to change, he actually creates change about himself. The world softens, literally, under his new gaze; that which had been lost, underground, betrayed—speechless and turned to stone—now begins to be heard.

After this point, the poem should hold few mysteries for the initiated. The eyes may fill with tears, but such weeping produces a wine that soothes even as it bursts into (purifying) flame, and the "undimming lattices of flame" that look out on the "Compulsion of the year" and regard it with acceptance and understanding—as an occurrence both creative and destructive—are a marked contrast to the "unyielding smile" of the windowsill bracketing the machinery. "Sable, slender boughs" are indistinguishable from "charred and riven stakes" because the very insight of the poem is that if one is able to accept the disruption in his life by responding to it forgivingly, then this activity is an immediate rebirth. The person who can do that holds "the grail / Of earth," an earthly grail that fulfills the promise of renewal here and now. One can integrate disruption into his life, and that is the immense strength appreciated in the course of this poem; by contrast, the inertia of the mill machinery is a form of weakness.

What is complicating in "Lachrymae Christi" is that Crane edges toward a firm belief in remaining open to the events around him which might challenge or frustrate him, but the poem itself assembles a complicated machinery that, in a way, protects the poet in his vulnerability, associating his own actions, for example, with the character of Christ. The poem should not, perhaps, be judged by the extent of courage that Crane displays; he will, in further work, amply display his own ability to confront himself truthfully. Rather, it should be remembered that "Lachrymae Christi" is a poem of transition, and it effectively spans what could have been a yawning gulf between his youthful and his mature work. The poem, as in his early work, upholds an ideal of sacrifice, of abandoning the individual personality in order to participate in a greater flow; and to that extent it clearly resembles his initial work on *The Bridge*, and "Possessions" and "Recitative." But it approaches that ideal in movements that are not broad and sweeping and energetic, designed to sweep the reader along, but just the opposite: it is a slow, thoughtful, brooding work, in which it seems that every line is taking the measure of the difficulty of the discovery underway. Intricately organized, striving to be both melodious and intellectual at the same time, it is marvelously unlike any other poem Crane had attempted, yet clearly the product of his youthful convictions.

2

"Lachrymae Christi" is a success not only as a transitional poem but as a poem; it is not only a cross section of Crane's divergent interests at this point in his career but it manages, however eccentrically, to hold them together. It is, quite simply, a feat of the impossible, a bridge between the poetry of self-abandonment and the poetry of self-analysis. "Passage," written in the summer of 1925, is not so successful, though it emphasizes a similar dual vision. It brings the two opposites together, though, only to split them off further. Written as a work of self-analysis, the poem measures the poetry of self-abandonment and finds it wanting.

But "Passage" is not simply a dismissive work. While it reflects Crane's new desire to use language as a way into understanding rather than as music, rather than as the basis for a free-flowing associational melody that overwhelms restraint, the poem also centers on the effort by Crane to extricate himself from the bondage of his past. This is an aggressive, exacerbating task, highly self-critical, which, after a certain point, leads into thoroughly uncharted territory. It is supposed to move in that direction, since the value of the poetry of analysis is that it discloses knowledge not within the grasp of the poet before undertaking his poem. But Crane's ability to find the words proper to his new understanding is so new as to fail to limit him clearly at the end of his poem, and the conclusion, which effectively catapults him into a new understanding, is undermined by the very novelty of the discovery. What makes the poem impressive, though, even in its conclusion, is that Crane carries into it that very air of bewilderment and bedazzlement. The poem is profoundly idiosyncratic and deeply personal—too much so to be a complete success—but it is marked by a stubborn integrity, a willingness to press through the ramifications of thought, that will be the signature of Crane's mature work.

In the opening four stanzas, the simplest part of the poem, Crane rehearses—in a language that is analytical and inquiring without being merely surgical or dismissive—the efforts he had made in the past to be free of his own past. (This lays a groundwork for regarding this poem as an ultimate test: will this poem turn out to be the failure that his previous efforts to escape the past have been?) In search of an "Improved infancy," his first step (previously) had been deliberately to suppress his memory. Memory was an unbearable weight, and its hold over him is effectively conveyed in a series of ominous and murky images, as though he could only approach each one—so fearsome are they—for the briefest of instants. (A similarly oblique approach toward memory will be featured in the later poem "Repose of Rivers," though in that work Crane is boasting of his new control over his memories.) Memory, for example, "aprons rock," and turns mothers into stone. It wakens alleys with a hidden cough, suggesting the murderous depths that skulk within a neglected darkness. And it "congregates pears / In moonlit bushels," stifling their individual sweetness, inviting the ripeness of decay as they rot below a patina of silver moonlight. Memory is the "Casual louse that tissues the buckwheat"—the unwanted, unpredictable, disruptive force that confutes one's efforts to rise and be free; a parasite eating away at what should be whole and natural.

Or so memory appeared to him in his past. For if Crane is confessing to his deepest needs in this poem, he is also rigorously questioning the aptness with which he accommodates his needs. Is an "Improved infancy" a truly desirable goal, or is it a new form of an old weakness? A fierce irony is never far distant from this first half of the poem. What is exposed here is not simply the terrible pressures of memory; equally under fire is the alternative he pursued as he sought to be free of his memory. The notion of childhood regained, the ideal of a wholeness achieved by dwelling apart from pressure of any kind, is subjected to an intense scrutiny.

In rehearsing these past episodes, he is able to uncover the illusions that drive him. For example, burying his memory in a crevice, he is able to join the "entrainments of the wind." This, however, proves to be a short flight, productive of nothing. Rain dries at once on his overheated, sun-bronzed cheeks; this bronzed superman, who wanted to render him-

self utterly free, is utterly infertile. Come harvest time there is nothing
for him in the "red and black / Vine-stanchioned valleys." He has become like the wind which must eventually exhaust itself, turning into a
smoke that emanates from the "chimney-sooted heart of man," as though
he had been only burning himself up all along.

"Passages" acknowledges Crane's discovery of the limitations of "visionary" poetry, at least as he had practiced it in his earlier days. But the
poem becomes more than elaborate autobiography precisely because
Crane poses and resolves the problem of what kind of poetry to write to
supplant that visionary verse. The poetry of analysis, which regards the
actions of the past to learn from them, to measure failure and redirect
oneself accordingly, offers the new alternative—an alternative so new at
this point that Crane can only plunge ahead with it, not fully in control of
all it offers. There is a freedom to pick and choose images in this poem
which is both energizing and unsettling; it seems entirely appropriate
that the poem should take this form, but it makes for arduous reading.

In the second half of the poem, Crane understands that the reason for
his failure stems from his original intent to separate himself from the
pressures of memory. And his quest truly grows unsettling when he turns
back to his own past effort to suppress his past, and he attempts to confront that which he had once hoped to place behind him. To return
at evening to the gorge of abandoned memory requires considerable
courage:

> The evening was a spear in the ravine
> That throve through very oak. And had I walked
> The dozen particular decimal points of time?
> Touching an opening laurel, I found
> A thief beneath, my stolen book in hand.
>
> "Why are you back here—smiling an iron coffin?"
> "To argue with the laurel," I replied:
> "Am justified in transience, fleeing
> Under the constant wonder of your eyes—."

The gorge is overgrown with darkness, rampant in shadow, a place of lost
time, more of a dark wood than ever. Abandoning memory has only
caused it to flourish in uncontrolled ways. Under a laurel which opens
with deceptive ease (as though everything now depends on Crane's every
gesture), he is confronted by the thief—an emblem not just of memory

but of memory grown powerful through neglect—who holds the poet's stolen book in his hand. That book surely represents to Crane his true biography, not the "too well-known biography" of defeat; but it is also a book that he had, in the past, thrown away. It is now in the possession of the thief, who is unlikely to relinquish it. As the book is associated with the repression of memory, Crane is recognizing that he has jeopardized his own creativity by deliberately trying to escape from the conflicts within him.

One of the remarkable things in this poem is that Crane remains true to his own sense of hesitation and anxiety; he uses the poem to explore his weaknesses rather than as an occasion to resolve all problems in a blaze of light. The "thief," for example, confronts him challengingly, as though Crane were the interloper, the one out of synchronization, trying to manage his own life. The thief's question emerges derisively, and his speech, unlike Crane's flawed stammer, is threateningly direct. Are you here to smile your way back to your own coffinlike existence? the thief inquires, suggesting by his derisive tone that only the greatest of fools would believe that one can easily return to the past. Instead of routing his interlocutor, Crane can only stammer an evasive, defensive reply— and he is interrupted before he can prolong his defense. It seems plain that he has not risen to the direct speech that the tense occasion demands; he cravenly places the burden for his flight on one other than himself, refusing to bear responsibility. The thief, then, in a gesture that is a dismissive snap of the wrist, cuts him off: "He closed the book."

With this alarmingly abrupt gesture, Crane is plunged into a crisis, pitched into a chaotic and troubled new dimension that is not the breakthrough one might have expected (and Crane had surely hoped for), though it is the new understanding that the poem reveals. If this new dimension can be identified with anything, it must be the present, the present of this poem at this moment, with the insights grasped in its course brought together in a summary fashion. Abandoned by the thief, cut off from the possibility of an easy return to a simpler past, Crane is even more disoriented than ever:

> He closed the book. And from the Ptolemies
> Sand troughed us in a glittering abyss.
> A serpent swam a vertex to the sun.
> —On unpaced beaches leaned its tongue and drummed.
> What fountains did I hear? What icy speeches?
> Memory, committed to the page, had broke.

This bizarre conclusion is, in fact, a stunning insight. Crane, having precipitated this crisis that sets his ultimate problem so clearly before him, fuses together his sense of failure with a burst of understanding that illuminates that failure. Thus the scene widens into a vista that stretches all the way "from the Ptolemies"—a drastic change from the claustral atmosphere of the dark wood—at the same time as poet and thief remain swamped in a "glittering abyss" that is similar to the terrible ravine. The poet is locked with the thief in the ravine, but now it is blazingly illuminated. This new light reveals that Crane's problem is not his past as such, not his memories, but his attitude toward memory. In compact imagery, the whole poem unfolds again: the serpent swims freely to the sun (as the poet had joined the wind) but once there finds it can only drum its tongue emptily; it has arrived at nothing. The sleek freedom of the serpent that swims in the sky is a hollow freedom because it is a freedom from any kind of complicating involvement rather than a freedom won through engagement and confrontation. With this awareness blazing before him, Crane's insight is that it is impossible to divide one's life into simple positives and negatives, into "fountains" versus "icy speeches," into expansive spaciousness versus contemptuous dismissals. (As in "Lachrymae Christi," where Crane moves to the awareness that death and life are inextricably intertwined, so in this ending there is the implication that free-flowing fountains cannot exist without the tautness of icy speech.) If memory can be committed to the page, integrated into the poem, its fearful, obsessive hold will be broken; but this knowledge, though it occurs in an instant of illumination, is darkly tinged with dismay at the new demands now placed on the poet. That blend of darkness and illumination is, of course, the complex integration the poet requires, but it is proffered here as a necessity that has been grasped but not realized in this poem.

Idiosyncratic as it is, "Passage" clearly displays the strength of Crane's revised understanding of what a poem should be. A poem can be a way of working back toward problems, not for purposes of therapy or release but actually to gain a hold on oneself, to accrue self-knowledge, and to demonstrate that one can understand precisely the remedy his analysis requires. It is not surprising that the poem should be so eccentric; it is necessary, indeed, that the gnomic images in the poem retain a sense of the distorted menace of a nightmare, for Crane is working his way toward subterranean aspects of himself, articulating his feelings without simplifying them, scrutinizing himself without resorting to surgery. "Passage" is not at all what it has been described as—a failed attempt to deliver a narrative that might have been revised into a straightforward story—nor is it a narrative of obfuscation marred by an unwavering commitment to momentous and portentous language.[7] The language is essential to the poem: it is a way of capturing insights into oneself through a ring of images felt as personal extensions which cannot be lopped off or rapidly labeled or allegorically summed up. Crane's impulse to suppress or in some way distort his memory is countermanded in the very way the poem is written.

The "Passage" of the poem is the determined struggle to articulate inner problems without viewing them in isolation but by feeling out the complications and entanglements as they actually exist. It surely marks how far he has come, in two short years, from his earlier work. By contrast, a poem such as "Possessions" is the act of a man wishing to join the "entrainments of the wind," hoping to swim to the sun without interference. One who swims to the sun, Crane realizes now, is liable to find only a void when he arrives, because he is purposely trying to leave everything behind him. The alternative is to work through that which sends one into a headlong flight, to discover the origins that create the need for a hasty momentum, and to grasp the limitations that one prefers to evade and break from their bondage by fronting them.

3

"The Wine Menagerie," the most undeniably impressive of these three works of initial maturity, has been read as a poem of autobiographical confession in which Crane exposes the ephemeral joy of alcoholic intoxication.[8] According to this reading, he confesses that he turns to drink in hopes of arousing visionary impressions that cannot appear to him in his sobriety; but wine is a vicious ally, and its moments of ecstasy cannot be prolonged. When its effects wear off, he is plunged into a bleakness that is nearly paralyzing. What critics have found to praise in the poem is, then, its air of remorseless objectivity. Crane charts his (illusory) moment of ecstasy, then annotates his inevitable slide downhill. Though Crane may have been helpless to resist the blandishments of alcohol, he at least confesses to his weakness with a manly strength.

Such a reading is not so much wrong as incomplete, and a similar kind of partial reading may have been the motive behind Marianne Moore's extensive revision of the poem. As editor of *The Dial*, she tamed the whole menagerie by revising the poem into eighteen elliptical lines.[9] As an exceptionally private person herself—none of her poems could be considered as in the least confessional—she may have been appalled by a work that seemed so candidly to confess to such desperate measures. Her revision (much resented by Crane, frequently maligned by others) may have been a gesture of friendship—a rewriting of such radical obfuscation as to protect Crane from his own impulse for candor, an impulse that could only have struck her as truly desperate. Her response —though opposite to that of the critics who dwell upon the poem as a confession of the desperate risks the visionary cultivates in the pursuit of his derangement of the senses—is no less inadequate and incomplete; both positions, one minimizing Crane's desperation, the other emphasizing it, ignore the difficult, serious struggle Crane undertakes in what is essentially a poem of loneliness and love.

Though "The Wine Menagerie" is one of Crane's most self-critical works, it is not a confession of weakness but a judgment and appraisal of his failure to rise to a meaningful challenge. Crane's condemnation of his own actions, that is, is made from a position of strength. Instead of being reduced to helplessness by the close of his poem, he is acutely aware of the reasons for his own failure. Rather than simply exposing himself, he is judging his actions, and the difference is that by the end of the poem he is not uncertain, isolated, or disoriented but keenly aware—all too keenly, as it happens—of why he has failed. It is a crucial difference: the missing element in all commentaries on the poem is the acknowledgment that Crane understands precisely the reasons for and the extent of his own most thorough failure.

"The Wine Menagerie" claims attention not as a confession of alcoholic abuse but as a poem of loneliness. While the poem is definitely concerned with the price that intoxication exacts, it is a price measured not against some standard of visionary absorption but against the value of encountering another person. From the very beginning, Crane appears as one who depends on wine to release a sense of positive well-being; but at the same time, he takes pains to show that this position of comfort, in which one so easily extends feelings of sympathy to others, is not any genuine achievement. Indeed, it is difficult to say, even at the start, whether wine is attractive because it gives the illusion of sympathy with others or attractive because it allows one to become thoroughly lost in shadows, dissolved entirely. What is clear, however, is that a striking contrast emerges early in the poem, virtually redirecting its course. The contrast is that between the visionary alcoholic's squinting glimpses of intricate facets of the speakeasy and the profoundly ambiguous and challenging and potentially fearful encounter—possibly destructive, possibly creative—between two persons, both of whom are exchanging looks with one another and using their eyes in a way that involves their entire bodies. This encounter or exchange—it is not yet clear which it will be and it never becomes clear—is the ideal at the center of the poem, an ideal perceived by Crane under the influence of alcohol, an influence that disbars him from participating in it except as observer:

> Against the imitation onyx wainscoting
> (Painted emulsion of snow, eggs, yarn, coal, manure)
> Regard the forceps of the smile that takes her.
> Percussive sweat is spreading to his hair. Mallets,
> Her eyes, unmake an instant of the world.

This ambiguous encounter, by its very nature, eludes any clear-cut resolution. The scene opens neatly enough, framed as it is by the "imitation onyx wainscoting." But this proscenium arch or window frame quickly dissolves into a combination of objects reflected in the imitation onyx. In a parallel way, Crane's attempt to frame the scene and place it onstage, to make it manageable and coherent, to bring it into crisp focus, breaks down into uncertainty because it is not possible to sum up the relationship of the observed couple. What appears from one perspective as a scene of blatant seduction in which a smile calculatedly "takes" another sexually (and in which the flirtatious flutterings of eyelids are "Mallets" that spread "Percussive sweat" on the other's brow) appears from another perspective as a scene vibrant with new life, as that smile is a "forceps" that brings another to birth in a new world and as the eyes of the other contain a world so precious that one cannot bear to lose an instant of it with a blink.

Though the relationship between this couple cannot be resolved, their significance is that they are in a relationship that cannot be resolved. The power they display between themselves is the center of the poem. The great thing is to be strong enough to stare deeply into the eyes of another—so deeply that the stare becomes a gaze and one feels that his vision has been returned. But the terrible risk of such an encounter is that one's own stare may be rebuffed; the ambiguity inherent in the couple, as Crane observes them regarding each other, is an ambiguity inherent in the very notion of daring to regard another openly, nakedly, in anticipation of a response. You may be met with a stare of contempt or you may fall prey to the manipulations of the other. And while it is clear that this couple is involved in this essentially ambiguous, risky relationship, it is equally clear that Crane, as the drunken observer, is allowing no one to regard him. He is the sympathetic observer looking from deep within protective shadows, invisible to others. In this respect, "The Wine Menagerie" looks back to *Voyages:* it is *Voyages* from the viewpoint of one of the "brilliant kids on the shore" who cannot bear to enter the sea, even as it is a "Voyages VII," written by one who longs to enter the sea but cannot because he is overriden by the fears, the risks, the challenges he knows lie before him.

In her memoirs of Crane, Susan Jenkins Brown, while commenting on a letter in which Crane mentioned submitting "The Wine Menagerie" to *The Criterion*, remembered "The Poncino Palazzo, or Punchino Palace, as we called it, a grim six-by-eight foot hole behind a delicatessen on West Fourth Street, where for fifteen or twenty cents we drank lethal speak-easy 'rum' in hot water, made almost potable by a twist of lemon peel." [10] Whether or not this was the setting of the poem, it is appropriate for "The Wine Menagerie" to trigger thoughts of an actual location, for at the opening of the poem, it is crucial that a reader envision the specific interior of the speakeasy. Crane is seated at the bar, and his back is turned to the other inhabitants, some of whom occupy the booths behind him. To these others, he is virtually invisible, an anonymous figure in the shadows; to him, however, these others are vividly, even violently, exposed in the mirror behind the bar, the mirror in which he can observe them circumspectly. If, at the opening of the poem, his eyes seem at times literally to be roving, moving freely about the interior, it is because of the freedom granted him by observing others in a mirror: he has the enormous advantage of viewing them without permitting them to know they are watched—or allowing them the chance to regard him.

If the first stanza is a welcome affirmation of a familiar sense of relaxation, of elation, of freedom, then the second stanza at once introduces the convolutions necessary for the exercise of this freedom. The bar mirror is bordered by a row of decanters underneath that reflect the street (visible through at least one window which is by, or in, the door). These bottles replicate his face endlessly as he adjusts himself to block out the street scene and stare into them; he returns his own stare (in a parody of the actual encounter he will soon witness), and he is granted the sensation of being center stage (though he is in fact entirely self-absorbed):

"Slow / Applause flows into liquid cynosures." Again adjusting his angle, the multiplied reflections of his face dwindle to minute points of light, and as he looks beyond the decanters into the mirror behind, he is "conscripted" to the "shadows' glow" as he enters the role of observer. (In a sense, he is watching the inhabitants of the speakeasy as though he were witnessing a play; the moral danger, so to speak, of always remaining an observer is that persons become puppets, subject to one's own fantasies. Later in the poem Crane likens the creations before him, the men and women observed, to marionettes, and he ends with a pointed reference to the marionettes in Stravinsky's *Petrouchka*.)

The form of "The Wine Menagerie" is a series of interruptions, with each stanza giving rise to some new, alarming swerve that radically alters the course of the poem. With his own anonymity thoroughly established in the first three stanzas, his hidden watch is, of course, in sharp contrast to the ambiguous encounter he observes between the man and the woman. The question of whether or not they are staring each other down or returning each other's gaze is the question Crane stalls over in his fourth stanza. Is the scene to be brushed away with contempt (his first inclination), as just the sort of hasty pickup one would expect to find in this "heap" where the serpent "pries"? (The prying serpent nicely emphasizes Crane's role as voyeur.) Or is there the higher possibility that love and sex can intermingle—that the serpent can shed its skin and be reborn again?

> What is it in this heap the serpent pries—
> Whose skin, facsimile of time, unskeins
> Octagon, sapphire transepts round the eyes;
> —From whom some whispered carillon assures
> Speed to the arrow into feathered skies?

The stanza erratically, anxiously, pauses between these two opposites though Crane's inclination is to lean toward the idea that the very act of disrobing, of unskeining, of exposing, can actually enhance the eyes with "Octagon, sapphire transepts." Then the arrow of lust will open out onto "feathered skies," skies that are delicate, graceful, and (with the idea of "feathered" as evoking the balancing feathers at the tail of the arrow) able to guide the arrow as though it could speed forward forever.

But Crane's wishful speculation closes down actual possibilities because his very revery is itself a retreat from the kind of active encounter

the couple demonstrates. One cannot attain an ideal without having
risked himself in the process of attaining it. (The advice offered in "Legend" is once more appropriate.) In the next stanza, as he suddenly realizes the gulf that lies between the enclosed innocence of the child and
the ambiguous interchanges of the adult, he is equally aware of the un-
bridgeable gap between him, the anonymous observer, and the couple,
the engaged participants. In the most intricate and dramatic and dense
stanza of the poem, he sees that he is closer to the child than to the
adults:

> Sharp to the windowpane guile drags a face,
> And as the alcove of her jealousy recedes,
> An urchin who has left the snow
> Nudges a cannister across the bar
> While August meadows somewhere clasp his brows.

The first two lines display the intricacy of adult relationships. The man,
breaking from the impassioned circle he has shared with the woman,
turns away from her eyes and toward the window, causing her jealousy to
flare. But her face instantly recomposes itself—the "alcove of her jealousy recedes"—as she identifies the face by the window as simply that
of a child. (With the face identified and the problem resolved, the tension immediately drains out of the poem, and intricately convoluted syntax gives way to the simplest line in the poem: "An urchin who has left
the snow.") The simplicity of the urchin's entrance, though, throws a
strong light on the complexity of adult relationships, and an array of questions linger unanswered from the first two lines. Why does "guile" drag a
face sharp to the windowpane? The man may be acting with guile when
he turns abruptly toward the new face, anticipating the resulting flare of
jealousy; or Crane, who has been acting with guile himself, may draw
attention to his identity with the child, who is peering in at his elders,
looking in at the forbidden speakeasy, off limits to the child. What is
both dramatic and deflating in this sudden entrance, though, is the appearance of a face "sharp to the windowpane"—a face that is openly
looking at others yet not expecting to receive an answering gaze. Com-
pared to the faces of the man and the woman, both of which are complex,
full of shadows that emerge and vanish, recesses that wax and wane, the
urchin's visage is virtually blank; he has no eyes to see. The passion and
the heat of the speakeasy only evoke, for him, a memory of summer past
("August meadows somewhere clasp his brow"). He is so far out of this

atmosphere that he does not even breathe the same air as the adults do: to a reader in 1926, with the Great War only seven years distant, "cannister" would immediately evoke its new meaning of "gas-mask." The urchin's brow is clear; as yet it has not developed that brow within which a leopard must range, always seeking freedom.

The ideal that sex and love should intermingle as equals is never under fire in "The Wine Menagerie": that ideal is the possibility Crane recognizes that he longs for but fails to rise toward. What is under fire, remorselessly, is the notion that a person can participate in such an ideal without heavily risking himself. An adult walls himself in his privacy but does so willingly, unlike a child who is walled up by his own impenetrable innocence. The difference between adult and child is that the adult can let down his defenses if he dares to do so, and in the process invite others to do the same, but the child must always be playacting, at best nudging a cannister across the bar in an imitation of a gesture he has viewed in adults. If one is an adult who acts like a child—who is too fearful to be open—then he is liable, by the way he views others, to condemn everyone else to an isolation identical to his own, simply by refusing to drop his defenses. That is precisely Crane's understanding as reflected in the next stanza, which spins out of his recognition that he has no occasion to which to risc. All the adults in the speakeasy appear to be locked protectively and even aggressively in their own privacy. They only look to rebuff each other, to guard their individual territory: "Each chamber, transept, coins some squint, / Remorseless line, minting their separate wills." And persons hapless enough to fall under their "squint" are glanced at only to be rejected, dismissed in the blink of a squinting eye that squeezes the view down to "Poor streaked bodies wreathing up and out." Every twist of dismissal, Crane sees, is an effort to reject the stigma which, if shared, might have bound the adults together: the stigma of another's judgment suffered but overcome through an encounter with an open eye not defensive. The hard truth is compressed into one dense line: "Between black tusks the roses shine!" It is the moral axiom of this poem that in order to find the gleaming roses one must be prepared to look into a fearful maw, a ferocious void. To turn a stare into a gaze one must first encounter the fearful unknown of another's face; the tongue becomes a rose but only to the one who looks beyond the forbidding visage. (The image is also specifically homoerotic.)

R. P. Blackmur, in his pioneering study of 1935, maintained that the seventh stanza—

> New thresholds, new anatomies! Wine talons
> Build freedom up about me and distill
> This competence—to travel in a tear
> Sparkling alone, within another's will.

—was not only the centerpiece of the poem but also illustrated "both the substance and aspirations of Crane's poetry." "We see that thresholds open out upon anatomies," Blackmur wrote; "upon things to be explored and understood and felt freshly as an adventure; and we see that anatomies, what is to be explored, are known from a new vantage, and that vantage is part of the anatomy."[11] But in his attempt to come up with an overarching view of all Crane's poetry, Blackmur lost sight of the particular moment in which this stanza appears. By interpreting "anatomies" as an embellishment on "thresholds," as though Crane were only bent on spinning his next word luxuriantly out of his last, he views the language as a spontaneous flow of free, if thoughtful, association, some of which is comprehensible, some of which is not. His conclusion matches the assumption that everywhere and always Crane is aiming for sheer ebullience. But in this stanza, Crane is not soaring out, he is flinching inwardly. He now regards himself with the judgmental squint that he had just viewed in others. It is, he now states outrightly, his own elaborate protectiveness that prevents the spontaneous encounter; though wine builds freedom and creates in him a sympathetic response for others, it also builds a freedom that is a cage (as "Wine talons" hold him in their grip) and prevents his sympathies from extending any further than the tears he sheds—"Sparkling alone, within another's will" but hidden completely from that other. Every threshold thus collapses, under the influence of wine, into its dread opposite, an anatomy, a hollow shell, a puppet. What he had arranged to be a threshold, a lure drawing him out of his restraint, is at once, by virtue of its elaborate stage management that places him only in the shadows, a frame that keeps him at a safe remove from others. The entire stanza, far from being the celebratory burble running aground on its own momentum that Blackmur characterized, is a rigorously painful moment of self-analysis. It casts him into the hell of despair in the next stanza.

An immense and bitter irony underlies the concluding stanzas, for in the severity with which he completes his poem, Crane actually stares at himself with the stare of remorseless dismissal that he had been fearful of receiving from another. His reference to Holofernes and Baptist John are especially vindictive to himself, since these men were at least un-done by passions, while he has been undone by his inability to risk even the possibility of passion. The beheading they suffer is what he had feared: the individual will be destroyed when he discovers that what he had thought, or hoped, to be love turns out to be not love but a form of manipulation. Yet though the heads are severed, they continue to live on and talk and even seem to mock him—"Their whispering begins." So destruction, when it actually occurs, is not so fearful as he had believed.

It is proper that at the end of the poem he remains frozen, pivoting helplessly as a puppet. Having withstood his own withering gaze, he cannot but be aware, too late, that he could have sought out another and perhaps borne even dismissal. As the Petrouchka-Pierrot who knows so much but is unable to act, as an individual who turns out to be closer to Prufrock than he would have guessed, he must hear a ghostly, scornful laughter—as at the end of Stravinsky's music—mocking him in the last lines.

What makes "The Wine Menagerie" so compelling is not simply that it demonstrates Crane's sense of his own isolation or reveals him endur-ing an exposure that he dreads: it also evokes a living ideal that emerges from the actuality of the poem and stands over and against his own ac-tions throughout—the ideal of mutually implicatory eyes that meet and exchange regards, overcoming the distance between individuals. The speaker never rises to such an ideal but by the end of the poem he has felt every possible permutation of it. He begins, perhaps hoping for a visionary breakthrough, but he finds himself instead; it is as though the mature Crane looked back upon the early Crane, the Crane intent upon soaring above problems rather than confronting them. Visionary intox-ication is a symptom of a grave timidity that constrains him from taking the very actions he most desires. At the end of the poem he is painfully aware of what he must do to move beyond his isolation, though no more certain than ever of his capacity to rise to the challenge.

5

Crane as Critic

Crane's commentary on his own work—whether it takes the form of letters to his friend or patron, or of quasi-public statements such as "General Aims & Theories," or of his reply to certain questions posed by Harriet Monroe, editor of *Poetry*—has not been subjected to rigorous questioning. Sympathetic critics have used parts of Crane's documents as an adjunct to their own commentary, citing passages on the "logic of metaphor," for example, to offer a general overview of his strategies, while hostile critics have isolated identical passages to indict Crane for his muddled thinking, for his tendency to promote grandiose schemes he could not fulfill.[1]

To a large extent, these documents themselves encourage such casual usage. In them, Crane may speculate at length about matters of theory but only briefly light on illustrations drawn from his own work. An exception, however, is his letter to Harriet Monroe, a reply prompted when she hesitated to publish "At Melville's Tomb" (written in the fall and winter of 1925) because it struck her as so thoroughly obscure. Though more than half of Crane's reply is taken up with a general defense of the "logic of metaphor," in its conclusion he turns to focus on some of the actual lines of his poem.

Perhaps because direct commentary by Crane on his own work is so rare, critics have been especially receptive to his interpretations. Virtually every commentator begins his approach to "At Melville's Tomb" by citing, in some detail, Crane's reply to Monroe. It forms the basis of what can only be called an established reading of the poem, so many unite in agreement over it. According to this reading, the poem displays the poet in the act of identifying with a powerful presence, only this time the presence is not Helen or the Bridge but a fellow poet, Melville. By adopting Melville's insight, Crane is guided into a visionary realm the wondrousness of which is registered in a show of language designed to appear radiant and dazzling. Crane is striving to present his own mystical view of the infinitely numerous correspondences that exist in the world. Both he and Melville pierce beneath the surface of things and celebrate the dynamic flux they perceive: the subtle interpenetrations, the curious overlappings—the way in which, for example, drowned men's bones resemble dice. The poem is, therefore, the revelation of a series of such intertwinings; what Alvarez said about "Voyages II," that it is a "mixer" which brings in conjunction related feelings about the sea and love, could also be applied here: the poem brings in conjunction feelings about the sea and death, and, in homage to Melville, echoes some of his imagery and concerns.

This interpretation of the poem has enjoyed remarkable staying power, prevailing throughout the critical literature on Crane.[2] But this may be because it originates less in a reading of the poem itself than in a reading of the document, the reply to Monroe, which circulates along with it. In truth, the poem is a complex work which the document simplifies considerably. Moreover, the preeminence of the document creates a distinct disadvantage: it not only acts as a barrier to the actual poem, simplifying its motives considerably, but it encourages readers to regard its poet as a mystic, as one who focuses primarily on bizarre connections, who leaps casually from one discrete realm to another. This final impression was not what Crane set out to create when composing "At Melville's Tomb" but it is the impression that has lasted.

1

"At Melville's Tomb" was begun in October 1925, when Crane was in one of his blackest moods, and the poem emerges from this darkness. It insists that men must find the courage to live even in the face of a universe that is blank, entirely unresponsive to their needs. Shortly thereafter, as if in reaction against the bleakness of his own poem, Crane set out dramatically to change the course of his own living. He applied to the financier Otto Kahn for a loan that would free him to devote all his time to work on *The Bridge*, a poem that he had been neglecting for the last two years, writing *Voyages* instead, then assembling his short poems into a first book, then completing additional lyrics to fill the book. In contrast to his previous mood of despair—a mood that had fostered the impressive poems of 1925—he now recommitted himself to his old optimism. He received the loan, and his troubles began to vanish. An outline of *The Bridge* composed in March of 1926 indicates that the sequence was planned to proceed through a series of trials but would end in the sweeping affirmation of the 1923 "Finale."

In fact, this positive thinking was premature. Through the spring of 1926, Crane proved unable to revive his enthusiasm for *The Bridge*, though a series of events allowed him to display some of his newly recovered optimism in one short poem, "Repose of Rivers," composed in April of 1926. After receiving the first of Kahn's loan installments, Crane had retired to the country near Patterson, New York, where he had been invited to stay with Allen Tate and Caroline Gordon. By springtime, when it was evident that work on his long poem had stopped entirely, a quarrel erupted between Crane and the Tates, dissolving the household. Abruptly unhoused, Crane had no other option but to shift his residence to his family's cottage on the Isle of Pines in the Caribbean—a place he had long wished to revisit but to which his mother had prevented him from going, usually by claiming that the property was about to be sold. Under his new emergency conditions, he applied the necessary pressure and received permission to visit. "Repose of Rivers" records his joy at leaving Patterson and heading for the Caribbean. It is a poem in which he relishes the chance to state that now his past is firmly behind him and his future beckons promisingly, and it restores some of the optimism that must have been eroded in the winter and spring of 1926. His reply to Harriet Monroe may have been written at this time, or later in the summer of 1926, but whether the reply dates from late spring or early summer, the point remains: by the time of his reply, he had undergone a considerable change in attitude since completing "At Melville's Tomb."[3]

One of the complications in matching his reply to Monroe with the poem on which that reply centers is that he has already, by 1926, grown distant from the very poem he was asked to defend. Moreover, "At Melville's Tomb" belonged to a distinctly different phase of his own thinking, a bleak and pessimistic phase that he had taken deliberate steps to place behind him. That is complication enough, but an additional complication is that the optimistic mode of "Repose of Rivers" is still uppermost in his mind, and at least a portion of his reply to Monroe is appropriate as a response to this most recent of his poems. A final complication is that in his reply (as in his letters of the same period) Crane displays a considerable animus against Monroe. He had submitted "At Melville's Tomb" to the *Calendar*, a short-lived but influential English journal edited by Edgell Rickword, and the poem had been accepted immediately. On June 19, 1926, he wrote to Waldo Frank: "*The Calendar* is a decent quarterly, and I'm glad to get the 'Melville' in print—not one magazine in America would take it."[4] *Poetry*, however, would publish the poem only if Crane consented to explain a number of its lines. This provisional acceptance was reason enough for dismay: it was disheartening as it was to have his work readily accepted by an English editor while continually rejected by American editors, but it must have been truly dismaying to be asked to justify so many of the lines in his poem, as though his work were hopelessly, immitigably obscure.

These complications must be borne in mind while examining his reply to Monroe. It is a reply that, at first, seems eminently straightforward, divisible into three related sections. The first is introductory, a general defense of what Crane called the "logic of metaphor"; the second comments on examples of that use of metaphor by other, more established poets (with Eliot as the prime example); and the third section specifically addresses the questions Monroe raised about Crane's individual lines. A closer look, though, reveals that none of these sections fits together harmoniously. In the first section, Crane displays his irritation at Monroe for asking such elementary questions (though he masks his irritation somewhat in a ponderous gallantry). In the second section, while offering an example from Eliot, he actually sketches out a reasonable approach to "Repose of Rivers." And in his third section, while purporting to comment on specific lines, he is largely concerned with insisting, more or less defensively, that his meanings are quite obvious, almost self-evident. His reply, then, is actually a strange mixture of animosity and defensiveness, with some useful hints thrown in for a poem, "Repose of Rivers," which is never mentioned. The principal victim of this complication is not Harriet Monroe but "At Melville's Tomb."

One of the major obstacles to considering his reply as a thoughtful defense is that he contradicts himself, reversing his stand in the third section on the very values he had taken pains to establish in his first section. The first section is, in essence, a stinging lecture that chastizes Monroe for constraining the modern poet unnecessarily. (Monroe had left herself open by prefacing her questions with the unfortunate plea: "Take me for a hard-boiled unimaginative reader," and Crane complies with a vengeance.) His overall reaction to her inquiry takes the form of a bristling address to one who is both a "hard-boiled unimaginative reader" and also the editor of *Poetry*: "The nuances of feeling and observation in a poem may well call for certain liberties which you claim the poet has

no right to take. I am simply making the claim that the poet does have
that authority, and that to deny it is to limit the scope of the medium so
considerably as to outlaw some of the richest genius of the past." If
Monroe had been in charge of the Globe Theater, we would have no *King
Lear.* Crane's general defense of his poem hinges on the right of the poet
to risk obscurity; that is a privilege that cannot be abrogated without distressing consequences: "If the poet is held to the already evolved and
exploited sequences of imagery and logic—what field of added consciousness and increased perceptions (the actual province of poetry, if
not lullabies) can be expected when one has to relatively return to the
alphabet every breath or so?" As a polemic, the first third of his reply is
a stirring performance, defending the poet's authority to be an adven-
turous pioneer.

In the final third of his discussion, however, when explaining his own
lines, he diverges markedly from his first approach. There are two problems with his exegetical strategy. The first is that he stops too soon: instead of closely examining and carefully defending his decisions, he offers handy explanations that only serve to raise more questions. He
glosses "Frosted eyes lift altars" by stating that the movement of eyes
raised skyward projects an altar for the deity for which they are searching—and that is his final word. There is no attempt to amplify, no effort
to suggest why a man should be searching for a deity at this point in the
poem. The second problem stems from this first: by refusing to amplify,
he suggests that his meanings are more or less readily available, if not
transparently obvious. His asides and parenthetical remarks help to further that suggestion. Crane continually reminds Monroe that her questions serve only to amaze him: "(Haven't you ever done it?)" he asks at
one point, and notes that one explanation "Refers simply to a conviction
that . . ." and still later he wonders "Hasn't it often occurred that . . . ?"
His tactic in his third section is to maintain that what is obscure to
Monroe is lucid to Crane and, by extension, most readers of poetry. But
are these ostensibly self-evident metaphors the best example of the poet's
right, so eloquently defended by Crane at the outset, to pursue new fields
of inquiry, to provide readers with "added consciousness and increased
perceptions"? Starting out with wonderfully high standards, Crane has
set them aside completely by the close of his piece. If his animus against
Monroe sparked some of the fiery statements in his first section, by his
third section his ire has degenerated into condescension. Through insist-

ing that his lines are not all that complex, he may embarrass Monroe, but he also simplifies his poem drastically.

Monroe asks Crane to explain how one word in his text can possibly lead to another; how can "calyx" give rise to a "scattered chapter"? In reply, Crane maintains that the connections are not as farfetched as they might first appear. A calyx, in the context of the poem, is the whirlpool of a sinking ship, he explains, and that whirlpool casts up detritus which, becauses it is nothing more than the remnants of a ship, makes "a *scattered chapter* so far as any complete record of the recent ship and her crew are concerned." The reader, that is, must supply a missing link— in this case, the drama of a shipwrecked vessel, which perhaps might be deduced from linking the title and its reference to Melville with episodes in Melville's work. Judging from this example and others, the reader is to accept the fact that Crane's poetry has yawning gaps in it, gaps the reader can only hope to negotiate through a forthright exercise of the imagination. Or as Blackmur grumbled in his 1935 essay, Crane's poetry "requires of the reader that he supply from outside the poem, and with the help of clues only, the important, *controlling* part of what we may loosely call the meaning."[5]

Because Crane as critic slides so handily over these gaps, as though completely oblivious to the distances he is leaping, it is easy to assume that his entire poem is built upon a chain of such free associations. This assumption, readily encouraged by Crane's own example, has been generalized into the method for understanding this poem. If Crane builds his poems out of the connotations released in his mind as he sets down his words, then Blackmur is correct when he states, speaking of the seventh stanza of "The Wine Menagerie": "The separate meanings of the words fairly rush at each other; the right ones join and those irrelevant to the juncture are for the moment—the whole time of the poem—lost in limbo." This means, as Blackmur insinuates, that the connotations are liable to be somewhat unusual. The reader, intent on applying this method, is faced with a challenging proposal. Crane, it is believed, leads himself into a construction with its own labyrinthine logic, because Crane attends not to the primary or even the secondary but often the tertiary meanings of his words. (As an alarming example of the method in action, Blackmur cites "talons" as a reference to the playing cards left over after a hand has been dealt.) If the reader can make the identical choices Crane made, hearing in each word the exact inflection that

Crane heard, the reader will be rapidly dispatched forward to the next
word where the process will begin again; if the reader is sidetracked,
however, by hearing the wrong inflection, the poem may simply pass
him by.

Crane's reply invites readers to judge him as a mystic on the loose (as
Gorham Munson described him at this time). To anyone who read his
reply hastily, it would seem certain that, in the third section, his defense
was to insist that the wide gaps between words were not really wide at
all. It all strikes him as perfectly simple. For the reader to conclude,
then, that Crane is very much in another world requires little extra
thought: what is baffling to others is crystal-clear to him. He seems to
espouse those short circuits in thinking that are the stock-in-trade of the
mystic.

To a more thoughtful reader, to a Blackmur, a similar impression
would emerge. If the poet moves by association from one word to the
next, then the only way for the reader to follow him is not by adopting
the usual course—by studying the overall movement or repeated imagery or shifts in rhythm—but by meditating on the reader's own response
to the associations triggered in his mind by Crane's novel word combinations. Sometimes this works, sometimes not. But to understand a Crane
poem, one must give oneself up to it, floating on the surface of its language, encouraging the words to tumble about till they combine in a way
that unlocks a vault in the reader's mind. The puzzlement of Monroe,
who wanted to know "how *dice* can *bequeath* an embassy," can be as-
suaged by meditating on just what Crane might have heard in the secondary, or more likely tertiary, meanings of "dice" and "bequeath" and
"embassy." Awash in a variety of ambiguities, readers and critics have
been led to conclude that this very sense of an extreme disorientation—
of plumbing the depths of words, of establishing novel combinations
(even near-arbitrary combinations)—must have been precisely what
Crane intended to celebrate. Therefore, the established reading consistently emerges, down through generations, as though preserved forever
by the clues deduced from "A Reply to Harriet Monroe": the poem self-
reflexively celebrates its own act of creating new correspondences through
envisioning unlikely possibilities; Crane is a mystic, or a visionary, who
conveys to his readers the vital confusion of the mystical.

2

In the second section of his reply, Crane is neither concerned with defending his own lines nor intent upon embarrassing Monroe; he is concentrating on examples of strained metaphors as they appear in the work of other poets, notably Eliot. In the process, he offers a useful insight for readers who are momentarily baffled by metaphors that seem to be disconcertingly obscure. "You ask me," he begins, paraphrasing Monroe's questions, "how *compass, quadrant and sextant* 'contrive' tides. I ask you how Eliot can possibly believe that 'Every street *lamp* that I pass *beats* like a fatalistic *drum!*'" And he answers his own question obliquely. "There are plenty of people who have never accumulated a sufficient series of reflections (and these of a rather special nature) to perceive the relation between a *drum* and a *street lamp*—*via* the *unmentioned* throbbing of the heart and nerves in a distraught man which *tacitly* creates the reason and 'logic' of the Eliot metaphor." The missing link that binds together the seemingly disparate is, in the case of "Rhapsody on a Windy Night," not a dramatic event to be supplied from outside the poem (such as a vessel undergoing a shipwreck) but the individual personality of the speaker of the poem, the sensibility that is, in the example from Eliot, "distraught." The entire poem, then, could conceivably add up to an intimate portrait of a particular sensibility at a certain time, the whole evoked with an inner clarity impossible in a less compressed form.

"Repose of Rivers" is such a portrait. Images that, by themselves, seem extraordinarily confused come together in the course of the poem to add up to a whole presentation of a personality. In stanzas 2, 3, and 4 of the poem, a group of images abruptly appear, apparently unrelated to each other. "Mammoth turtles" climb "sulphur dreams" in one stanza; in the next, there is a "black gorge" "Where beavers learn stitch and tooth"; and in the last, a city appears "With scalding unguents spread and smoking darts." What is anyone to make of this onslaught of distinctly different landscapes?

The answer is that each landscape is redolent with specific feelings that reflect the sensibility of the speaker. To see the landscape the poet describes is to see into his thoughts, and the images in the landscape all point to an implicit sensibility. Or as Crane says, with regard to Eliot: "It is of course understood that a street-lamp simply can't beat with a sound like a drum; but it often happens that images, themselves totally dissoci-

ated, when joined in the circuit of a particular emotion located with specific relation to both of them, conduce to great vividness and accuracy of
statement in defining that emotion." Read in this light, "Repose of
Rivers" virtually invites the reader to peer into its depths. The opening
landscape, in which "The willows carried a slow sound," suggests a stability, a measure of calm and restraint, that the poet cherishes. It stands
in sharp contrast to the disorderly landscapes of the following stanzas,
each of which the poet is remembering and associating with the past.
Because he is now supported emotionally by the calm of the willows, he
is able to confront these other landscapes which represent difficult memories from troubled times.

One possible complaint that "Repose of Rivers" could provoke is that
the passages in the poem that relate to the past are imprecise and murky
and hectic. They appear, that is, as though they were not fully disclosed
but as flashes from a remote distance, obscure and dark at the edges,
with their implications undeveloped:

> Flags, weeds. And remembrance of steep alcoves
> Where cypresses shared the noon's
> Tyranny; they drew me into hades almost.
> And mammoth turtles climbing sulphur dreams
> Yielded, while sun-silt rippled them
> Asunder . . .

Here it becomes useful to recall that images, "when joined in the circuit
of a particular emotion . . . conduce to great vividness and accuracy in
defining that emotion." The obscurity in the imagery makes sense if the
past which Crane would leave behind him is ugly and fearful. The memory
of that past may cast up haunting, demonic, nightmarish images—images
of "steep alcoves" that invite a perilous fall, or images of shadowless thin
cypresses that offer no respite from the heat of the "noon's / Tyranny"—
but the poet attends to them with a long view, protected by his new sense
of restraint announced at the start, and they lose their stinging quality.
The particular frame of mind being revealed is that of meditating on a
painful, tormenting past, but from a great distance: it is a triumph to be
able to regard these memories at all, so nightmarish are they, and one
cannot peer too closely for the spell of restraint with which the poem
opens may be broken.

If there is any progress to the poem, it is that these images grow increasingly remote and framed and fixed at a distance. Thus the first image, which culminates in "mammoth turtles climbing sulphur dreams," is a nightmarish portrayal of a scene in which objects are being drawn down and sucked under. To plunge into the water might offer itself as a way of escaping from the blistering heat of the sun but, as it turns out, even underwater "sun-silt" appears, as though the tormenting heat was impossible to avoid. It is just as though this very image reflects Crane's relation to it: this past would draw him back, down into its fearful depths where there is no escape. The next stanza, however, of the "black gorge" and the "nestings in the hills" and the winsome, self-contained pond, is viewed by the poet with a control that is reflected in the interactions of the images. The objects are rather primly set apart from one another—the gorge here, the pond there, the nest elsewhere. And the gorge, though black, is not especially fearful: it has become domesticated. The fearful fluidity in the first stanza has become steadily crystallized in the second stanza, and the final stanza, with its distant view of the city, is quickly regarded as though in a frame, summed up in a dismissive fashion that indicates Crane's desire to be utterly remote from it. Though the precise significance and exact emotional weight of the three groups of landscapes can never be adduced, we sense first that each landscape represents a memory that the poet would place behind him, and second that his freedom from their grip is cumulative. The impression is of passing through a recapitulation which leads toward the poised assumption of a new life.

What is striking about the poem is its self-control and serenity, its assured confidence. From the start, it invites revery, musing, speculation. The willows, which might have been cumbersome, turn graceful and stately in the calm way they respond to the wind; the minuet of their movement recalls art framing life in an orderly fashion. Crane takes his measure from their restraint. Their mood, which frames the poet, encourages him to frame images from his past, images that increasingly lose their fearful and frenetic quality.

Accordingly, the conclusion simply affirms a new life filled with promise, a life no longer based upon hectic struggle but grounded in attendance to some inner sense of pausing and pondering:

> There, beyond the dykes,
> I heard wind flaking sapphire, like this summer,
> And willows could not hold more steady sound.

This attractive final statement presents the most intricate landscape so far, a blend of the ocean and the willows. Crane, after his journey through the past, which was also a journey in which he threw off the past, now looks forward to a new serenity such as that offered by the example of the willows—but in addition he enjoys a new sense of sweeping powers continually at work, of the jewels tossed off so effortlessly as the edge of the wind graces the deep oceanic surges. That combination of wind and waves, of the surfaces of air and water meeting to break into "sapphire," offers us a firm view of bright possibility.

Focused entirely on the sensibility of the speaker, the poet who experiences the feelings reflected in these inner landscapes, the images fall into place as proper and appropriate. The disturbance in the landscapes from the past is not to be explained by looking for some suggested incident that is only hinted at in the poetry and needs to be worked up from the random clues offered obliquely. The disturbance, rather, is precisely what Crane wants to convey; viewed in this way, "Repose of Rivers" becomes one of Crane's more accessible poems.[6]

3

"At Melville's Tomb," however, is a far more complex work than "Repose of Rivers." In "Repose," Crane recounts the incidents of a past that is now behind him; persuaded that he is free of that past, he foresees a promising future. The poem is relatively straightforward as it moves toward its resolution; none of the problems touched upon are pressing on him—they are reduced to fragments from the past. Just how the poet endured these conflicts of the past in order to arrive at his new poise is not explored, and in fact the overall form of the poem, along with the cavalier attitude it displays toward past conflicts and future resolutions, resembles that optimistic outline charting the course of *The Bridge* in March 1926.[7]

In "At Melville's Tomb" Crane actually undergoes a trial and finds his integrity tested; the conflict in the poem is not of the past but a continuing, persistent conflict that requires a certain courage to endure. The poem dramatizes the integrity of Melville—and of all mariners and, ultimately, all individuals—who come up against the brutal, blind, impervious waste of the sea. On the sea, men make contact with that which they are usually protected from in the centers of civilization found on land: the total indifference of the universe. That indifference is felt intimately when at sea, not remotely, not as a distant threat. And what that contact reveals is that men cannot bear that indifference: rather than yielding to it, rather than becoming indifferent themselves, they press back against it and define themselves over and beyond it. Though the sea remains forever a blind and ignorant force—casually destroying men, grinding their bones to dust, leveling them indiscriminately into anonymity—Crane insists that men refuse to succumb to an indifference equivalent to that of the sea. Yet the sea always wins. The "frosted eyes" of mariners lift "altars," but they receive not so much as a glimpse of heaven in reply. They peer into the heartless empty depths of the universe, and find there only the reflections of other men (like Melville). Only the sea keeps; men experience loss. And out of such an awareness emerges (in the final lines) both the sense of a universe unfathomably vast in its emptiness as well as the sense of mankind's ardent desire to project human needs and aspirations over and against such emptiness. Crane's urge is to hold Melville as a "fabulous shadow," as one of the giant men who peered into the blankness, even as his spirit fades back into that sea which eventually must claim all.

Since Crane's reply to Monroe stresses none of these themes in "At Melville's Tomb," it is apt that the one critic who has maintained that Crane displays impressive strength of character in his poem is Sherman Paul, who dispenses entirely with the crutch of "A Reply to Harriet Monroe" and interprets the work in the light of his own knowledge of Melville.[8] Yet a knowledge of Melville, while it is an aid to understanding, is not essential for the poem; Crane conveys as much as needs to be known through the rhythmic patterns in each line. And this brings up the final misleading note in Crane's reply to Monroe: in answering her questions, Crane concentrates exclusively on the poem's metaphors, but in this poem the crucial conflicts are conveyed and even resolved through the interactions of meter and rhythm.

Samuel Hazo remarked that "the metrical variations and the skillful manipulation of tonal and alliterative effects contribute . . . functionally to the poem's meaning."[9] Indeed, the entire work is organized around a recurrent rhythmic pattern of a trochee, two iambs, and a caesura, which Crane sets forward in his opening lines, then loses, and eventually recovers in his conclusion. This rhythmic pattern is what guides one through the imagery and helps orient one's understanding; not to hear it

is to misunderstand essential movements in the poem. Exclusive emphasis on metaphor, then, as in Monroe's questions, is almost certain to lead
in erroneous directions.

The rhythms of the opening stanzas reveal the essential drama of the
poem. Though one might arrive at this work knowing nothing of Melville,
by the end of the first stanza he would have experienced all that was
needed for the purpose of this poem:

> Often beneath the wave, wide from this ledge,
> The dice of drowned men's bones he saw bequeath
> An embassy. Their numbers as he watched
> Beat on the dusty shore and were obscured.[10]

The sea appears most attractively, in the first line, as an alluring vista.
The flexing, lilting rhythms of the opening line—in blank verse with a
trochee substituted in the first and fourth feet—evoke a spaciousness
and freedom in a promising expanse. The caesura, enforced syntactically
by the comma, provides a sure pause between the two successive beats of
"wave, wide," and there is a springing step, a lilt to this movement.

This initial impression, strong as it is, is at once threatened; in the
abrupt plunge to the second line, the lilting rhythmical pattern is not
merely interrupted, it is ground down. The difference between the rhythm
in the first line and that of the second line is the difference between the
surface of the sea and its depths. The expectation aroused by the first
line is that a pattern of lilting, spacious rhythms will be established; what
is given instead is the ugly alliteration of "dice of drowned men's bones."
Beneath its romantic vista, the ocean is a graveyard that churns the bones
of dead men about as men might toss dice. Beneath its waves, the ocean
has no lilt, only the rumbling, grinding force of the sea which levels
down all. While the first line distributes its accents so as to create a
specific rhythm, the second line is so much a jumble that one is tempted
to accent "men's" as well as "drowned" and "bones." There is no apparent rhythm to the second line—or so it appears: in fact, the line
brilliantly evokes that leveling press of the ocean which obscures all
individuality.

Against that leveling force, however, a caesura intervenes, a breathing
space between "bones" and "he saw." This is the moment in which the
"he" of the poem—the poet or the poet influenced by Melville's spirit or
Melville himself—exerts himself against the leveling brutality of the
sea. "He saw" is not only an active retort; it is also an assertion that

works against the leveling rhythm and sets in motion again a pattern of steady accents. What it is that "he saw" is inspired by a revulsion against this indiscriminate sea, and the sound of the words alone is almost enough to convey their meaning—they are deliberate and precise, articulately discriminated especially in contrast to the alliterative rumble that precedes them. The thrust against the ocean in these five words— "he saw bequeath / An embassy"—affirms human involvement in contrast to the blank and destructive indifference of the ocean. Melville, knowing that we all come to death—and knowing this vividly, harrowingly, as befits one experienced with the sea—insists that we should take this knowledge of our commonality and use it to conceive of ourselves as united against a shared enemy. His vision of the death of so many men, the death of all men, gives rise to a counter-vision. If the bones of the dead mingle freely, surely men should be free to mingle in a living brotherhood. It's a joint-stock world in all meridians. An "embassy" is free ground, an ideal creation forged by men acting in concert, a place where men choose to suspend the barriers that ordinarily separate them. That idea of an embassy is the heritage that an awareness of the brutal sea bequeaths, an exemplary ideal plucked out of and elevated against the indifference of the waste-sea.

This intense perception lasts only a moment. From the height of activity and participation of "he saw," there is an immediate descent to the helpless passivity of "he watched." The truth emphasized by this abrupt shift is that his ideal, his active insight, his participation, simply has no effect on the indifferent ocean; though he draws out his counterthrust for as long as he can, extending it over the line break so that "bequeath" hovers for a long moment, the ocean is unheeding. It has no effect. The waves roll on, and he must now watch helplessly as his ideal of an "embassy" turns into the "numbers" of endless waves, all of them equally anonymous. The waves may "Beat on the dusty shore" as though they were individual hands beating on a door, but to no avail. The ocean is oblivious, and each wave dies into obscurity, like all the men the ocean has claimed, with another wave ready to supplant the one just broken, and no one wave indistinguishable from any other. Thus the effort to return to the lilting and spacious opening rhythm, the pattern of a trochee with two iambs and a caesura, which actually takes shape in "Beat on the dusty shore," is cruelly dissolved as the line continues into the fuzzy, smudged off-rhyme of "were" and "obscured." The stanza ends disheartening, in what amounts to a mutter or a mumble, and it recalls the dissolution that intervened in the turn from the first line to the second line.

It should be clear that to try to answer the question which Monroe addressed to this stanza—how can dice bequeath an embassy?—is to be led into serious confusion; her question itself is misleading. It is not "Dice" that "bequeath an embassy"; it is the man who sees (perhaps but not necessarily Melville) who bequeathes an embassy by the way in which he looks longingly and posits an ideal in defiant contrast to the dismemberment of dead men's bones that the sea haphazardly tosses about. The drama of the first stanza, expressed completely enough in the poem (though nowhere in Crane's reply) is that, within the enormity of the ocean, itself a vivid evocation of an uncaring universe, Melville stands, projecting his own aspirations, in revulsion from the sea, only to learn how fragile those aspirations are.

Is the sea more powerful than man? Crane's answer is no, but with this proviso: men need courage to stand against the indifference of the sea. An example of such courage appears in a later stanza of the poem, but the key line—"And silent answers crept across the stars"—has been subject to extensive misunderstanding. The majority of commentators, following the lead of R. W. B. Lewis, take this line to be an awesome climax for the poem, a moment in which the religious vision of the mystic-poet discovers an answering response, a silent answer viewed in the heavens; Sherman Paul's commentary is the single exception.[11] For Lewis, the "And" that begins the line is a positive construction; this "And" outweighs the negative connotations of "crept," a word that Paul, to the contrary, associates with Eliot's "A rat crept softly through the vegetation." Paul's sense of the "And" is that it leads into the dead end of "silent" answers. For him, the "And" is in reality a "But," even though the mariners hope for a genuine "And." Lewis believes that answers are answers, whether audible or not: they could be awesome and beatific rather than mute or blank. Can a study of the rhythm in this stanza resolve this dispute?

The rhythm suggests that Lewis is in error. In the third stanza the recurrent pattern of trochee with two iambs gathers itself again, with a strong accent on "Then" in the first line:

> Then in the circuit calm of one vast coil,
> Its lashings charmed and malice reconciled,
> Frosted eyes there were that lifted altars,
> And silent answers crept across the stars.

In the preceding stanza, the detritus of a shipwreck had been thrust to the surface, as though the tendency of the sea is to reject anything human. As the whirlpool winds down, there is a momentary uplift of spirit—but it is only momentary. Though there is a pause after "calm," nothing springs out of it. Indeed, the rhythm of dissolution once again becomes apparent, since "one vast coil" (with its wavering accent on "vast," an accent just strong enough to muddy the rhythm) stretches end-lessly outward, conveying the emptiness of the sea. "Vast" receives a beat almost as strong as the accent on "coil," and this recalls the dis-solute rhythm of "dice of drowned men's bones," in which "men's" re-ceived a beat almost as strong as that on "bones."

But it is against such a dissolution that men must act. The calm of the whirlpool is not a resolution but an empty, mocking calm—no more than the effect of inertia. If it is "charmed" for the moment, it is no more placid than a cobra coiled in sleep. Yet men, unable to endure this emp-tiness, press against it, moving actively forward. Every foot is trochaic in "Frosted eyes there were that lifted altars," and the effect is that of heav-ing, pushing, thrusting. Crane conveys the willful exertion of men as they attempt to lift themselves up from the dragging weight of the ocean and look beyond the flattening level of the horizon. What they seek, those "altars" they project, remains poised as a pinnacle of self-assertion.

Therefore, in the final line, when the steady iambic pentameter forms itself again—in contrast to the pushing, heaving trochaic feet—there is an extraordinary sense of deflation, of letdown. "Silent" answers can only be non-answers, a lack of response rather than a hushed response. And the occurrence of "answers" in the plural cannot indicate a wealth of replies but only that there is no single satisfying response presented to uplifted eyes; what is experienced is the chilling reach of an empty uni-verse. Beyond the flat horizon that rings them round, there is an empty heaven of cold stars. Mariners may plot their course by the stars and even body forth constellations to populate the night sky, but no answer-ing order is present in those lines that creep across the stars. The con-stellations are projections across the void, man-made creations, a sign of man's need for order, not a discovery of an inherent order or supernatural beneficence.

The poem can stretch no further. It has revealed men straining to pro-ject themselves upon the universe at the same time as it has recognized that the universe encroaches upon them, delivering them a stinging mes-sage of their own smallness. Yet despite this agonizing awareness, there is more than ever a keen sense that men are distinguished from the indifference of the universe. Flattened out on an empty horizon, wreckage around them, they instinctively look to the stars, searching at the very instant when they are most leveled.

It is, finally, Crane's belief in an undying human spirit that pervades the climax of the poem, and releases at last that winging, expansive rhythm first heard (then lost) in the opening lines. More important, Crane not only recovers that rhythm but sustains it in a pattern: it occurs not once but twice, sprung by the comma and the line break: "High in the azure steeps, / Monody shall not wake the mariner." The recovery of this pattern takes some of the sting out of the bitter ending of the poem; but the sting is still there: the dominant rhythm remains that of the ground bass of the sea, which always has the last word and which always reminds us of the inevitable dissolution. With two strong beats on "sea keeps," the poem slams shut. As it always will, the sea wins out in the end. But before it wins, Crane affirms the eternal desire of men to continue denying, with their individual actions, with their looking skyward and persistent need for order, its brutal indifference. It is as though no one, individual dream ever comes to pass, yet men never cease from dreaming. If the ending is bitter, it is also swept with grandeur, the grandeur of men who are as fleeting as a "shadow" but also titanic, also "fabulous"—creatures who are creators, who may end in dust and bones but who always stand against that anonymity into which they are driven.

It may be proper that, soon after beginning "At Melville's Tomb," Crane swung back with a new determination, rededicating himself to *The Bridge*. For the poem can also be read as Crane's staunch retort to "Death by Water," section IV of *The Waste Land*. Eliot's sea is the sea of death as sleep; meditating upon that sea, life on earth seems transient and vain. Crane's sea is Melville's tomb; meditating on that sea arouses men to act in concert, to pursue their destinies, however hopeless they may seem. Europe, represented by Phlebas the Phoenician, is an ancient culture which succumbs to its despair; a younger culture, represented by Melville, is animated by the prospect of an insurmountable challenge.

6

The Two Versions of "O Carib Isle!"

Crane frequently tinkered with his poems after they had been accepted by journals, but his usual policy was to restrict revision to a matter of a word or two, or a change in detail. The final version of "Lachrymae Christi," for instance, differs only slightly from the earlier version as it appeared in *The Fugitive:* punctuation has been altered, line breaks shifted, three words eliminated, and one word replaced by another. In a similar way, Crane neatened up a few details in "The Tunnel" after Eliot accepted it for *The Criterion.* "The Harbor Dawn" underwent the most extensive revision of all the *Bridge* poems previously published in journals, but even then there were no substantive changes. A half-dozen lines were rewritten, and some new images were introduced; though the poem clearly benefited from these changes, its overall movement was not altered in any radical way. As a rule, minor changes were all Crane permitted himself once a poem had appeared in print; and for every published poem he could not resist touching up, there is another that he left entirely unchanged.[1]

The exception to this policy of restraint is "O Carib Isle!" and it is, by any standard, a most striking exception. For of all the poems Crane submitted to journals, this one, in its original version, had proved the most popular. It was, for example, the first of his poems to be translated. Prior to founding *transition* Eugene Jolas solicited new work from Crane for an anthology, in French, of contemporary poetry, and his somewhat literal translation of "O Ile des Antilles" appeared in 1928.[2] By then he had asked permission to print the poem in its original English for the first issue of *transition.* Meanwhile, the poem had been submitted to Harriet Monroe at *Poetry,* and she had accepted it without hesitation—a remarkable change from her earlier position which a few months earlier had subjected "At Melville's Tomb" to a third-degree grilling.[3] Finally, the poem had also been submitted, along with two others, to the short-lived English publication, the *Calendar*, where it would almost surely have appeared had not the journal ceased publication. Before word reached him of the demise of the *Calendar*, Crane wrote jubilantly to Yvor Winters: "I think *transition* is a good wedge to use—and I hope it appeals to you somewhat as it does to me. The version of Carib Isle which has appeared therein is slightly different than the version which appears in Poetry— which is again slightly different from the version as it will appear in the Calendar! Hurricanes seem to take with editors—or is it Carib mathematics—at any rate if there were only more Anglicized countries in the world that poems might pay my way around it!"[4] If the *Calendar* had not folded, the original version of "O Carib Isle!" (with very minor modifications from publication to publication) would have appeared on three continents as well as in a French translation.

Yet Crane decided not only to revise it but to revise it substantively. In every stanza, he found details to alter and sometimes whole passages to rewrite. The emphasis of his conclusion was changed, and the meaning of a key word ("shell") was totally redefined. And the first four stanzas were heavily revised to provide a virtually new introduction. The revisions clearly sent the poem in a new direction; they were not minor matters of clarification. Indeed, he had already fussed with the poem in his usual restrained manner, touching up details here and there; the versions submitted to journals, as he mentions to Winters, reflect a few afterthoughts, each of them resulting in minute adjustments.[5]

The two versions of the poem hold special interest, however, not simply because they are evidence of a rare act of revision. Their special interest lies in the fact that Crane almost certainly undertook his revisions after most of *The Bridge* had been completed. When Crane first mentioned to Waldo Frank, in June of 1926, that he was thinking of poems with a Caribbean setting, the only portions of *The Bridge* he had completed were the "Finale" (circa 1923) and the opening stanzas of "Ave Maria." By late March or early April of 1927, when he most likely began his final version, he had completed nearly three-fourths of *The Bridge*.[6] To study the two versions, then, is to examine poetry which may well reflect the change that had come over Crane, enabling him to begin and sustain work on *The Bridge*.

1

When Crane first sent a prospectus to his would-be patron, Otto Kahn, on December 3, 1925, and described his projected long poem as "aiming . . . to enunciate a new cultural synthesis of values in terms of our America," he was using words almost identical to those in remarks addressed to correspondents as long ago as February 20, 1923: "I'm on a synthesis of America and its cultural identity now, called *The Bridge*," and February 18, 1923: "Very roughly, it concerns a mystical synthesis of 'America.'" If these letters are any indication, in the course of nearly three years he had not advanced his thinking about his long poem in any noteworthy way. It is not surprising, then, that after Kahn's generosity freed him to devote full time to his writing, he found he could not write.

The original idea for *The Bridge*, in 1923, had been supported by his newfound enthusiasm for the ideas of Waldo Frank, as explained by Gorham Munson; additional substance came from the excitement of living again in New York City and meeting Frank, Stieglitz, O'Neill, and others. This excitement and enthusiasm was bound to wane. Moreover, he had been writing a group of poems all through 1925, each of which was based on the poet's rigorous questioning of himself—poetry markedly different from his 1923 verse in which the poet held the role of unquestioned seer.

After Crane received the first installment of his "loan" from Otto Kahn, he immediately left the city and, at the invitation of Allen Tate and Caroline Gordon, joined their household in Patterson, New York. Living with the Tates in the country probably protected him from experiencing too many doubts about his project. If, in their conversations, Tate adopted a position opposite to Crane's, this adversary relationship might have only strengthened Crane the harder to cling to his old formulas. But when he abruptly broke with Tate in April of 1926 and removed himself to the remoteness of the Isle of Pines in the Caribbean, he had the opportunity to be his own devil's advocate. Left alone to question his own convictions, he began to inquire into the reasons for his baffling failure to begin his epic; and at this early stage in his thinking, he assigned blame not to himself but to the culture he had been born into. "I have not been able to write one line since I came here," he complained to William Wright, an old high school friend with whom he frequently shared his troubling thoughts. He recommended Spengler's *Decline of the West* and

added: "I get awfully exhausted sometimes, trying to achieve some kind
of consistent vision of things. But I don't seem able to relax—and knowing quite well all the time that most of my energy is wasted in a kind of
inward combustion that is sheer nonsense. All else seems boresome,
however,—so I must continue to kill myself in my own way."[7] Things
seem out of focus, writing poetry is a mechanical task, an alternative to
boredom but perhaps a waste of energy. Out of this dispirited, lethargic
mood emerges the first version of "O Carib Isle!"—a poem that attempts
to identify the source of Crane's lethargy as outside his own control.

The document which encouraged him to focus on why things seemed
so out of focus (and permitted him to write if not *The Bridge* at least
"O Carib Isle!") is a little-known essay by I. A. Richards which was, in
fact, the "admirable essay" he strongly recommended to Harriet Monroe
when publicly corresponding with her over "At Melville's Tomb." Published in the July 1925 *Criterion*, the essay was titled "A Background for
Contemporary Poetry,"[8] and Crane was almost certainly familiar with it
prior to his crisis in the early summer of 1926, for Richards touches on
contentions that Crane amplified to some extent in "At Melville's Tomb,"
begun in October 1925.[9]

In his essay, Richards singles out for merit the poetry of Thomas
Hardy. Hardy alone, in contrast to Walter de la Mare, W. B. Yeats, and
D. H. Lawrence, rises to face squarely the unique dilemma of the modern poet: "He is the poet who has most steadily refused to be comforted.
The comfort of forgetfulness, the comfort of beliefs, he has put these
both away. Hence his singular preoccupation with Death; because it is in
the contemplation of Death that the necessity for human attitudes to
become self-supporting, in the face of an indifferent universe, is felt
most poignantly. Only the greatest tragic poets have achieved an equally
self-reliant and immitigable acceptance." "At Melville's Tomb" offers
Melville as an American counterpart to Hardy; Crane may have been
moved by Richards's parochialism (Richards deals exclusively with British poets, though he reserves a footnote for Eliot) to recognize an equivalent strength in American poetry.

Crane brought to his Melville poem not only his own experience of
Melville but his own experience of the burdens of the poet, and "At
Melville's Tomb" leaves Richards's essay far behind. Not so, however,
with the original "O Carib Isle!" which seems directly indebted to the
essay: in his poem, Crane enacts a crisis that was first sketched out by
Richards. At a time in the far past, Richards argues, poetry was allied

with magic. The natural world could be viewed as a sympathetic presence because men thought it could be controlled by a mastery of language: "By the Magical View I mean, roughly, the belief in a world of spirits and powers which control events, and which can be invoked and, to some extent, controlled themselves by human practices. The belief in Inspiration and the beliefs underlying ritual are representative parts of this view." The reason this magical view proved so enduring, Richards claims, is that it could afford an outlet for the emotional needs of men. The universe, in other words, was not an alien entity but responsive to human wishes. Of course we know today, Richards says, that this was an illusion, but to ancient men it had the status of a necessary fiction:

> the Magical View, being an integration of nature in terms of man's most intimate and most important affairs, very soon came to suit man's emotional make-up better than any other view possibly could. The attraction of the Magical View lay very little in the actual command over nature which it gave. . . . No, what gave the Magical View its standing was the ease and adequacy with which the universe therein presented could be emotionally handled, the scope offered for man's love and hatred, for his terror as well as for his hope and his despair. It gave life a shape, a sharpness, and a coherence that no other means could so easily secure.

What disjoins the alliance between nature and man is modern scientific knowledge. At present, dispassionate analysis is the sole satisfactory means of attaining the truth, and the truth, by contemporary scientific standards, always excludes the emotions. As a result, Richards says, "we have the universe of the mathematician." Though men still long for a god, there is no place for one in the modern universe. The god who can be accommodated to "Einstein's General Theory of Relativity does not make an emotional appeal." And various "emergent deities" proposed by well-meaning scientists and concerned philosophers are inadequate because they are so obviously makeshift and mundane. These invented deities "are there to meet a demand, not to make one; they do not do the work for which they were invented."

Hardy's bleak poetry, Richards maintains, is noteworthy for at least acknowledging this new awareness. By insisting that men must band together "to become self-supporting," Hardy responds to the revolutionary disruptions of the present without resorting to nostalgia. The same cannot be said of de la Mare, who tends "to seek shelter in the warmth of his familiar thickets of dream." Yeats and Lawrence also, according to

Richards, are guilty of "dodging the difficulties," one by retreating to a hermetic realm of "symbolic phantasmagoria," the other by attempting to induce "the mentality of the Bushmen." All four poets together register the same shock of recognition, but Hardy alone refuses to succumb to a form of withdrawal.

2

In the original, 1926 version of "O Carib Isle!," Crane is replaying Richards's summarization of the plight of the modern poet. But he does not respond, as he had earlier in his Melville poem, by affirming that men must grow together; his plight, at this moment, is far too crucial and far too personal for him to endure the thought of a long-range solution. Though he does refuse to display any of the ingenuity for which Richards indicts Yeats and Lawrence, he simply pronounces himself unable to rise to the call. The days of the seer, the profoundly dynamic poet animated by something akin to Richards's "Magical View," are over; everything is now a waste.

The poem begins somewhat hopefully and moves to its apocalyptic conclusion only after a series of disappointments. It opens with the poet in an island graveyard:

> The tarantula rattling at the lily's foot
> Across the feet of the dead, laid in white sand
> Near the coral beach; the small and ruddy crabs
> Stilting out of sight, that reverse your name—
>
> And above, the lyric palsy of eucalypti, seeping
> A silver swash of something unvisited . . .

As bleak as this is, the immediate inclination of the poet is to light on the one detail that will vivify the abysmal scene. Man, it turns out, is sharply distinguished from the aimless island creatures, for someone has made an attempt, however pathetic, to decorate the graves of the dead. And this arouses his interest:

> Suppose
> I count these clean enamel frames of death,
> Brutal necklaces of shells around each grave,
> Laid out so carefully. This pity can be told . . .

Unlike creatures, men mourn. Graves are decorated, even in this remote outpost of civilization. The tarantula, by contrast, rattles witlessly, pro-

faning the feet of the dead upon which it scrabbles unknowingly. Crane
sees that it has heedlessly uprooted or thrust aside a lily, that emblem of
human remembrance, of mourning. The poet can still side with mankind, in its inclination to ritualize death and bring order to chaos, and he
invites himself to "count"—to give weight to—"these clean enamel
frames of death, / Brutal necklaces of shells around each grave / Laid out
so carefully." Though the shells make up a "Brutal" necklace, they are
only brutal because they cannot entirely disguise their origin in nature—
yet men have tried to shape them purposefully and that is what counts.
Someone has polished them to a gloss like "clean enamel frames," and
someone has arranged them so they appear "Laid out so carefully."
Crane, noticing all this, registering these signs of mourning, murmurs
"This pity can be told," and moves apart from the heedlessness of the
tarantula and the crabs.

In these efforts, his agency is the wind, a traditional ally between
the human and the natural worlds. The wind ruffles the fronds of the
eucalypti, making them wave in a "lyric palsy," as though they were
partly alive, though diseased. In this deserted graveyard, the wind is a
breath of air that offers pity to the visitor, just as the visitor offers his own
pity as he searches the graves for a name, a further sign of the human
need to take an individual stand against death:

> And in the white sand I can find a name, albeit
> In another tongue. Tree-name, flower-name deliberate,
> Gainsay the unknown death. . . . The wind,
> Sweeping the scrub palms, also is almost kind.

Here is Inspiration responding to Ritual, Richards might say: the poet is
moved to "find a name" by acknowledging the human desire to act in a
way distinct from the indifference of nature. The urge to mark a grave, or
to identify a particular tree or flower, is in some way creative, a mark of
individualizing identity. It militates against death in all its anonymity.
Man uses his language to give a shape to nature.

But the poem now begins to register Crane's acute awareness of the
inadequacy of such gestures; the magical view, one might say, is no
longer efficacious. Though he makes his effort at naming, how feeble and
slight it seems, how little an impact it makes upon the scene. Instead of
a rousing, passionate wind, what swirls in? "The wind, sweeping the scrub
palms, also is almost kind." The wind may appear to join with the poet in
expressing pity for those laid out in death, but the wind is perceived at

once to be enervated and exhausted. Worse yet, the wind is "almost kind" (with a pun here on kindred), as though it took pity on the poet much as the poet, in passing, was inclined to take pity on the dead. The wind is patronizing the poet just as the poet is patronizing the dead. Rather than the poet being in control of the wind, the wind appears to mimic the poet—or so it seems: for the inescapable truth underlying this is that the modern poet must know that his words have no real effect, that he is only playing a game, that he can speak all he wants but he will never "Gainsay the unknown death." The modern poet, in truth, is just a kind of sweeper, tidying up as best he can.

The truth is that the modern poet resides within a new, bleak universe of "Carib mathematics" in which "to count" no longer means anything but simply adding numbers. There is no overarching, attentive god with whom to commune (meditating on death in a deserted graveyard had been a classic theme for the poet), and there is no principle of emotional order which can be shared with nature. There are only the paltry efforts of men trying, as Crane wrote William Wright, "to achieve some kind of consistent vision of things." But the game is exhausting:

> But who is Captain of this doubloon isle
> Without a turnstile? Nought but catchword crabs
> Plaguing the hot groins of the underbrush? Who
> The Commissioner of mildew throughout the senses?
> His Carib mathematics dull the bright new lenses.

Here he lashes out with irony at this new, vastated universe. He would, if he could, act brightly—but he disparages this, above all, as a delusion, as a donning of "bright new lenses" that might make the world seem radiant. His own effort at counting the pitiful shells turns those lenses "dull," for it makes him sense that his gestures are no more than a game, a pale echo of what poets once truly believed: that the world was animated by the poet's language, made fertile and fecund by his speech. Now, mockingly, "catchword crabs" are "Plaguing the hot groins of the underbrush." His longing for a "Captain," a figure of authority, is a genuine longing for an overarching god, but he mocks that possibility too. Indeed, mockery is the one avenue open to the individual grown suddenly aware of the extent of his helplessness. The world is a "doubloon isle / Without a turnstile": nature no longer accepts the coin of language to make the moves men wish. "Catchword crabs" now dominate, spreading disease and sterility, implying that nature may be a harlot, exacting payment in coin but repaying with disease.

From this point on, Crane deliberately dramatizes his own collapse, relinquishing all responsibility, locked in a deepening bitterness. He yearns to escape from the island, rising "White and black along the air" until he "joins the blue's comedian host." Here is an image of defeat and withdrawal—of going up in smoke to dissolve in thin air—articulated in an arch and deprecating manner. He pledges never to involve himself again in the fruitless struggle epitomized by "the dozen turtles" who are "Bound . . . on the wharf / Each twilight—still undead," "Huge, over-turned: such thunder in their strain!" These are like old gods who live on absurdly though they are long obsolete—as out-of-date as "pilgrims" beginning a spiritual journey, or as out-of-date as epic poets (the modern versions of pilgrims). Crane regards them with some of the pitying admiration reserved for misguided souls, and then he firmly withdraws. He has consigned himself to the sidelines, there to dawdle as a spectator, "satin and vacant." It is not for him to be involved. The days of the great poet are passed. As a shell of his former self, he prefers to fade out, becoming "the ember, / Carbolic, of the sun exploded in the sea."

The very idea of the great poet, as he had once cherished it (and attempted to live it in his earlier plans for *The Bridge*), now appears to him as hopelessly anachronistic. Richards's essay supports his conclusion; a reading of *The Decline of the West* offers additional evidence. And most likely he was remembering the decision of Rimbaud after he had completed *A Season in Hell* and abandoned poetry forever. In a letter to Waldo Frank on June 20, 1926, he attempted to justify his despair:

> The validity of a work of art is situated in contemporary reality to the extent that the artist must honestly anticipate the realization of his vision in "action" (as an actively operating principle of communal works and faith), and I don't mean by this that his procedure requires any bona fide evidences directly and personally signalled, nor even any physical signs or portents. The darkness is part of his business. It has always been taken for granted, however, that his intuitions were salutary and that his vision either sowed or epitomized "experience" (in the Blakeian sense). Even the rapturous and explosive destructivism of Rimbaud presupposes this, even his lonely hauteur demands it for any estimation or appreciation. (The romantic attitude must at least have the background of an age of faith, whether approved or disproved no matter.)

Just as this letter is an effort to justify the inertia of the modern poet, focusing the blame on the lack of an "age of faith," so the 1926 "O Carib Isle!" is an avowal of the hopelessness of the modern poet's task. He anticipates "the realization of his vision in 'action'" by moving from his pitying view of the graves toward an effort to speak a "tree-name, flower-name," wishing to transform the sterility that engulfs him. When he has no response, he recognizes that he is simply invoking a "Magical View" which can no longer be credited; the wind does not serve at his plea-sure—the wind reflects his own state of mind: it is a bitter mirror. At one time, it had been taken for granted that the poet's "intuitions were salu-tary." But now his perceptions sow nothing, they fall on barren ground because there is no one to believe them. He has lost the attention of an audience, an attention he once believed he had or could have, in writing "Faustus and Helen," when he felt literally possessed by an insight that he believed his audience needed. Now, in his isolated position, as the single human in the cemetery of the dead, he typifies the modern poet's relation to the world, to an unheeding, oblivious audience. Rimbaud's violent raptures depended on an audience that could be shaken (and per-haps secretly wished to be shocked) out of its moribund lethargy. When Rimbaud wrote (in the T. Sturge Moore translation that accompanied Edgell Rickword's *Rimbaud: The Boy and the Poet,* the volume through which Crane knew Rimbaud)

> Never a hope,
> Not a petition,
> Skill and patience
> Torment is certain.
>
> No tomorrows,
> Satin embers,
> Your ardour
> Is Duty.
>
> I have recovered it.
> —What? Eternity.
> It is the sea merged
> With the sun.[10]

—he was insisting on the poet's right to bring forward, however much it might cost him, a shattering dynamic vision that would (ideally) forever after alter the way the world was viewed. But Crane can no longer imag-ine recovering such elemental confidence in self-expression. In his poem he ends by postponing all effort. Rimbaud had rejected "tomorrows" of "Satin embers" in his actions, because his new ardor is a duty; Crane lapses into satin vacancy because the days of greatness are over. He has been virtually marooned on an isolated island, abandoned to a cemetery, in a way that is not at all unique but in fact characteristic of the place of the poet in modern culture.

3

In the 1927 version, the words of the poet are attended to critically, in such a way as to expose that it is the poet himself—not his "situation"— that is responsible for the sterility in which he feels trapped. The earlier poem is an act of justification, and what intricacy it displays is the result of carrying forward a complex argument in a somewhat indirect manner. The later poem is an exposure of the poet in the act of attempting his act of justification, and its genuine intricacy stems from the poet working his way toward an understanding of how he has created his own sterile situation.

The most dramatic difference between the two versions centers on the meaning of the word "shell." In the 1926 version, a "shell" is a husk, a hollowed-out, enfeebled form of that which had once been vital and alive. The poet himself has become such a shell, and he concludes:

> Slagged of the hurricane, cast within its flow,
> I congeal by afternoons here, satin and vacant.
> You have given me the shell, Satan—the ember,
> Carbolic, of the sun exploded in the sea.

He regards himself as the cooled slag cast off from that hurricane force which used to surge through all poetry. Typically, the romantic poet sold his soul, desiring to gain knowledge, to break past the boundaries of convention. For the sake of his own potency he was willing to risk his alienation. The modern poet, venturing the same, discovers he has been given an empty shell, a brittle husk, a fading ember. Without an audience bound by convention, believing in a single faith, there is no satanic majesty or meaningful rebellion possible. Thus the rhythm in these last lines, with accents on "of" and "in," is appropriately frail and feeble.

By contrast, Crane ends his 1927 version in an explosion of pent-up fury:

> You have given me the shell, Satan—carbonic amulet
> Sere of the sun exploded in the sea.

The hissing "s" predominates, mimicking the boiling waters of the sun exploding the sea into steam, the sea surging around the sun. The rhythm now bristles with energy: after the alliteration (and rocking trochee and iamb) of "Sere of the sun," there is the outburst of "exploded in the sea." It is as though enormous emotions, suppressed or misdirected in the course of the poem, are suddenly released apocalyptically. What is the source of this new energy and wrath?

In 1927, Crane notices a new, significant detail: all the creatures on the island possess a tough, protective shell, from fiddler crabs to terrapin. On this grim island, it is fearful to be exposed. And the crabs and terrapin have cause to fear for their flesh is prized: their soft insides will be torn from their tough, protective carapaces, if they are caught. In 1927, Crane notices the resemblance not only between the creatures but also between himself and the creatures; he is striving to throw up protective barriers between himself and the island life around him, using words as counters or spells, distancing himself by claiming a certain authority. Appalled as he is by the brutality of the island life and its creatures, he acts deliberately in the hope of distinguishing himself from them. But in this version, he recognizes a startling truth: the more he toughens himself against those creatures, the more like them he becomes, and the result of his toughening is to draw him back toward that which he had tried to evade. He becomes one more tough island creature, fearful of being gutted.

At the end of his poem, he realizes with some horror what he has become. His casting, which takes him apart from the flow, is in itself a most acute form of evisceration. By creating a shell for himself he has gutted himself, and his moment of damnation occurs when he turns his back on the image of the huge terrapins who are struggling, against all odds, to live. Fearful of seeing himself in them, helpless yet persevering, he chooses instead to "congeal by afternoons here," remote and distant from their reminders of his plight; as deeply touched as he is by the vision of the undying terrapins, he refuses to see himself in them, and as he cuts his ties, at that moment it is clear that he has lost all that he would want to preserve. By building a shell around himself he has lost the very soul, the very sensitivity, he had intended to protect. More precisely, shell and soul have congealed in one terrible fusion, into a "carbonic amulet." An amulet is a charm, intended to protect its bearer and to ward off evil—but the amulet he has adopted renders him immune from any involvement with the life around him. In suppressing his feelings, his pity and terror for the terrapins, in denying that they are a mirror of himself, he cuts himself off from his own humanity. And the amulet he bears is "carbonic"—burned out and useless: the protection it offers to him burns out the very soul it was intended to protect. The soul has fused with the shell, and when Crane realizes how perversely he has confounded himself, how he has played the Satan to himself by so successfully encasing himself in aloofness—he spins in rage and frustration. Is the sun comparable to the shell and the sea comparable to the soul? The suggestion is likely—but the point is, Crane senses in a flash how shell and soul have fused together and he recoils in horror. The seer is sere, withered and aged by his erroneous vision.

The 1927 version is a remarkable act of self-understanding in which Crane sees through the evasiveness that was at the base of the 1926 version. He now understands that his own fears trap him and push him toward that which he would recoil from. The first note of the major changes to come occurs in his revised description of the decorations around the graves:

> And yet suppose
> I count these nacreous frames of tropic death,
> Brutal necklaces of shells around each grave,
> Squared off so carefully. Then
>
> To the white sand I may speak a name, fertile
> Albeit in a stranger tongue. Tree names, flower names
> Deliberate, gainsay death's brittle crypt.

This version blurs the contrast between man and creature. The "Brutal necklaces of shells" are no longer "clean enamel frames" "Laid out so carefully," but "nacreous frames of tropic death," "Squared off so carefully." Instead of regarding the shells as decorative, tender, though pitifully crude examples of tidy care, as feeble yet somehow heartening emblems of the reverence men display for their dead, of the order men wish to create, he now views them as shrewd strategic placements, aggressively set in place so that their sharp edges discourage the casual tarantula from trespassing, from haplessly uprooting lilies. These necklaces are "Brutal" not because (as in the 1926 version) they remain a part of nature despite the efforts of men to polish them and order them in some sort of a pattern; rather, they are brutal because they have been turned back against nature by man. Any tarantula venturing to nest in the flowers of these graves will be razored by the "nacreous frames"; they

appear as "Squared off so carefully" because they are squared off for
combat. They protect territory—they are the graves' defense, the graves'
carapace, against intruders. As Crane says now in his revised first
stanza, "—No, nothing here / Below the palsy that one eucalyptus lifts /
In wrinkled shadows—mourns." Not even the men who care for these
graves of their dead. The great danger on this isle is that men, acting to
deny the life around them, will inadvertently become identical to that
which they would deny.

Crane's own actions are exposed as increasingly desperate. For example, the "Then" which hangs in midair at the close of the stanza
is ready to propel us forward, yet the word dangles there awkwardly,
stalling the poem. The bits of syllogistic reasoning which dot this version
stick out noticeably: "And yet suppose" also dangles in suspension
before a line break. These are revealed as calculated efforts, asserted
hastily, with no small degree of desperation. No pity animates his decision to "count" the shells. Here, to "count" verges close to manipulation. He hopes to use words aggressively to ward off the threat of brutality. And the very idea of uttering "Tree names, flower names" is
undertaken not in the hopeful intent of bringing fertility to the island;
rather, it appears as a strategy designed to erect a barrier around himself. He is uninterested in finding a name, as he had been earlier; he is
concerned only to speak a name. The promise to utter these fertile
names, then, sounds like a rumbling threat, an insistence of his own
control over his situation. (In this version, we notice that he never says
the names but only threatens to say them.) Instead of mourning in a
graveyard, this is more like whistling in the dark, and the formulaic
quality of the whole enterprise is underscored by the "Meanwhile" that
leads into the stanza's conclusion:

> Meanwhile
> The wind that knots itself in one great death
> Coils and withdraws. So syllables want breath.

As he blows himself up, the wind suddenly withdraws, as though as a
reminder of how little actual control he has over matters. Its withdrawal
is a stinging rebuke to him, utterly deflating to his purpose; it literally
steals his breath.

If the poet in 1926 was an isolated representative of humanity, affirming a desire for order against the oblivion of death, the poet in 1927 is
akin to a frantic sorcerer whose efforts to gain command over his sur-

roundings always collapse. The identity of the Captain in 1927 cannot be referred away to some missing God who should be present but who is unaccountably absent; the identity of the Captain in the new version belongs to this poet who fits the island so perfectly because he strives, like the other creatures on it, to evade any direct encounter:

> But where is the Captain of this doubloon isle
> Without a turnstile? Who but catchword crabs
> Patrols the dry groins of the underbrush?
> What man, or What
> Is Commissioner of mildew throughout the ambushed senses?
> His Carib mathematics web the eyes' baked lenses!

In 1926, when the harsh logic of nature proved insurmountable, he was simply alienated; the "bright new lenses" he had wished to don, to take note of the details such as "clean enamel frames," turned "dull," and he went off, limping, to sulk. In 1927, his own efforts to evade the island draw him back centrally to the island, leaving him stranded, choked, and constricted as never before. His "Where" and "Who" and "What man, or What" create a sour, wheezing, ironic wind that blows desperately through these lines. The more he struggles to escape, the more deeply he is implicated in entanglements that "web" even further the "eyes' baked lenses."

In 1926, following this stanza, Crane indulged himself in a posture of sheer withdrawal, trumpeting his escape from the conditions which he took as disdainful. The stanza is little changed in 1927, largely because it now fits so clearly into the deadly progress of the poem:

> Under the poinciana, of a noon or afternoon,
> Let fiery blossoms clot the light, render my ghost
> Sieved upward, white and black along the air
> Until it meets the blue's comedian host.

This now appears as a complex image of evisceration: the poet begs the "fiery blossoms" to fuse together and "clot the light" and become an umbrella for his inert body to collapse beneath while he journeys upward imaginatively in escape toward some realm of cool blue skies. It focuses all the evasive efforts in the first half of the poem and introduces the image of a soul escaping from a body. But it is an escape that is clearly unsuccessful. In 1926, his ghost was "black and white" as it sieved itself upward, in an easy catch phrase that helped to spring it skyward; in

1927, his ghost is the more cumbersome "white and black" and suggests that evasive action is not as simple as black and white. In 1926 he successfully "joins" with the host he imagines in the air, decadently merging with the oblivious reaches of an azure sky; in 1927, he "meets" the host, as though the sky itself had also grown into a barrier. Barriers within barriers, always forcing the poet back upon himself—that is the pattern established in 1927.

Most significant is the masterful change of details in the next stanza. In 1926, the "dozen turtles" were viewed at twilight:

> Let not the pilgrim see himself again
> Bound like the dozen turtles on the wharf
> Each twilight—still undead, and brine caked in their eyes,
> —Huge, overturned: such thunder in their strain!
> And clenched beaks coughing for the surge again!

The turtles at twilight accommodate themselves to the poetry of fading embers. Here are the last lingering remnants of an elemental strength, "Huge" but "overturned," in their final gasps. As these turtles echo the thunderous strains of a remote ocean, so this poem evokes the last gasps of great cosmic poetry. Here is a fleeting glimpse, from a great distance, of the surge that once animated all great poetry, back in the days of faith. Now it is stranded, beached, and will fade out as evening falls.

In 1927, the "huge terrapin" are not so easily or neatly accommodated. Their struggle is far more agonizing, enervating, and unavoidable because it is glimpsed at daybreak, at the very opening of what is to be a new day:

> Let not the pilgrim see himself again
> For slow evisceration bound like those huge terrapin
> Each daybreak on the wharf, their brine caked eyes;
> —Spiked, overturned; such thunder in their strain!
> And clenched beaks coughing for the surge again!

It is easier to turn away from the turtles in 1926 as evening falls; they are, for all their "thunder," about to fade away into the darkness. As it appears in 1927, the image is horrifying: at daybreak, the terrapin have been left cruelly and deliberately to bake in the sun, as part of the process of separating their soft insides from their hard outer shells. Yet their suffering is out in the open and impossible to avoid: daybreak for them is not a new dawn but the opening of long hours of torture. To deny this image of blatant suffering is to court one's own damnation: it is to adopt a very tough viewpoint indeed, and it is this denial, this ultimate betrayal—of the creatures and of himself—that hurls Crane into his final stanza to see in horror how his own toughness has eviscerated him. The terrapin are creatures who struggle awesomely against all odds; doomed to die, they still yearn to live, and their very strain cries out for a thunder that would promise rain—true fertility, not the pseudo-fertility of mouthing "Tree names, flower names." As creatures who are condemned to die but persist, even rage, to live, they indict the poet in his longing for aloof detachment. The 1926 turtles were an image of the poet fading out: he only hoped to pass away in a more civilized fashion, without a struggle, as a fading ember. The 1927 terrapins are an image of a courage that the poet has heretofore lacked; they serve to call him back to himself, to make him aware of how complete his corruption has become.

In 1927, Crane mercilessly reveals the cowardice in his own actions, a cowardice that had been masked in the 1926 version by his own assured self-pity. The two versions portray, in a summary fashion, Crane's attitudes before and after beginning *The Bridge*. In 1926, he was insisting, still, on the privileged status of the poet; the poet was the one responsible for stirring up the sluggish multitudes. And when his gestures proved ineffective or futile (as they had for many months) he had no other recourse but to turn and lash out at the deplorable conditions into which the world had fallen. Spengler was correct all along, and Richards had a handy diagnosis. When the poet fails, it is because the world no longer recognizes—and thus no longer deserves—great poetry, the uplifting sweep of the vital imagination that sees an underlying order and discovers an animating spirit.

In 1927, Crane looks back on this petulant withdrawal with dismay and with disgust, but with a measure of lucid understanding. He endows the poet not with great powers but with great responsibility. The poet is responsible for what he has made for himself, and Crane understands the extent to which his actions have consequence, responding to pressures from within the scene and creating new pressures. It is not the diffidence of an uncaring world that destroys the poet but the poet's failure to involve himself in the world around him, however grim and bleak it may at first appear. If one can comprehend the ways in which he is the source of his problems—that it is not the universe allied against him but his own poisoning weaknesses, even his own desires to erect a fiery, protective barrier around himself—then he is in a position to begin to change him-

self and thereby change his world. That is one of the fundamental under-
standings that will emerge when he begins at last to write *The Bridge*,
not from a center of towering strength but from a center of responsive
sympathy; it is an understanding he presses upon himself again in the
final version of "O Carib Isle!"

7

The Bridge in *The Bridge*

Before he left New York in the spring of 1926, Crane began his sojourn on the Isle of Pines by dashing off "Repose of Rivers" and posting it to Marianne Moore at *The Dial*.[1] The very act of submitting this poem to Moore appears to be a gesture of defiance as well as a reassertion of authority. Certainly he still sounds defiant a month later: "Yes, Marianne took the little specialty I wrote for her," he commented, "and even proof has been corrected and sent back. This time she didn't even suggest running the last line backwards."[2] Moore, after all, had been responsible for dismembering "The Wine Menagerie," as if to flaunt to Crane his inability even to control the messages in his own poetry. To submit "Repose of Rivers" to her is to declare that this poet is in control as never before. The poem is a firm, forthright statement, a commitment to a new strength of purpose, an assumption of a new responsibility. The past is emphatically set aside as the poet turns outward to the sea and sun, prepared to embark on new discoveries.

Yet a closer study of "Repose of Rivers" foreshadows the dilemma that will frustrate him soon enough. The poem generates no firm basis for its optimism. It registers, in its three middle stanzas, an increasingly detached and distant view of the confusions of the past, but the poet is simply gliding away from these confusions as though being reborn were simply a matter of a change of scene. Predictably, then, only a few weeks later, Crane is steeped in the doubts and uncertainties that had haunted him earlier. To slough off the past by looking ahead to the future is easy enough to entertain; to sustain that hopeful movement is more of a challenge. By the time of the first version of "O Carib Isle!," he is casting about for excuses to justify his considerable enervation; the first version evokes the atmosphere of sterility and diffidence with which he feels surrounded—the lack of participation, the indifference toward poetry, which mark him as isolated in the graveyard of the twentieth century.

Crane's problems on the Isle of Pines can be traced to many things, but foremost among them must be the outline he drafted for his epic sometime in March of 1926. The outline comes in the form of a progress report to Otto Kahn, in a letter of March 18, 1926; but since Crane had been unable to write for the last three months, there is little to report. When not writing, however, he had been at work—probably at the urging of Allen Tate—plotting the course of his epic. Tate's contribution seems almost certain, for this initial plan for *The Bridge* heavily emphasizes history, and one of Tate's persistent complaints, in his several essays on the poem, is that Crane passed too cavalierly over the history of America. In his original framework, this was not so: if anything, Crane relied heavily on American history—so much so that his epic, in its first overall format, seems as though it will be nothing more original than a panoramic overview of the course of America. It was to take place in six sections:

      I Columbus—Conquest of space, chaos
     II Pokahantus—The natural body of America-fertility, etc.
    III Whitman—The Spiritual body of America
         (A dialogue between Whitman and a dying soldier in a
         Washington hospital; the infraction of physical death,
         disunity, on the concept of immortality)
     IV John Brown
         (Negro porter on Calgary Express making up berths and
         singing to himself (a jazz form for this) of his
         sweetheart and the death of John Brown, alternately)
      V Subway—The encroachment of machinery on humanity; a kind
         of purgatory in relation to the open sky of last section
     VI The Bridge—A sweeping dithyramb in which the Bridge
         becomes the symbol of consciousness spanning time and
         space

This ambitious scheme is no less than the history of America; under the guise of writing about Whitman, in section III for example, Crane presumably hoped to evoke the disunity brought to the nation by the Civil War. (The influence of Tate once again seems strong.) The following poem, section IV, on John Brown, would possibly have intended to show that the wounds of the Civil War were still not healed. The virgin continent, discovered by Columbus and represented in all its ideality by Pokahantus, had been violated by strife between brothers. That strife, furthermore, not only persisted but seemed perhaps to be integrated permanently through the presence of the machine; in section V, the subway represents the "encroachment of machinery on humanity." What can restore unity to this immense scene of discord? Crane has his "Finale" on hand: the Bridge, symbol of "consciousness spanning time and space."

It is not the ambition of this poem that makes it seem bound to fail, at least as it is presented in the progress report to Kahn: it is its sheer impersonality and its stark conventionality. There is nothing in the material to discover; it is as though the poem is already familiar—as indeed it might be: it has the air of a pageant that might be organized for the centennial of a town or city. Crane, of course, already has his conclusion written; he needs only to discover why his conclusion is apt, but his approach to that problem has led him into a copybook version of American history which is a creative dead end. Staring at this rough outline for the winter and spring of 1926, it is not surprising he could write only a few lines. His frustration, which culminated in a fierce quarrel with the Tates, is perhaps understandable, even though the relief expressed in "Repose of Rivers" seems more a hopeful wish than ever.

The impossibility of ever writing an epic of America struck him most forcefully after a few weeks of isolation on the Isle of Pines. The easy solution he had plotted for himself in early 1926, and anticipated recovering again after breaking with the Tates, is no longer in sight. And in a sober letter of June 20, 1926, he virtually renounces his calling as an epic poet. The problem, he explains to Waldo Frank, is that he lacks an audience worthy of his efforts. The fault cannot be ascribed to an audience in particular—it is, he maintains, the fault of the age in which he is condemned to live, an age that lacks a common faith. As a poet he still aspires to write *The Bridge;* but he finds less and less support for doing so. "I had what I thought were authentic materials," he writes, but "These 'materials' were valid to me to the extent that I presumed them to be (articulate or not) at least organic and active factors in the experience and perceptions of our common race, time and belief." Now he senses that the very idea of a bridge, as conceived in the "Finale" of 1923, as a luminous object that stands within the present city and sums up all the possibilities available to those participating in its activities, "is an act of faith besides being a communication." With impressive eloquence, he resolutely demolishes the premise of his poem:

> The form of my poem rises out of a past that so overwhelms the present with its worth and vision that I'm at a loss to explain my delusion that there exist any real links between that past and a fu-

ture destiny worthy of it. The "destiny" is long since completed, perhaps the little last section of my poem is a hangover echo of it— but it hangs suspended somewhere in ether like an Absalom by his hair. The bridge as a symbol today has no significance beyond an economical approach to shorter hours, quicker lunches, behaviorism and toothpicks. And inasmuch as the bridge is a symbol of all such poetry as I am interested in writing it is my present fancy that a year from now I'll be more contented working in an office than before. Rimbaud was the last great poet that our civilization will see.

As John Unterecker has noted: "No one, in fact, has subsequently so efficiently attacked Crane's basic assumptions as Crane himself did here."[3] The poet is an anachronism, a holdover from an ancient time (when the concept of "destiny" still had meaning). Objectively viewed, the culture displays no interest in a poetry of destiny: it is a culture that is all efficiency, speed, and triviality.

Amplifying on this point, the first version of "O Carib Isle!" reveals that the isolated poet lacks the energy or enthusiasm to revitalize the sterility that surrounds him. As the poem suggests, the traditional role of the poet is to identify certain positive signs which other, less sensitive eyes might have overlooked. It is his eye, for example, which catches the detail of "clean enamel frames" around each grave. By counting on his superior insight, he recognizes the shells as necklaces, as offerings, that reveal men care for each other. Out of this tiny spark, his task is to cultivate a flame. But the enormity of this burden exhausts him; he senses that such extrapolations are mere automatic gestures which are, in actuality, self-delusions. Because no one any longer grants the validity of such expansive speculations as he would convey, he remains in isolation, in the graveyard. The spark of poetry fades to an ember. Even the discovery of an optimistic sign, a demonstration of care such as the arrangement of shells, becomes, in the first version of "O Carib Isle!," only a holdover from some distant past, a ritual the significance of which has been forgotten, the persistence of which is a matter of rote gesture. No matter how passionately the poet amplifies upon it, it remains of little consequence.

1

As Philip Horton was first to show in his 1937 biography, Crane had ample reasons for despair at this moment in his life. After more than six months of concerted effort, he had written only a handful of lines for *The Bridge*. His previous failure to get along with his project could be avoided or explained away by the demands of full-time jobs or the attractions of other, shorter poems; there were no such excuses left in the middle of the summer of 1926. Moreover, he had quarreled with an old friend, Allen Tate, and had perhaps cut meaningful ties with one facet of the New York literary community. On a more practical level, he had spent $1500 out of the $2000 promised to him by Kahn (and to be disbursed prudently in $500 installments); that was money gone chiefly to travel south to the Isle of Pines where he found himself still unproductive, out of funds, unwilling to ask for more, and with nowhere else to relocate. Finally, his first collection of poems, which had been in manuscript for better than a year, was still the subject of convoluted negotiations between his anticipated publisher Horace Liveright and Eugene O'Neill.[4]

Horton also shows, however, that within a few weeks in July of 1926, many of these problems simply evaporated. Though no new work was forthcoming on *The Bridge*, his earlier poetry suddenly began to appear in journals: four of the *Voyages* in the *Little Review*, "Repose of Rivers" in *The Dial*, "Praise for an Urn," "Passage," and "At Melville's Tomb" in the *Calendar*. In addition, the contract negotiations for his first book had been settled in an especially heartening way: Allen Tate, having learned that Liveright was holding up publication for a preface from O'Neill which O'Neill felt incapable of writing, unexpectedly volunteered to compose the preface himself and allow it to appear under O'Neill's signature. That could only strike Crane as a genuine sign of confidence in his poetry. Tate, who had every reason to bear a grudge, could still be so affected by the quality of Crane's work as to set aside personal differences in order to see that work into print. Finally, the letter containing the final contract from Liveright included a welcome $100.[5]

Thus a series of fortuitous circumstances combined to contribute to Crane's well-being. But these were, for all their importance, surface phenomena: his paralysis in the summer of 1926, though reinforced by anxiety over such things as his failure to publish a first volume, originated in something deeper—in his willful effort to reclaim the simple exuberance that he had possessed in 1923. In 1923, the role of the poet had been a relatively simple one. Since the multitudes were more dead than alive, victims of a drab routine, they needed a poet to address them in ringing tones that would arouse them to a new vitality. In 1926, Crane

no longer found this attitude toward his audience capable of spurring
him on to poetry.

R. W. B. Lewis is especially sensitive on Crane's need to modify his
original ambitions in order to begin his epic. Lewis cites M. H. Abrams
on a similar problem faced by the English romantic poets. The roman-
tics, living so close to the actual promise of the American and French
revolutions, were bound to be disappointed when the entire fabric of society resisted radical, revolutionary change. They channeled their disappointment, however, into a new kind of poetry: "the marriage between
the Lamb and the New Jerusalem," Lewis quotes out of Abrams, "has
been converted into a marriage between subject and object, mind and
nature, which creates a new world out of the old world of sense."[6] This
shift, argues Lewis, is similar to the shift Crane had to make. According
to Lewis, Crane could no longer look to the actual culture around him, as
Frank had done in *Our America* (and as Munson had increasingly urged
Frank to do with regard to the machine), but he had to turn "away from
historical actuality to formulate within the poems a new relation between
consciousness and reality." "The emergent subject of *The Bridge*," writes
Lewis, "was not the actual or even the latent greatness of the actual or
contemporary America. Its subject was hope, and its content a journey
toward hope: a hope reconstituted on the ground of the imagination in
action; while the thing hoped for was the creation in *poetry* of a new
world—forged out of the old and fallen world, which had failed him, by
the very vigor of the poet's own transfiguring vision."[7] Lewis's intelligent
rendering of the change necessary for Crane is obscured, however, by his
insistence that hope be instituted in the poems through a "transfiguring
vision." Lewis is right to claim that the poems are created out of nothing
more (but nothing less) than the poet's active pursuit of his own aspirations, but it is possible to be even more specific about Crane's evident
intentions.

In order to resolve his crisis completely and move beyond his stale-
mate, Crane needed to overcome his doubt that he lacked a worthy audience. Having resurrected his old idea that the poet is supreme—able to
identify those radiant details that can serve to inspire his audience—he
has come to believe that his audience lacks all interest in such things.
However, his analysis of why his audience cannot hear him is markedly
different at this moment than it had been earlier in 1923, and this difference is the first clear foreshadowing of the change in attitude which will
signal a breakthrough into *The Bridge*. The change is already evident in

his critical June 20, 1926, letter to Waldo Frank, though he is not ready to act upon its full significance. In his previous poetry, the multitudes had been lifeless and unenergetic; in "Faustus and Helen," at the close of day they all struck out for home, carrying the routine of their office existence into the substance of their personal lives, leaving the city empty at twilight. In the letter to Frank, however, Crane laments that "the bridge as a symbol today has no significance beyond an economical approach to shorter hours, quicker lunches, behaviorism and tooth-picks." Later he adds that "*Everybody* writes poetry now—and 'poets' for the first time are about to receive official social and economic recognition in America. It's really all the fashion, but a dead bore to anticipate."[8] The multitudes, that is, are no longer viewed as listless: if anything they are frenetic, racing over the bridge to whatever latest fad is at hand or in search of some bright idea of efficiency. Poetry is accepted now more than ever, though its acceptance, from Crane's viewpoint, is simply one more facet of an America suddenly, rapidly, heedlessly growing—an America on the go, though heading in twelve directions at once.

Once Crane has approached this new vision of the multitudes, he has brought himself to the critical point that will generate *The Bridge*—but it will not be the epic he had been promising to write for the last several years: it will be a new, unexpected sequence of work that will spring from a sudden reversal of attitude initiated by this crisis of 1926. The problem of modern culture, as expressed in that new *Bridge*, is not that the persons in it are listless shells, content with their torpid routine, lying as corpses in a graveyard awaiting a poet to resurrect them with his potent act of naming. The problem is, instead, that persons are anxious and restless and driven with outbursts of undirected energy; and no one pauses for a moment to ponder their situation, to consider why they are so fervently on the move. Everyone simply desires to escape from the difficulties that constrict them; they long to blur themselves into some dynamic activity that postpones all conflict. That is the fundamental insight that Crane must have grasped in July of 1926: out of attending to the strain and the falsity in his own effort to be affirmative at all costs, he discovers that his desire for a clear-cut, dynamic affirmation is precisely what he shares with the multitudes.

The breakthrough of 1926 springs from Crane's awareness that the multitudes have, as it were, adopted a position identical to that which he had advocated for himself in 1923. But he has the new advantage of looking back critically at this position. To be on the go is to wish to avoid any complicated involvement, any lasting relationship with another individual. With everyone on the move, engaged in a headlong flight, the modern city seems composed of isolated selves, each one intent on maintaining its own momentum. Just as a younger Crane had entranced himself with talismanic words, using language to stir events in motion, so the multitudes abuse the new mobility that is theirs in order to stream ahead in endless movement. Just as Crane matured, recognizing the emptiness that lay behind his own ingenious use of language, so the multitudes could be made to realize the hollowness behind their own infatuation with flight. In the poems of 1926, then, Crane is prepared to involve himself in his epic as he had not done before: not only does he uphold the notion of involvement as a countering effect to the lure of endless movement, surging momentum, soaring flight, but he is involved with his own earlier self even as he turns to address the multitudes. At one and the same time, he discovers that he has an audience for his poetry, that he himself is both intimately connected with that audience yet also in touch with an answer to its problems. The new sequence of poems rises directly out of his new ability to turn and view himself as he was in the past, as he would not be in the future—and to see the action necessary in the present in order to link his past and his future.

Throughout the weeks of creativity that ultimately gave rise to more than three-fourths of the poems in *The Bridge*, Crane displays no real certainty as to where his new insights will lead him. In the summer of 1926, one poem simply leads to another, each one a response to its predecessor. Freed from all his ponderous plans and ambitious outlines, he is able, at least momentarily, to concentrate on following out the new leads that open up in each poem, to allow his poems to develop according to their own tendencies. And in the ten poems of that summer, Crane brought together the experience of the last several years and composed a single long sequence virtually flawless in its execution, a sequence with its own accumulating momentum, a personal epic that does not "enunciate a cultural synthesis of values in terms of our America" (as Crane had once promised) but reveals instead something more pertinent to both him and his audience: it reveals how it is possible for an individual to take bearings within a culture that offers no immediate support for such a task.

2

The essential difficulty Crane faced in *The Bridge* was prophesied by Allen Tate in his 1926 introduction to *White Buildings*.[9] Crane's future importance, Tate predicted, would be measured by the way he encountered the central dilemma of the modern epic poet—a dilemma incidentally shared by all modern poets, though the epic poet would feel it most directly: the absence from the culture of any orderly matrix of values. Any poet, according to Tate, who tries to speak for a whole culture has no ground on which to stand since the culture is no longer whole but infinitely fragmented. "The important contemporary poet," he wrote, "has the rapidly diminishing privilege of reorganizing the subjects of the past. He must construct and assimilate his own subjects. Dante had only to assimilate his."[10] Because the Middle Ages were already interpreted, so to speak, by the living authority of the Catholic Church, the *Divine Comedy* could be written, a poem that mirrored abundantly the terms necessary for organizing a civilization. But the absence of any guiding authority—an absence which Eliot might be said to have exploited brilliantly in *The Waste Land* by proliferating possible guidelines and touchstones so profusely as to make no one of them seem more important than any other—is the key to understanding modern times.

Tate was ultimately to decide that Crane had failed in his heroic task of combining Eliot with Dante. In an essay published in 1937 (and drawing on earlier essays of his own), he argued that *The Bridge* mirrored chaotically the dispersiveness of the times, with Crane neither coming to terms with the limitations of modern culture nor accepting his alienation from it. Typical of his failure, according to Tate, was his vacillating approach to the Bridge of the title. "The single symbolic image in which the whole poem centers," Tate complained, "is at one moment the actual Brooklyn Bridge; at another, it is any bridge or 'connection'; at still another, it is a philosophical pun and becomes the basis for a series of analogies."[11] He suggests that the Bridge was finally chosen for no better reason than that it was "'modern' and a fine piece of 'mechanics.'" In Tate's view, this very choice illustrates his contention that all options today are merely personal; no objects remain, in this flawed pluralistic culture, upon the significance of which persons can agree. "Crane's poetry has incalculable moral value," he concludes drily: "it reveals our defects in their extremity."

What should Crane have avoided? Tate is disturbed by the vastness of Crane's enterprise: by focusing on a subject as grand, but amorphous, as "America," he was bound to risk a certain diffusion:

> America stands for a passage into new truths. Is this the meaning of American history? The poet has every right to answer yes, and this he has done. But just what in America or about America stands for this? Which American history? The historical plot of the poem, which is the groundwork on which the symbolic bridge stands, is arbitrary and broken, where the poet would have gained an overwhelming advantage by choosing a single period or episode, a concrete event with all its dramatic causes, and by following it up minutely, and being bound to it. In short, he would have gained an advantage could he have found a subject to stick to.

Tate himself in fact had already benefited from the advice he was offering here. In the spring of 1926 or shortly thereafter, at the time he and Crane were sharing intense discussions over *The Bridge*, he began his own version of a cultural epic, a version that closely subscribed to his own rules, the "Ode to the Confederate Dead."[12] Tate's poem is not about a huge topic, not about America, but it is concerned with the quality of modern culture. It takes for its subject one specific incident in American history, the Civil War, and it focuses on a special instance of it. Here, then, is a poem contemporary with *The Bridge*—a poem, furthermore, on which Tate himself has written an extensive commentary within which there appears a pointed comment by Crane. No better example exists of the essential contrast between the two poets, and a proper introduction to *The Bridge* should begin with a study of the "Ode to the Confederate Dead." Tate's poem reveals what Crane's poem will not be.

In Tate's "Ode," men of the present are essentially frantic, moving uncertainly in no specific direction. Above all, there is only the wind, ceaselessly rustling. The poignancy of the "Ode"—Tate explains that it had been originally conceived as an elegy but he preferred the "irony" of depicting "a lone man by a gate" as though that isolated expression could issue in the public celebration announced by an ode[13]—is that the individual only has one option: to explore with regret what has been lost, then to turn away stoically to face up to the isolation of the present. The regret is deeply meaningful, but harrowing, because it takes shape from what has become a lost moment, a time in the past that is now utterly remote—the unity, the coherence of the South at the time of the Civil

War. Commenting on his poem in 1938, he states firmly that the heroism of the South, as recollected in his poem, was not poetic fancy but a matter of record: "a formal ebullience of the human spirit in an entire society, not private, romantic illusion."

Tate's use of the old South as a pivotal ideal, as an actual culture in which heroism could flourish, however briefly (and in which death thereby had a meaning, unlike the present culture in which death is simply disintegration, the presence of the wind blowing through the leaves), contrasts quite sharply to Crane's choice of the Bridge. The Bridge is a personal symbol whose clear meaning is not evident at all. Tate's old South is historically demonstrable—it existed, the chivalry of that time is no illusion but a matter of record; he is on firm ground. But such solidity is purchased, as Crane delicately remarked in a January 7, 1927, letter to Tate, at the expense of the present. According to Crane, the theme of the "Ode" is the "theme of chivalry, a tradition of excess (not literally excess, rather active faith) which cannot be perpetuated in the fragmentary cosmos of today—'those desires which should be yours tomorrow,' but which, you know, will not persist nor find any way into action." [14] This is tactfully put and serves to mark the distance between the two men. From Tate's viewpoint, his poet is acting realistically, if with sombre bitterness: the notion of finding in the present any equivalent to the unified, heroic civilization of the past is unthinkable, the very kind of "private, romantic illusion" from which he turns in disgust, preferring his own brand of grim stoicism. But from Crane's viewpoint, Tate's paralysis is unthinkable: Tate's poet cannot act, only meditate and mourn. To be weighed down by a perfected past is to be thoroughly constricted, unable to move in the present, unable to create a future.

There is no room in Tate's poem for that hope which R. W. B. Lewis identifies as one of the crucial elements in *The Bridge*. The old South, to a large extent, already existed prior to Tate's poem, but the Bridge of "Proem" must be created by Crane as he writes. In the "Ode," Tate's search for that which profoundly engages him takes place outside the poem, in the actual span of time before the poem was written; once he finds his ideal moment, he then is ready to begin his poem. With Crane, however, the search and the discovery are indistinguishable from the poem; what value the Bridge has is learned in the course of writing about it, as the occasion of the poem gains its stature, becoming more than a whim or a notion, as the poem unfolds in a search that becomes successful. Significantly, the Bridge that is discovered in this act of search-

ing further reflects the value of searching, the very act that allowed it to
be discovered.

Tate and Crane share one common premise in their separate poems:
that contemporary culture lacks a center. The great distinction between
them hinges on their opposite responses to this essential perception. Tate
looks to the past nostalgically, honoring a time when there had been a
center, when heroism was possible. Crane insists on struggling to act in
the present, believing that the search for value is itself not only of ines-
timable value but virtually creates that which it sets out to find. No poem
more clearly demonstrates the advantages of such an approach than
"Proem: To Brooklyn Bridge," the work whose sudden appearance in the
summer of 1926 allowed him to begin *The Bridge* at last.

3

For many readers, "To Brooklyn Bridge" is only a prelude to the epic,
a poem of flickering, suggestive imagery providing fragmentary glimpses
of themes to be taken up later in *The Bridge*. "The main function of the
'Proem,' in terms of the whole, is to set the background of the poem,"
Thomas A. Vogler writes: "despair with the present, a longing for freedom, the possibility that the vision will prove as 'apparitional' as a 'panoramic sleight,' and the desire to find a hopeful organization of experience, a myth that will enable the poet to avoid the 'bedlamite's' end." [15]
In accord with other critics, Vogler concentrates on the range of material
quickly introduced in the proem, and he anticipates no more than a
rapid scanning of a variety of topics, all of which are to be treated more
extensively in later sections. A much closer look at the proem, however,
reveals that Crane is not simply ranging about spaciously; he is, in fact,
demonstrating, in each of his examples, the propriety and the necessity
of his actions. Rather than being an overture touching on a few important
themes, the proem embodies what Crane takes to be an essential way of
acting.

Especially in the first four stanzas, Crane gives the Bridge an identity
very different from that which it had in the 1923 "Finale." In 1923, the
Bridge was an answer, capable of resolving all dilemmas. In "Proem"
the Bridge is an action, a way of moving which also turns responsibility
back to those who learn from it and which is always inviting them to see
that the genuine answer to any dilemma lies in their own hands. It is
important to note that Crane does not open his poem's first lines with the

Bridge, because the thrust of these opening stanzas is to lead him to the point at which he can truly see the Bridge; until he has reached a certain stage, the Bridge is only present as one more object in the cityscape. In fact, "Proem" opens with a false start. It suggests that we should be following the graceful curve of the "seagull's wings"—except that those wings vanish abruptly and leave us suspended in frustration:

> How many dawns, chill from his rippling rest,
> The seagull's wings shall dip and pivot him,
> Shedding white rings of tumult, building high
> Over the chained bay waters Liberty—
>
> Then, with inviolate curve, forsake our eyes
> As apparitional as sails that cross
> Some page of figures to be filed away;
> —Till elevators drop us from our day.

No matter how gloriously the wings flash, no matter how closely one follows their "dip and pivot," they ultimately vanish, soaring up and out of sight, and they lead us into the long, dismaying downward spiral of the second stanza as we are returned to the confinement of office routine. What began, in line 1, as a vision of utter freedom, a vision unbounded and defined only by the play of the white wings, has become by lines 7 and 8 a glimpse enjoyed for a tantalizing moment from an office window, a glance that breaks up the routine of filing for only an instant. The liberty of the gull is in striking contrast to the bondage of the office. Persistently, everything that is expansive and free is squeezed down into the confined, the orderly, the rigid. Memory, for example, which allows the attractive image of the white wings to persist, is gradually being undermined: in the office, memory is a matter of filing cabinets. The drop of the elevator at the close of day may signal a release from routine, but even that release is compromised: the persons dropped in that elevator are being treated no differently than the "figures" rolled back into the file drawer.

Within the modern city, it is actually painful to dream of unfettered freedom, just because that dream is so certain to fade, dropping one back to his routine surroundings but with an even greater sense of his bondage than before. Yet despite the pain of this longing for freedom, Crane also sees that everyone is driven to search for it:

> I think of cinemas, panoramic sleights
> With multitudes bent toward some flashing scene,

         Never disclosed, but hastened to again
         Foretold to other eyes on the same screen.

The third stanza recapitulates the movement of the first two. The white
wings reappear in the "flashing scene" of the cinema, and the multitudes
bend eagerly toward them, only to find that the scene longed for is
"Never disclosed," and must be sought out again. The crowds remain,
as the poet had been in the opening stanzas, left in a state of frustration.
Yet the major change in this third stanza is subtle enough that its significance is not clear at once. The poet, in thinking of the multitudes,
has curved away from his thoughts of frustration to find a similar frustration in others. Instead of the poet remaining fixed on his own dilemma,
he has shifted his attention to see that others also hunger for a need similar to his own. The downward spiral of the second stanza is actually
checked in the firm opening of this third stanza which begins actively: "I
think . . ."

    Instead of reaching out to ephemeral white wings, instead of longing to
soar up and away, the poet has reached out to the tangible presence of
others. He has made a striking connection, realizing that the crowds in a
cinema—crowds vulnerable to a scathing dismissal (as indeed they are
scathingly dismissed by meretricious filmmakers who provide them with
"panoramic sleights")—share his own frustrations. He has seen his own
actions reflected in theirs, and though the two are different, they share a
common longing. It is at this point, then, that the Bridge dramatically
enters:

         And Thee, across the harbor, silver-paced
         As though the sun took step of thee, yet left
         Some motion ever unspent in thy stride,—
         Implicitly thy freedom staying thee!

After the darkness of the cinema, with the eyes straining for a glimpse of
"some flashing scene," this entrance of the Bridge bathed in silver moonlight is almost blinding. But its sudden appearance is not an intrusion; it
is the culmination of all his actions so far. The Bridge only appears, as
the muse appears, when the poet is worthy of beholding. Now that the
poet is worthy, he understands the significance of what had so far been
an intuitive series of steps. He has himself just taken a flashing step; his
own moment of silver-pacing occurred when he turned outward with
his own problems and saw them revealed in the longing of the crowds.

Turning toward other persons, he found himself reflected in them, and the poem opens up, at this point, because he has opened himself up. Indeed, by turning toward others instead of simply clinging to his vision of soaring up and away, he discovers a motion in himself as uplifting as identifying with the white wings. This new turning, moreover, is a motion that can be sustained, a motion that can extend itself and develop; it is unlike the motion of the white wings which can vanish into their "inviolate curve," leaving him painfully aware of his isolation. In seeing the Bridge suddenly, in a new light, as though for the first time, Crane is seeing the importance of his own actions, and the particular beauty of the Bridge is that it reflects back on its surroundings, giving more than it takes. It soars, but within the city, not up and out of it—it soars as Crane did by turning in the city toward others, recognizing himself in them. This act of awareness is the soaring that is not ephemeral.

This intricate identification never absents itself from the movements in "Proem": the poet gives value to what is before him by the way he regards it. Though the next stanza is shocking in its abruptness, it underscores this essential point: the Bridge appears only momentarily, in its perfect form, as long as one's actions are such that they recreate it. If persons act unconscionably, then the Bridge simply vanishes:

> Out of some subway scuttle, cell or loft
> A bedlamite speeds to thy parapets,
> Tilting there momently, shrill shirt ballooning,
> A jest falls from the speechless caravan.

The bedlamite falls, as though the Bridge had disappeared out from under him, precisely because a "jest" escapes from the lips of the "speechless caravan." In refusing to respond except scornfully to the bedlamite's threat of suicide, the crowd literally pulls support out from under him. The ambiguous syntax hinges on this: the jest that falls "from the speechless caravan" is simultaneously a jeer from the crowd ("speechless" because it only jeers) at the same time as it is the bedlamite, the victim of that jeer who, derided, finds the "ballooning" of his "shrill shirt" deflated by the disdainful crowd. If, in the first four stanzas, Crane is able to see the Bridge in all its excellence because he has recognized the correctness of his own actions, in the fifth stanza he is urging others to recognize the power each has within himself—a power with the potential to bring life or death, to connect with others or to dismiss them, to see the Bridge as an ideal, as an exemplary lure to action or as a mere "piece of 'mechanics,'" a cold artifact of iron.

One has the choice, as an individual, to change for good or for ill. From this advantage, the sixth stanza, which may at first appear as a series of descriptive details, divulges its own miniature plot, with thesis, antithesis, and synthesis:

> Down Wall, from girder into street noon leaks,
> A rip-tooth of the sky's acetylene;
> All afternoon the cloud-flown derricks turn . . .
> Thy cables breathe the North Atlantic still.

The stifling, narrow depths of the city—more pointedly, the financial center at Wall Street—make it impossible to look any great distance, and the sun, the source of life, is squeezed into a "rip-tooth of the sky's acetylene" as it finds a narrow passageway down only at noontime. Left to itself, the city is bent on roofing itself over, building higher and higher walls that serve all the more to isolate persons. As a revulsion from this narrowness, the inclination is to turn away and loft oneself on high, above it all: "All afternoon the cloud-flown derricks turn." But that lofty overview is only the dead opposite of the constrictions of Wall Street: aimless pleasant drifting. What is required is a capacity that reaches out beyond the encircling narrowness not in order to escape but to introduce a spaciousness into the constricting coils: "Thy cables breathe the North Atlantic still." The magisterial strength of the cables, which calms the stormy North Atlantic sea, also brings into the city a breath of those windswept, expansive waters. As in the previous stanza, where Crane pivoted on twin meanings of "jest," he here uses "still" as the pivoting word. The complex doubleness of the last line, which resolves the conflicts that had been unfolding, stands in contrast to the straightforwardness of the previous three lines.

The breathing cables, responding as a vast Aeolian harp both to the North Atlantic and to the city, produce a recognition of enormous strength, and Crane's direct praise of the Bridge as a "terrific threshold of the prophet's pledge, / Prayer of pariah, and the lover's cry," reflects back on the poem so far. Instead of regarding the Bridge as, at one occasion, the domain of the prophet and at another occasion the domain of the pariah, Crane now suggests that it can be a "terrific threshold" in which all are, at once, pariah, lover, and prophet. To recognize that one is a pariah, a misfit whose wants have gone unmet, is to articulate those wishes with the fierce passion of a lover and thereby become a prophet who pledges to fulfill those needs. (Another way to view the grouping is to see that the pariah overcomes his banishment by becoming the lover who sympathizes with the weaknesses displayed by others and then turns into the prophet bent upon changing the world for the benefit of all.) And as the lights of motorcars and trolleys, in the next stanza, move beyond the crest of the Bridge but, instead of vanishing, appear to break into the stars in the sky—as though the glittering stars were a living expression of a true "flashing scene"—there is the sensation that the prayer and the cry will be fused in the pledge that can bring about a new future.

The proem Crane is writing does not set about resolving the conflicts of the city. What it stresses, though, is that such conflicts have their origin in individual decisions. The conflicts are not hopeless, but redeemable. The "jest" falls because a jeer escapes from someone's lips; one can choose to wander in the Wall Street canyons or loft himself aloofly on high—or pause and breathe a new air of stillness. There are false aspirations and true aspirations. False aspirations are those evasions, those swerves, those jests, that twist one away from others and encourage isolation and flight. True aspirations are those turning movements that reach within oneself and out to others, taking up problems to counteract them and literally creating, in the process, a new direction for the future. The contrast between what is ephemeral and what is genuine is enhanced in the final stanzas:

> Under thy shadows by the piers I waited;
> Only in darkness is thy shadow clear.
> The City's fiery parcels all undone,
> Already snow submerges an iron year.
>
> O Sleepless as the river under thee,
> Vaulting the sea, the prairies' dreaming sod,
> Unto us lowliest sometime sweep, descend
> And of the curveship lend a myth to God.

To one who looks from within the shadow of the Bridge, the ephemera of false, material promises are evident. When the "fiery parcels" of the skyscraper lights blink out, the city seems undone, plunged in darkness, but the Bridge possesses a shadow even in the dark and does not depend upon ephemeral illuminations. Though a purifying snow "submerges an iron year," softening the harsh outlines of the city and inducing an illusory repose, Crane persists in following the shadow the Bridge casts upon the unfrozen waters of the river. The shadow of the Bridge, unlike the darkness that accompanies the submerging snow, does not muffle or mute what it covers but emphasizes it. The shadow touches its surface and transforms it, embracingly, unfolding differences rather than suppressing them. That is why its shadow extends so easily outward to evoke the sleeping continent.

"Curveship," as distinct from craftsmanship, is Crane's neologism for the kind of writing the Bridge requires.[16] As generated in the course of "Proem," the Bridge can lend a myth to God—the secular city may lack a common faith that could provide all its inhabitants with an overall sense of purpose and direction in their lives, but precisely because of the restlessness and the frustration that all recognize in themselves, it should be possible to channel that energy expended in pursuit of false aspirations toward a new direction. By making himself aware of what he lacks, Crane can understand what it is he needs, and "Proem" is illuminated by turns in which what is registered as a felt absence at one moment becomes a way of understanding how to move in the next moment. As Crane presents the situation, Tate's fears, while real, are unfounded; there need not be anything paralyzing about one's own sense of being lost—that very sense of loss can become a spur to significant action, if one is prepared to work through his thoughts.

The Bridge, if it can only be seen, stands as a testimony to the sweeping grandeur that exists latently in one and all. It is an affirmation of the power individuals have to shape their own lives in a meaningful fashion by becoming responsive to the lives of others. The curve of the Bridge is man-made, a revelation of the truest longing in people, the desire to reach out to others, to span distances, to build relationships that endure. But the power of the Bridge is genuine only if individuals act to sustain it. The "myth" is always temporarily on loan, dependent on the willingness of men and women to deploy their own potential. In a secular world, it is the premier myth, and perhaps the only myth to which all can enjoy access. Its possibilities are limited only by the willingness of persons to tap their own possibilities.

8
The Bridge in 1926 (I)

If Crane's attitude toward his own role as epic poet has changed dramatically with the writing of "Proem," then his attitude toward Columbus, the great man who stands at the very beginning of the poem, should reflect that change. To begin an American epic with Columbus was an almost inevitable decision, and it puzzled Crane that this part of his poem should prove so intractable. Through the winter and early spring of 1926, he had managed only a version of the two opening stanzas.[1] In an April 5, 1926, letter to Gorham Munson, he lamented: "I'm afraid I've so systematically objectivized my theme and its details that the necessary 'subjective lymph and sinew' is frozen."

What did Crane overcome in order to move to the writing of "Ave Maria"? In planning his poem, initially titled "Columbus," he had the support of Waldo Frank's *Virgin Spain*, the last chapter of which is a dialogue between Columbus and Cervantes. That chapter, Crane wrote to Waldo Frank on March 20, 1926, shortly after he had first outlined his epic in detail, "is truly something of a prelude to my intentions in *The Bridge*." In Frank's dialogue, Cervantes is cast in the role of the ironic analyst who uncovers the flaws of modern America; as Helge Nilsen summarizes: "Cervantes sees a city of white towers that present a 'glittering order,' a front which hides the real chaos of race and traditions. The people have lost sight of their gods and yet are full of 'God-hunger,' so they turn to their own works and worship these."[2] The foil to Cervantes is Columbus, the visionary who peers beyond the analyst and believes that a new world will inevitably emerge from this restlessness: "all the towers and all the machines and all the gold on earth can not crush down this unborn need in them for a true New World."[3]

In early 1926, in the drafts of "Columbus," Crane must have conceived of Columbus as a noble prophet, an image whose original was found in Frank's portrait. Furthermore, this Columbus would be an ana-log to the poet: both men were to maintain steadfastly a glorious image of spiritual riches. In his March 1926 outline, he hinted at the centrality of Columbus, for *The Bridge* is to be "based on the conquest of space and knowledge. The theme of 'Cathay' (its riches, etc.) ultimately is trans-muted into a symbol of consciousness, knowledge, spiritual unity."[4] But in the summer of 1926, when "Columbus" suddenly turned into "Ave Maria," Crane carefully modified Frank's portrait. The new Columbus, instead of playing the optimistic seer to Cervantes's pessimistic analyst, is now himself part Cervantes. Indeed, the very flaws that Frank's Cer-vantes had sensed in the multitudes of the new world are flaws that Crane's Columbus displays himself, precisely in order to counteract them and move beyond them. In "Ave Maria," the definition of the great man is not simply that he is a seer; rather, the great man owes his great-ness to his ability to recognize the flaws in himself, to realize that he is the source of his conflict, and to change course in mid-direction if necessary.

In "Ave Maria," Columbus undergoes a severe testing and emerges as an exceptionally strong individual, capable of understanding the con-flicts within him. In this respect, he differs most sharply from another portrait of Columbus in current use at this time, in William Carlos Wil-liams's *In the American Grain*. Crane often betrayed some anxiety over the apparent similarities in themes and subjects in his long poem and in Williams's prose epic, but the differences between the two writers are displayed most dramatically in their two versions of the Columbus story.[5] In Williams's "Discovery of the Indies" (originally published in *Broom* for March 1923), Columbus recovers peace of mind, and the joy that had hitherto eluded him, by happening upon a lush island inhabited by primitives. After the long series of tribulations, all detailed by Williams, which marked his wrangles with old-world administrators, princes, and governors, Columbus finds his paradise momentarily in this interlude when he can walk alone on the shore in radiant simplicity. Williams gives Columbus the last words:

> On shore I sent the people for water, some with arms, and others with casks; and as it was some little distance, I waited two hours for them.
> During that time I walked among the trees which was the most beautiful thing which I had ever seen . . ."[6]

In this Eden, prayer merges with thought: *"O Clemens, O pia, O dulce Maria."* The simplicity of Columbus's words endows them with the purity for which he had been longing; here is the virginal beauty of America, in all its clear simplicity. (It will be violated in Williams's next chapter, "The Destruction of Tenochtitlan.")

"Ave Maria" is at odds with this definition of virtue. Crane locates his Columbus struggling to return home; rather than escaping successfully into an utterly new world, even momentarily, his Columbus must focus on returning to the source of conflict. Like the poet in "Proem" who cannot follow the inviolate curve of the white wings but must double back to that city from which his first inclination is to escape, Columbus is in the process of doubling back. With this curious emphasis not on discovery but on return, Crane immediately places his work in relation to the new ideas of July 1926: the multitudes endlessly on the go testify to the ease with which Americans are ready to pull up what few roots they have and light out for an unsullied wilderness, motivated by some inner vision of a pure green place. Williams's Columbus is square in this tradition. But Crane views that longing for purity as a form of flight, an evasion of responsibility; he would urge persons to work with what they have at hand, to discover what is before them as they seek to resolve their own anxieties.

Crane's Columbus is worthy of emulation because he moves through a disorder whose origin he recognizes in himself; out of his new insight into himself, he redirects his own thinking, mentally changing course, and with his return to Europe vouchsafed, he is granted a vision of the universe as a jewel beyond value. The virtue he demonstrates—though as a man of the fifteenth century, he ascribes it to an intervention by the Virgin Mary—is the ability to rise above disorder by recognizing the part he had played in contributing to disorder. Crane wrote to Waldo Frank in excitement, insisting that his Columbus was "REAL," and one of the things he must have meant was that he had not shrunk from portraying Columbus in an unbecoming role, at least at the outset of his poem. For it is necessary that Columbus appear in all his weakness so that he himself can understand how the storm that assails him originates in his own pride, his boastfulness, his possessiveness.

1

The dramatic monologue of "Ave Maria" begins with Columbus crowing like a braggart, congratulating himself on his own superiority. Though

he is in the midst of a pounding storm, his concentration is turned toward
the accolades he expects at his triumphant return. He is eager to sweep
into the king's court and rout all those experts and critics who had
scorned him, and he invokes his two staunchest advocates: "Be with me,
Luis de San Angel, now—"

> For I have seen now what no perjured breath
> Of clown nor sage can riddle or gainsay;—
> To you, too, Juan Perez, whose counsel fear
> And greed adjourned,—I bring you back Cathay!

The note of defiance here is unmistakable, but it masks a profound misunderstanding: Columbus's error, as he will realize, is that he believes
that "Cathay" is his to bring back. As long as he is convinced of this, or
clings to that belief, he will be truly lost, assailed by a fierce storm that
is a parallel to the tempest within him. In truth, his vindictive boasting
and his determination to clutch Cathay is a form of greed that should be
more alarming to him than death by water. In the beginning, however,
the storm he is enduring only prods him into greater boastfulness; he
does not yet know that the storm outside and the storm inside are one
and the same thing.

   To convince himself of the rightness of his mission and to assuage the
fear that he may lose all in his storm, he clings to a vision that assigns
him a central role of the highest importance. There is a desperate shrill-
ness in his assertions, swathed as they are in an unmistakable pride:

> It is morning there—
> O where our Indian emperies lie revealed,
> Yet lost, all, let this keel one instant yield!

> I thought of Genoa; and this truth, now proved,
> That made me exile in her streets, stood me
> More absolute than ever.

The emphasis is on the fatal flaw of an unyielding pride. If his truth has
been vindicated, why then is he subject to this "tempest-lash"? This is
the question that gnaws at him throughout the storm and leads him to
rehearse his moments of triumph, both those of the past in the discovery
of Cathay and those to come in the future in the return to the court. To
steady himself, he relives again his moment of glory, the instant when
the natives, seeing his boats and men for the first time, addressed them
as gods: "And they came out to us crying, / 'The Great White Birds!'"

With this memory, Columbus is suddenly abashed; he turns at once to address "Madre Maria," as though he had indeed stepped over the mark. He hears the boastful note in his own voice. And from his own shock at realizing that he had been thinking of himself as a god, he understands that his own word has been tested and found wanting. He is, in reality, "between two worlds" where "another, harsh, // This third of water, tests the word." The awed praise he had received from the natives had been exactly what he had been anticipating from those contemptible "clowns" and "sages" on his return home, when he could state dramatically and unequivocally: "I bring you back Cathay!"

Cathay is not his to possess. Chastened by the gulf that has opened between his perilous actual position in the waters and his pompous, vainglorious ambition, he experiences the storm dying down (for the storm had been inside him from the start): "Some inmost sob, half-heard, dissuades the abyss, / Merges the wind in measure to the waves, // Series on series, infinite." To Columbus, the amelioration of the tempest appears as divine intervention; to the modern reader, it is the new confession of humility, that "inmost sob, half-heard," that calms the waters. The abrupt shift in Columbus's fortunes originates in his ability to take the measure of his own vanity, to recoil from it, then rise above it. The reason, then, that his prophecy seems to carry such undeniable authority—

> This turning rondure whole, this crescent ring
> Sun-cusped and zoned with modulated fire
> Like pearls that whisper through the Doge's hands
> —Yet no delirium of jewels! O Fernando,
> Take of that eastern shore, this western sea,
> Yet yield thy God's, thy Virgin's charity!
>
> —Rush down the plenitude, and you shall see
> Isaiah counting famine on this lee!

—is that we sense it is his own previous greed and possessiveness and ambition, not simply Fernando's, that he is pushing away from in these climactic lines. The passage is not simply a condemnation of Fernando but a condemnation of what he himself had become; his assertion is not just a prophetic warning but a chastening message to himself. Even the noblest of men can slip into vainglorious pride.

The end result of Columbus's increased self-awareness is a total sense of the dynamic harmony of the universe, a universe in which he plays a small but crucial part. The concluding stanzas, which to him appear as a vision of the presence of Elohim, to the modern reader appear as a reflection of his new magnanimity. His own assertive ego has been set aside, and he relives with a new understanding his passage westward; it is a test in which God "Cruelly with love" sounds the "parable of man." Like Job he is beset by trials, but he can rise above them by his refusal to yield to pride or ambition. The parable of man is that he has the freedom to fall or, if he takes the courage to face himself, the freedom to soar. The endlessness of such testing is only to be welcomed, for to be challenged, to be brought up short, is to be made aware of one's own frailty and falsity, and to be given the opportunity to rise to even greater heights. Though the poem ends with no land in sight but "still one shore beyond desire!," the conclusion is an affirmative cry. The testing "Hand of Fire" offers the hope of a joyful self-renewal.

It is perhaps an obvious exercise to point out the many similarities between Crane's own position, at the point of beginning *The Bridge*, and that of his Columbus. The same sudden reversal that had occurred to Crane, shifting him away from his own assertive belief in the role of the seer, is essentially dramatized in the change that overcomes Columbus. Like his Columbus, Crane had been boastful and possessive, insistent on the rightness of his vision; he had learned to modulate his ambition, and in the process had begun to find answers which had eluded him for years. "Ave Maria" extends and amplifies the understanding at the base of "Proem," and it establishes what will in fact be a pattern for many of the 1926 poems, a pattern in which the narrator recognizes the falsity in his own original position, is brought up short, and must reorient himself in a new direction.

2

It is perhaps not surprising that a few days after completing "Ave Maria" Crane could be at work on a new, entirely unexpected poem, "Cutty Sark." For the Columbus in "Ave Maria" exemplifies Crane's new attitude: he no longer lays claim to powers that other persons lack but instead sees that he is gifted with an awareness that anyone can develop. What Crane's work now begins to display prominently is an effort to free others by making them able to examine themselves so that they generate their own living ideal, much as Columbus had discovered what he truly valued in the course of his poem.

The derelict mariner featured in the "Cutty Sark" speakeasy is as remote as can be from Columbus. To function at all, the derelict must put
rum between himself and the world. As long as he is staring through the
bottom of an uplifted glass, he is in his element, not water but alcohol,
as though he is himself preserved, a holdover from a lost time. When the
glass is drained, however, his eyes dart about helplessly, floundering in
the dry air:

> I met a man in South Street, tall—
> A nervous shark tooth swung on his chain.
> His eyes pressed through green glass
> —green glasses, or bar lights made them
> so—
> > shine—
> > > GREEN—
> > > > eyes—
> stepped out—forgot to look at you
> or left you several blocks away—

But the poem is not designed to mock the derelict or to reveal a debased
present in contrast to a glorious past; it is a study of a man who holds
persistently to a dream that is destructive, a dream that is no longer possible (the great days of the clipper ships are gone forever) but which lingers in his mind, both preserving him for now as well as bottling him up
in another time. The mariner is a derelict because he clings to a dream
which may once have challenged him and roused him to action, but
which he has failed to grow out of. As a result, he is lost in time, with
time on his hands, and Crane runs through a series of wordplays that
embellish on that: "his bony hands / got to beating time . . ."

Yet Crane is never merely dismissive toward his derelict, for he is
struck by his remarkable resilience, his ability to stay alive even though
out of his element, living in an atmosphere that is inimical to him. He is
a testament to the persistent power of dreams; and while there is something unbearably frail about him, there is also something powerful, intense, and demanding that holds him together. Even as his own scattered
tales turn out to be disasters, turn into ashes in his mouth ("'have you
seen Popocatepetl—birdless mouth / with ashes sifting down—?'"), he
still springs back, however desperately:

> "—that spiracle!" he shot a finger out the door . . .
> "O life's a geyser—beautiful—my lungs—
> No, I can't live on land!"

As shattered as the derelict is, there remains something haunting in his presence; he endures even though he is merely a shell. He is a curious blend of the fragile with the resilient, the ghostly with the enduring:

> A wind worried those wicker-neat lapels, the
> swinging summer entrances to cooler hells . . .
> Outside a wharf truck nearly ran him down
> —he lunged up Bowery way while the dawn
> was putting the Statue of Liberty out—that
> torch of hers you know—

He is so light that the wind threatens to take hold of him, as though his "wicker-neat lapels" (the mark of the precision and tidiness of the sailor: a badge of his profession guaranteeing him safe conduct through the South Street speakeasies) were sails. The rising winds of dawn appear to unmoor him from the bar, a ghostly visitation condemned to his round of visits to "cooler hells" before he returns to his grave. Though the wharf truck nearly runs him down, he appears, phantomlike, as indestructible, lunging up the Bowery. He is like a neglected relic that, however ill-used and ignored, somehow persists in living—like the overlooked, taken-for-granted Statue of Liberty "the dawn was putting . . . out" as though a shady lover hastened her out the door. Liberty's torch remains ambiguously upheld, not dimmed by the dawn but emerging from the gathering morning light. "That / torch of hers you know" is a line spoken quizzically, hovering midway between flippant dismissal and surprised recognition. Is the statue more impressive in the dawn, or does it fade into the oblivion of a casual presence? Can the rich dreams of the night persist in the bright air of the day?

These are not immaterial questions: Crane addresses himself to them in the final turn of the poem, the long reverie on the golden age of clippers. Out of the disjointed fragments gleaned from the derelict's tales, Crane reconstructs what must have been his youthful dream, and in the process also composes an elegy for him as well as an elegy for everyone still haunted by the bright dreams of his early youth. The regatta of ghost ships he envisions below him as he starts walking home across the Bridge in the misty dawn is not simply that world of the past which the derelict had once inhabited: it is that world as the sailor must have imagined it in his youth, as a bright dream of dazzling promise. It has a beauty about it that is all ravishing motion:

> Blithe Yankee vanities, turreted sprites, winged
> > British repartees, skil-
> ful savage sea-girls
> that bloomed in the spring—Heave, weave
> those bright designs the trade winds drive . . .

It is a fantastic realm of castles and stilettos and duels and "savage sea-girls," as divine in its way as Williams's paradise was for Columbus, but all of it tinged with a glow of its sheer impossibility, as though one needed to recall the books of his youth in order to recover it again. This divine world is achingly unreal even to itself, for what do the clippers trade in but "sweet opium and tea"? Using his own encyclopedic knowledge of nautical slang, Crane concocts a ballad that implies the ships run on rum as much as wind:

> At Java Head freshened the nip
> (sweet opium and tea!)
> and turned and left us on the lee . . .

A "nip" is not only a portion of rum but also the point at which a rope is wound taut, and the "lee" suggests not only the shipside away from windward but also the dregs of wine in a cup.

As one moves away from youth, intoxication inevitably wears off. The ships themselves prove evanescent, in bondage to the wind, locked "in wind-humors." Since their only goal is the intoxication of speed, once they reach their port they literally cease to exist, collapsing into a note in a log: "(91 days, 20 hours and anchored!)". Yet so compelling is their graceful flight that one is pained to let them go and even the morsels of their names are to be savored. This poem closes in a way that is strikingly different from that surge of energy Columbus had been granted in "Ave Maria":

> *Rainbow, Leander*
> (last trip a tragedy)—where can you be
> *Nimbus?* and you rivals two—
>
> > a long tack keeping—
> > > *Taeping?*
> > > *Ariel?*

For if Crane is acutely aware of the evanescence of these youthful dreams —of the way in which they are unable to be sustained—he is no less aware of their haunting power, of the way in which they remain unforgettable and moving. At the same time as the derelict sailor's vision is revealed as a lure that is destructive, a dream that is impossible, it remains ravishingly alluring, overwhelmingly attractive.

But the wrong dream can be killing. It can leave one beached, helplessly entangled in a memory so pure and bright that one cannot bear to leave it.[7] "Cutty Sark" has been derided as a self-indulgent poem, a stray insertion that deviates from more important themes; in fact, it fits precisely with other themes developed in the 1926 *Bridge*. It is a false ideal, and it can be a destructive one, as the example of the derelict so clearly reveals, yet it attests to the power of something so apparently insubstantial as a youthful dream. It is unthinkable to conceive of not having dreams; one must make promises to oneself. But the crucial question is: what dreams are positive? What dreams will not fade at dawn but will persist into the clear light of day?

3

One good reason for the success of "Southern Cross," the work next to be completed (again in an unexpected deviation from the original scheme), is that the poem most likely mirrors feelings that Crane had to work his way out of in order to begin *The Bridge*. For the poem is an examination of nostalgia, of the bitterness a nostalgic and backward-looking vision breeds. A hatred for the present, based on a reverence for the past, is one of the positions advanced in "O Carib Isle!," but in "Southern Cross" it is directly at the center of what appears, at first, to be a nearly incoherent set of fragmented outcries.

"Southern Cross" is not as obscure as it seems. It conveys an experience which Crane has had to work through, an experience he knows full well to be a powerful and attractive lure pulling against the sense of reaching out to others, the sense of moving beyond oneself, that Crane realizes in the course of *The Bridge*. And with the force of "Cutty Sark" borne in mind, Crane writes this poem in the hope that such an incisive exposure will release others trapped in the same position. For it is a terrible position to be in. A nostalgia for what is past and gone, like the desire for anything so remote it cannot be attained, leads only to bitterness and contempt. One comes to cherish his ideal, the past, based only on the substantiality of his hatred for the actual, the present. The posi-

tion is destructive, bound to break again into hatred and contempt, as
does the end of "Southern Cross." There, everything is lost:

> All night the water combed you with black
> Insolence. You crept out simmering, accomplished.
> Water rattled that stinging coil, your
> Rehearsed hair—docile, alas, from many arms.
> Yes, Eve—wraith of my unloved seed!

> The Cross, a phantom, buckled—dropped below the dawn.
> Light drowned the lithic trillions of your spawn.

The stars have turned to stone, to "lithic trillions," masses of dead rock,
because the mariner must bitterly insist that his Southern Cross, his
ideal from the past, is but a phantom, nonexistent. His ideal, that which
has traditionally given light and direction to those at sea, buckles as he
buckles under to his own hatred. Though it moves toward a dawn,
"Southern Cross" is not a poem of dawning but a poem of morning written by a man who wants to be back in the evening, back in the time
before Eve has fallen, when the air was rich and sweet with memory. If
there can be no evocative evening, then Eve must turn into the Medusa,
just as the mariner will turn himself to unresponsive stone rather than
give up his love for the past based on his contempt for the present.[8]

The agony of desiring a pure ideal only serves to invest the Cross with
its air of untouchability. It becomes "Still more alone," like the speaker,
even as it is seen as performing the hauntingly beautiful act of making
love to the evening. This lovemaking, however, is scarred by the intrusion of the speaker who comments with a snarl at the "lower heavens"—
heavens he would have strictly dissociated from his Cross. Evoking an
alluring image, he mars it at once with a sneer of hatred:

> The Southern Cross takes night
> And lifts her girdles from her, one by one—
> High, cool,
>   wide from the slowly smoldering fire
> Of lower heavens,—
>   vaporous scars!

Clinging to the supernal beauty of the star making love to the night provokes the bitterest contempt for the "slowly smoldering fire / Of lower
heavens." The nostalgia for perfection is based on contempt.

The most unsettling lines are those which capture a bittersweet awareness of a love that has irretrievably fallen, yet to which one still desperately holds:

> Eve! Magdalene!
> > or Mary, you?
>
> Whatever call—falls vainly on the wave.
> O simian Venus, homeless Eve,
> Unwedded, stumbling gardenless to grieve
> Windswept guitars on lonely decks forever;
> Finally to answer all within one grave!

If he could, this man would become as disembodied as a grieving windswept guitar, but he cannot lapse comfortably into that illusion, for in
order to sustain it he must curl back in hatred against his plight:

> And this long wake of phosphor,
> > > iridescent
> Furrow of all our travel—trailed derision!
> Eyes crumble at its kiss. Its long-drawn spell
> Incites a yell. Slid on that backward vision
> The mind is churned to spittle, whispering hell.

To keep the notion of a windswept guitar alluring, he requires this stinging sense of a present that is utterly inadequate. And this fruitless self-
derision leads to an even more excruciating awareness of all the comfort
the Southern Cross could bring if only it were capable of being possessed
forever, recovered in all its purity:

> > The embers of the Cross
> Climbed aslant and huddling aromatically.
> It is blood to remember; it is fire
> To stammer back. . . . It is
> God—your namelessness.

This man cherishes those glowing embers, those ghostly memories, as
being all that still holds fragrance, but he cannot even broach them.
They gain their allure from the fact that they remain nameless, unable to
be reconciled with the wash that lies around them. This mariner lives
within a constant stream of pain as he forges an evanescent (and agonizing)
beauty by exacerbating the ugliness around him. Unattainable beauty, or
the ideal of it, depends on its creator lashing out at the life around him,
viewing the present as utterly vain and worthless. The idea of a perfect

past, an impossible ideal, lives parasitically on the creation of an imperfect present—a present that the ideal rends and violates to foster itself all the more preeningly.

There is a clear relation between "Cutty Sark" and "Southern Cross"; crossing from one poem to the next is possible because the same feelings are revealed in both. The derelict clings to his youthful dream, and he serves as a keen reminder that some dreams are destructive, drawing one back into a past, instituting an ideal that becomes more and more unreal at the same time as it is grows lavish and alluring and evocative. The isolated mariner exemplifies a similar situation, but in his case all the anguish of feeling utterly at one with a love that is past, with a remote ideal, is brought forward. "Southern Cross," however, is more than a recapitulation, from another, more intimate angle, of "Cutty Sark": it is, in fact, a pivotal poem, as it leads to the following two works which bring Crane close to answering the questions he had raised in "Cutty Sark."

Following the lead of an influential article by John R. Willingham, critics have usually characterized "Three Songs" as a deliberately unflattering group portrait of the modern woman. Crane's true feminine ideal, it is argued, is represented by Pocahontas in "The Dance." And it is true that if each of the women in "Three Songs" is held up against Pocahontas, who is usually felt to represent the purity of virgin America before it was sullied by entrepreneurs, gold diggers, and conquistadors, then the only conclusion is that the modern woman is lacking in dignity and grace and delicacy.[9] Such an approach is too simple for these poems. Perhaps because critics are intent upon using the modern women in "Three Songs" as a way of idealizing Pocahontas, they miss the very point of these sketches, each of which presents a woman who is being idealized by men. It is the process of idealization that Crane finds so distorting, since it actually prevents men and women from developing a genuine relationship.

The essential problem Crane is struggling to delineate is that of the emptiness which stems from longing for an impossibly remote ideal. Such yearning lures persons into deliberately cultivating imaginary, illusory relationships that do not meet desires but rather keep desires intact, unfulfilled, unexpressed. "Southern Cross" is a dramatically exaggerated version, no doubt felt from personal experience, of such an idea, which is to be developed less autobiographically in the other two songs. On its surface, modern culture may look freewheeling, with the mariner's ideal of a remote purity long eclipsed by shrewd secretaries who keep smiling the boss away and burlesque queens who tie men in knots. But in fact the mariner's self-enclosed frustration is an accurate index of the relations between men and women in modern culture. Persons long for such impossible ideals that they turn to stone pursuing what is so remote as to be untouchable. Meanwhile, Crane wants them to realize, genuine possibilities pass them by.

At the center of "National Winter Garden" is a manless woman surrounded by womenless men. At first, Crane appears to regard the entire situation only with contempt. The dance is simply reductive and deserves only a flick of attention; ingenious puns dominate the opening and help convey an air of dismissal:

> Outspoken buttocks in pink beads
> Invite the necessary cloudy clinch
> Of bandy eyes. . . . No extra mufflings here:
> The world's one flagrant, sweating cinch.

Without degrading his own language, Crane suggests that to describe this audience it would be best to deal in a language stripped of any and all intricacy. The reductive edge of the dancer's routine is paralleled by the quality of speech that lingers after her gestures begin. Dancer and audience both share a world where it is best to be "Outspoken," where words are bandied about, where "It's a cinch!" is a proven password. "Before the final ring . . . begins / A tom-tom scrimmage" brings the world of the prizefight into the burlesque hall, reminding us that this is predominantly a masculine world we are involved in.

But as the routine develops, and as Crane draws his attention closer, the poem becomes no longer dismissive. This dance, it turns out, is like a prizefight, with the men eager to see the woman fall from her height, defeated and destroyed:

> We wait that writhing pool, her pearls collapsed,
> —All but her belly buried in the floor;
> And the lewd trounce of a final muted beat!
> We flee her spasms through a fleshless door. . . .

This aspect of the dance is emphasized gradually. Crane's first inclination is to think that what is so disturbing is the way the mock-availability of the dancer encourages the men to create an ideal fantasy image:

> And while legs waken salads in your brain
> You pick your blonde out neatly through the smoke.

> Always you wait for someone else though, always
> (Then rush the nearest exit through the smoke).

The dance, then, is always dissatisfying, always unfulfilling. Why are men drawn to it? Perhaps because it is so simple, so unreal: the woman is like a jewel, "Sprayed first with ruby, then with emerald sheen." But everyone knows that the jewel is an illusion: "A caught slide shows her sandstone grey between." The real answer is that the men enjoy seeing the woman punished, humiliated, destroyed. The "trounce" of a "muted beat" is what holds their attention, and the spectacle revolves around a humiliation: "Pearls whip her hips, a drench of whirling strands. / Her silly snake rings begin to mount, surmount / Each other—turquoise fakes on tinselled hands."

In seeing the woman "die," and apparently enjoying it, the men confess to a desire forecast in the simplistic language noted at the beginning: the men want to die out of the complexity of life, out of the actual confrontation with another woman. The more the dancer invites their attention and proves alluring, the more gratified they are to see that she is being punished, rejected, villified. The peculiar warp of this violent sexuality is that it is such an expression of misery. With eyes focused on the womb, as though it were about to give birth, the men confess their own wish both to return to the safety of that enclosure and to be born over again into a better life. But this womb is an "empty trapeze" upon which one swings casually, and it issues in nothing; it leads them back to their dead world, themselves victims of the violence they had willed upon the dancer. Agape at the womb exposed, "the burlesque of our lust—and faith," they stare into an emptiness that simultaneously denies the hope of new birth.

In all three of the songs, the contortions people create for themselves are efforts to avoid pain which only create additional pain. At this point in his writing, Crane wants to give a sense of persons as they are but as they need not be: men and women involved in relationships that they themselves have depersonalized. While each of the "Songs" presents a different aspect of the contemporary, all are united by this common thread. But an additional achievement is that in each poem Crane alters his approach by adopting a way of talking that he hopes his subjects can hear. That is one reason the songs are so dissimilar from one another, and in this respect the seemingly frivolous lyric "Virginia" is one of his most successful poems. The singsong rhythms of "Virginia" are not that different from the kinds of pop tunes a person such as Mary is likely to admire, and, indeed, Susan Jenkins Brown remembers well the words to a tune from the 1920s that was the inspiration for "Virginia."[10] Crane adopts such rhythms, hoping to go through them in a spirit both critical and involved, to show Mary how she is falsifying her life.

In "Virginia," Crane keeps the relation between Mary and her young man hard to pin down, in deference to Mary herself: she is so much up in the air about her own feelings. "Mary (what are you going to do?)" is a legitimate question that wants an answer throughout the song. Mary seems to want a Prince, but she is surrounded by Princes who would urge her to "Let down your golden hair!" not as Rapunzel but as any ordinary flapper. There are many seductive forms that suggest desires should be gratified immediately, and Mary is correct to "keep smiling the boss away." But what Crane wants Mary to see is that her own dream of a Prince is tinged with the same false smile she gives to her boss.

In the background of "Virginia" lies the masculine world of modern business, but Crane points out that it too lacks substantiality. It has the feel of a place where riches are supposed to lie just around the corner, yet it is a world of the five-and-ten, built on nickels and dimes. The "Way-up nickel-dime tower" of frugal penury is the counterpart to the random energies of a dice game where all richness rides on the lucky break: only some lucky break frees one from that tower. And the counterpart of the dice game is Mary's belief in a spring with a Prince Charming. The creed of the lucky break keeps returning in the song, along with Crane's wish to expose what is so tragic in that creed: it keeps persons waiting for unimaginable riches instead of alerting them to discover a richness of their own, in the present, within their grasp. The creed, in short, is no better than a concoction: it is as satisfying as popcorn and it is bolstered by the corny themes of pop tunes that conspire to turn the multitudes into "Pigeons by the millions" lured by the "high carillon / From the popcorn bells!"

By the time of this third song, Crane is incisively aware of the tendency in persons to turn away from their own longing for contact with others. To deny this drift, Crane presents Mary's world so that it remains intact yet appears open to criticism. The opening—

> O rain at seven,
> Paycheck at eleven—
> Keep smiling the boss away,
> Mary (what are you going to do?)

> Gone seven—gone eleven—
> And I'm still waiting you—

presents Mary as sidling through her workweek, entering a rainstorm as a loss which can be countered by her Friday pay as a gain, and all the while waiting for the lucky break. But "Gone seven—gone eleven," the week is past, nothing has changed, and the invisible, ineffable voice of popular songs which we hear crooning below these rickety rhythms still hasn't brought much of a future. That voice claims to be "waiting" but, as in all the puns and double meanings which suffuse this song, we hear it as weighting her down, still weighting you. At the end, she is more virginal, more remote, more untouched, than ever. Though the decorations seem light and airy, the walls are building around her:

> High in the noon of May
> On cornices of daffodils
> The slender violets stray.
> Crap-shooting gangs on Bleecker reign,
> Peonies with pony manes—
> Forget-me-nots at windowpanes:

> Out of the way-up nickel-dime tower shine,
>   Cathedral Mary,
>   shine!

Mary is "High in the noon of May"—drunk ("High"), that is, at the dead center ("noon") of all her possibilities ("May"). Will a slender violet stray, or will a forget-me-not linger wistfully at a closed window? It is the decision to be made every weekend. The moment is at hand, but she has no way to choose. The haze of pop songs offers no insight. Meanwhile, the flowers are bound to fade, and the identity of "Cathedral Mary" is unpromising: her postponements may keep her a nun in a narrow room, not a June bride.

"Three Songs" may be the most unjustly neglected segment of *The Bridge*. The poems reveal Crane touching on others, using appropriately varied tones of voice that each person might best be able to hear, so as to reveal to them the falsity they carry in their own lives, the falsity they use to create their own misery. If only because the poems are not condemnatory, they are a wonder. Crane emphasizes the sadness, not the repugnance, of the men who wish to punish the dancer, and the torment, not the weakness, of the mariner who longs for a pure woman, a guiding light. And most important of all, Crane is striving to free persons from their obsessions so they can actually attend to the deep desires they have within themselves but fail to acknowledge or act upon, thereby creating the distortions that these poems explore. Each poem is surprisingly delicate, adopting a different tone in each case, as Crane speaks in just the way needed for the other to hear him. The modern culture may encourage the formation of distant and remote ideals, forms that allow for an escape from the actual interchange among individuals, forms that divide the masculine from the feminine. But if that is the case, the same culture can be transformed by individuals made aware of the falsity in their lives, made alert to the distorted way they handle their feelings. By writing with others in mind, yet with problems that are close to his own, Crane fulfills the promise of that first transforming turn in "Proem," where he suddenly felt his kinship with the crowds at the cinema.

9

The Bridge in 1926 (II)

After completing "Proem," "Ave Maria," "Cutty Sark," and "Three Songs," Crane had created an impetus for his poem much different than that called for by his original outline, that chronological narrative of American history from Columbus through Pocahontas up to Whitman, John Brown, and the present. The new additions have made him even more attuned to the false aspirations held by himself and others, aspirations that he sees as self-destructive. If he has been critical, however, he has also been careful to imply that there remains within persons a deep desire for change, a profound need for promises that are not illusory but remain firm and positive. The immediate question faced by Crane, at this point in his suddenly expanding epic, is whether this need can be directed in a purposive way.

Crane's own uncertainty at this moment is indicated by the fact that, at the same time as he was completing "Three Songs," he was also attempting a return to the format of his original outline. The works on which he was engaged when "Three Songs," as he said, "just popped out,"[1] were two in number: a revision—for the nth time—of the finale to his poem, now entitled "Atlantis," and the section on Pocahontas, now entitled "Powhatan's Daughter." While new ideas were coming to him at an unprecedented speed and offering to draw his epic into uncharted territory, he was resisting.

Yet his resistance took a curious form. In his letters, he is jubilant at his unexpected progress, and he welcomes the chance to fly off in every direction at once. "I skip from one section to another now," he wrote to Waldo Frank on August 12, 1926, "like a sky-gack or girder-jack." By this time, he was working simultaneously on four segments of the poem: "Three Songs" (two of which were complete), "The Dance" (under the working title of "Powhatan's Daughter"), "Calgary Express" (the working title for the John Brown poem), and "The Tunnel" (the subway poem).

151

Since these last three poems correspond to segments sketched in his original scheme, he appears to be striving to integrate his new, unplanned work with his previous framework.[2]

To what extent was Crane aware of the divergence between his new work and his old plan? His letters from July and August of 1926 shed no light on the subject. They only serve to raise questions about the actual sequence in which the poems were written. For example, he wrote to Waldo Frank on August 12 and announced that "Even the subway and 'Calgary Express' are largely finished." But in fact "Calgary Express" would never be completed; a fragment of it, possibly all that was written, eventually surfaces as the concluding eight quatrains to "The River." The subway poem also raises a question. He announced two weeks after his August 12 letter that he had finished it, but he added that the process of composition was "rather ghastly, almost surgery—and, oddly almost all from the notes and stitches I have written while swinging on the strap at late midnights going home."[3] What, then, did he mean in his August 12 letter when he stated that "Even the subway" was largely finished? Did it seem finished because he had actually worked on it, or because he had suddenly realized the value of his "notes and stitches" gathered earlier? A final complication is that the exact identity of the poem he calls "Powhatan's Daughter" remains unclear. In *The Dial* for October 1927 "The Dance" was published as "Powhatan's Daughter." Is it only, then, "The Dance" which engages his attention at this time, or is it also "The Harbor Dawn" and "Van Winkle," two additional poems that later appeared in the final group of five poems entitled "Powhatan's Daughter"?[4]

None of these questions can be answered firmly. In general, it seems likely that Crane moved about considerably from section to section, shifting pieces of poetry about as they took shape, assigning them to whichever place they seemed to fit. Never an organized writer, he allowed his poems to develop on their own. He may have hoped to bring his burgeoning long poem back under the umbrella of his original framework, and he may have set out to compose "The Dance," under the title of "Powhatan's Daughter," in the hope of accomplishing that end. But the inclination to follow up the tendencies proliferating in his new work offered so tempting a prospect that he veered over to the deeper and more compelling problems he had brought to light in "Cutty Sark" and "Three Songs." And just as those two sections had emerged, serendipitously, out of reworking "Columbus" into "Ave Maria," so the decision to rework "Pocahontas" into "The Dance" gave rise to two new complementary poems, "The Harbor Dawn" and "Van Winkle." As a result, the newly emergent sequence which seemed to keep asserting itself spontaneously took on an even firmer shape than ever, a shape that was, moreover, distinctly different from a chronological and historical narrative.

1

If Crane was momentarily uncertain in August 1926 of which step to take next, was his confusion substantial enough to sabotage "The Dance"? "The Dance" had been intended as a cornerstone for the long poem, and Crane himself was adamantly convinced of its success. Writing to Yvor Winters in March 1927, he stated that while some poems in *The Bridge* were open to the criticism that "their viewpoint featured is too personal to the writer" (he had just sent Winters "Three Songs"), "no amount of ragging would ever convince me, for instance, that Ave Maria wasn't primarily solid and valid, and I could say the same of the Indian dance and certain other poems."[5]

But is "The Dance" so secure in its reputation? Winters eventually characterized the poem as "nervous and violent," containing both "some of the most brilliant lines in Crane and some of the most grotesque."[6] Since this comment by Winters, other critics have labored to defend the poem, but their apologies may have done more harm than good to Crane's reputation. For the common defense of "The Dance" is that the frenzied war dance of Maquokeeta, which is held to be an appropriate climax to the poem, is an analog to poetic creation as Crane experienced it. Writing poetry depends on unleashing demonic, primitive forces and the sacred rite of the poet is to be possessed by forces from beyond and consumed by a power which he has himself conjured up and to which he yields himself as sacrificial victim. If the bland emoluments of contemporary culture have caused people to forget this ancient, sacred role, Crane will remind one and all that the shaman and the seer and the medicine man are forerunners of the poet.[7]

From this interpretation, it might appear that Crane had returned to an earlier view of himself as poet: the poet as magician, a conductor of extraordinary natural forces which surge through him and which he translates into dazzling language. Yet if Crane is lapsing back into this older view, isn't he overthrowing his new insight into the multitudes as obsessed and frenzied? Isn't he rejecting his new belief in soaring within constraints? Either "The Dance" as read by most critics is an atavism, a throwback to an earlier self—and therefore a confusing interruption in the sequence, not an effective cornerstone—or critics have erred in their characterization and "The Dance" has not been read properly.

Another approach to "The Dance" resolves this problem and brings the poem in line with Crane's other new work. Rather than portraying Maquokeeta as an exemplary figure, Crane is presenting him in a critical light. His war dance is frenzied, extreme, out of control, and indulgent. In trying to view it as otherwise, commentators err, for it was written in such a way as to emphasize its grotesqueness; the passage is supposed to be, as Winters said, "nervous and violent." And its counterpart exists in another passage in the poem, a passage that is opposite but related: the languorous, decadent, and increasingly hysterical voyage downstream to the village of the war dance. Just as the war dance passage is deliberately overwrought, so the drifting and streaming passage is written to seem almost unbearably hazy and swoony.

Crane's purpose in composing these two parallel but opposite passages is so he can evoke a third, climactic passage in which the two opposites are resolved. This conclusion, which is the true "dance" of the title rather than the frenzied war dance of Maquokeeta, occurs in the final six stanzas, and it presents the essential value of the Indian world as Crane imagined it —a value with clear implications for the individuals of "Three Songs."

Commentators have frequently tried to pinpoint what Crane saw to admire in the Indian. R. W. B. Lewis, for example, while readily admitting that Crane's portrait seemed romanticized, recalls that in the minds of other American writers, Melville and Whitman and Poe and Emerson, there was a belief in a past "when the human situation was seen as informed by miracle and terror, when the natural landscape was regarded as hospitable to divinity, and human experience took the constant shape of significant ritual."[8] This angle on the past, however, is too backward-looking, too nostalgic, to suit Crane's present temperament. Crane's sense is that the primary knowledge the Indian held was a belief that the masculine and the feminine are absolutely dependent upon one another. When the two interact, there is harmony; if the two are kept apart, the result is disarray and confusion. The climax of the poem, the genuine dance, occurs when the masculine and the feminine act in relation to one another. The masculine has been identified throughout the poem with the sun and the sky, the feminine with the stream and the earth; sun and sky, stream and earth interact, on a cosmic scale, in the poem's conclusion. And when Crane realizes in his poetry this sublime interrelationship, he feels he has united time and space, serpent and eagle; everything is held together, in a harmonious balance. he feels both in touch with ancient Indian wisdom and that such wisdom has a message to address to his contemporaries who, in "Three Songs," are bent on avoiding such a commitment.

The reason Crane could be so enthusiastic about his achievement is that it is a genuine feat: it depends on the poet's ability not simply to recreate an Indian point of view but to imagine how the Indian might have experienced an anxiety similar to the anxiety felt by contemporaries in "Three Songs." The Indian, it turns out, lives in a world of strife similar to that of Crane's contemporaries. The anxiety displayed occurs when the woman is separated from her man, and when the man is separated from his woman. The primitive landscape, as the womanless man and the manless woman perceive it in their two individual passages, is tinged with the emotional stress felt by each. The positive qualities of the feminine are sensuality and fecundity and imagination; but these qualities require a masculine counterpart: lacking it, they degenerate, and women without men are apt to be coy and vague and flirtatious. The positive qualities of the masculine are leadership and strength and decisiveness; but men without women tend to be brutal, demonstratively dramatic, prone to excessive violence. The difficult feat Crane proposes for himself is to show a symbolic landscape (viewed by the Indian) as feminine in one passage and masculine in another, while at the same time conveying a sense that both landscapes are overdone, nerve-wracking, extreme— they each need the presence of their opposite. By emphasizing the underlying inadequacy that the Indian woman and Indian man feel while they move through each of their symbolic landscapes, Crane is then able to convey the pressure that the Indian must have felt to integrate the two.

"The Dance," then, is so simple a poem that its point has been easy to overlook. Yet it is a daring work, too, which accomplishes its aim not anthropologically, not through utilizing an actual myth, but poetically: it generates a necessary "myth" out of dramatizing the way the Indian sensed inadequacy. For it to work, Crane must write with an extraordinary subtlety. As in "Cutty Sark" where the clipper sequence was designed to appear as too achingly unreal, a destructive dream destined never to flourish, and as in each of the "Three Songs" where the viewpoints of the subjects were expressed only to be subtly undermined and questioned by the poet, Crane depends in "The Dance" on his skill in evoking an Indian's view of a landscape tinged with excess, a landscape too feminine or too masculine. This requires no small amount of confidence in one's prowess, and it is understandable why Crane should have been pleased with the result.

At the opening of the poem, his challenge is relatively simple. He wants to introduce the vision of harmony that he ascribes to the Indian but in a manner that, at first, conveys only its remoteness. Thus the harmony between man and woman, as reflected in the "mythic" interaction of sun and sky with earth and stream, is made to seem mystifying and strange, even quaint and dusty. Though he makes it clear enough that he is describing an Indian version of a winter sun melting snow, he withholds any appreciation for the Indian's habit of personifying nature. There is even the suggestion, in the lines "a winter king—/ Who squired the glacier woman down the sky," of something old-fashioned and outmoded in such gallantry. The "myth" is apprehended only for it to appear as that which is merely a primitive effort to explain natural phenomena; we know better today and respond patronizingly, if at all, to such tales. A barrier stands between this present and that past—"Now lie incorrigibly what years between"—but it hardly seems worth broaching.

One of the difficulties in the next segment which has caused misreading is that the poet, identifying fully with the Indian and addressing a "you" at certain moments in both the streaming passage and the war dance passage, is addressing the "you" that is felt to be missing in both cases; the "I" in the streaming passage is the poet reliving the experience of Pocahontas, longing for Maquokeeta, and the "I" in the war dance passage is the poet as Maquokeeta without his Pocahontas. The personages in the poem are fluid and shift about, as though the poet were in a trance as he writes, seeking to overcome the barriers between the past and the present. The "you" is not, in either case, an imaginary reader, as James McMichael has argued. As Crane, the feminized Indian, floats downstream, he is not luring the reader into an appreciation of minute details so ravishing that the reader, as McMichael believes, "can begin to participate with the details as immediately as we might with our lover."[9] Instead, Crane hopes to create in the reader a distaste for the dissolution he displays. There must be a sensuality described, but it must be a sensuality that is slightly overripe, fulsome, as in the luxuriant sound of "Feet nozzled the wat'ry webs of upper flows" with its unctuous "zzz" sound and the lip-smacking "wat'ry webs." There must be a feeling of ease and relaxation and acceptance (all of which are positive attributes of the feminine) but the passivity must verge on the languorous, it must attain the pitch of a decadent swoon:

> What laughing chains the water wove and threw!
> I learned to catch the trout's moon whisper; I
> Drifted how many hours I never knew . . .

The dainty languor of the "I," poised prettily over the line break, seems to mark indulgence, calling attention to its prominence. There must be a note of delicacy but fatally mixed in with a fluttering coyness: "I could see . . . the blue / First moth of evening take wing stealthily." (Crane deliberately uses many conventional "poetic" images, including those from his earlier poetry; this is a set piece, slightly hollow, echoing an outmoded kind of poetry.) Each of these details, though praised by McMichael for its fidelity to the actual, is in truth deliberately overdone, arch and mannered, not at all actual. Momentum hovers at the point of hysteria:

> I took the portage climb, then chose
> A further valley-shed; I could not stop.

Crane masterfully extends each moment just a bit too much. "Wisped of azure wands!"—how unbearably precious! The softness and delicacy of this deeply feminine landscape are running to seed.

Crane's portrayal of Maquokeeta is similarly exacerbated but in an opposite way: if the streams and valleys are haunted by the shade of genteel ladies' verse, the Indian council of war conveys a fantastic world of businessmen unleashed, a Rotarian club meeting gone wild. Maquokeeta is not commanding and authoritative but excessively dramatic; he is not simply forthright and decisive, he is brutally aggressive. If the feminine landscape is luxuriantly passive, alternating with spasms of wild hysteria, the masculine landscape is demonstrably active but its activity verges on pure frenzy, on displays of dazzling might:

> Now snaps the flint in every tooth; red fangs
> And splay tongues thinly busy the blue air.

This is a frightening world but one that is also filled with bluster. The lightning that flings its tongues about is part of a display of aggression as its sparks "thinly busy" the air. The triumphant edge of authority, the commanding aspect of true leadership, is right on the verge of slipping

into a show of pure bombast. "Medicine-man" catches up that echo of a
carnival showman displaying his wares, promising unbelievable cures,
offering wild threats and even wilder promises, working himself up to a
pitch of delusion:

> Sprout, horn!
> Spark, tooth! Medicine-man, relent, restore—
> Lie to us,—dance us back the tribal morn![10]

The sense that the storm is a sky out of control, the sun twisted into darts
of lightning (phallic, aggressive), is most clearly suggested in the scenes
of sacrifice that emphasize the frustrated violence underscoring this passage. "I could not pick the arrows from my side" is not some primitive
shout of joy as Crane becomes one of the participants in a vital ritual;
rather, this cry of pain and boasting confirms a confusion that reigns
once the masculine show of power gets out of hand, as though men go to
war and kill each other because their barbs of lust, their pointed arrows,
have no yielding object and so must fly indiscriminately, even twisting
back upon their owners. The excess is deliberate in this passage—power
is unleashed ferociously and the entire landscape is razed. Without their
loves, men turn at once to destruction, which culminates in an orgy of
self-destruction, the warped sensuality and boastful display of wrestling
with lava, and "stag teeth" that foam at a dark throat.

   Having lived out these two opposing landscape-atmospheres in their
quintessential forms, Crane is in a position to sense how each requires
the other as a complementary opposite. Now his language is purified of
its disorderly aspects and he adopts the "thou" and "Thy" that confer
respect. The interrelationship of sky and earth, of sun and stream, instead of being stated in a manner that is both stilted and patronizing (as
involving squires and priests and corn goddesses), is now presented in a
way that is effortlessly natural:

> High unto Labrador the sun strikes free
> Her speechless dream of snow, and stirred again,
> She is the torrent and the singing tree
> And she is virgin to the last of men . . .
>
> West, west and south! winds over Cumberland
> And winds across the llano grass resume
> Her hair's warm sibilance.

As the spring sun melts the winter snow, the earth is renewed in its purity. The wind playing among the grass—each interacting with the other so that the wind is visible within the grass as the grass is stirred to movement by the wind—is in striking contrast to that earlier weather when conquest was all: "A birch kneels. All her whistling fingers fly." In a similar way it is natural to envision "hair's warm sibilance" in the grass caressed by shifting winds; before, there had been strain and urgency in the idea of glimpsing hair in a froth of water:

> By the canoe
> Tugging below the mill-race I could see
> Your hair's keen crescent running.

The transformation now come over the landscape conveys the knowledge Crane values in the Indian: the perfect union of man and woman, a union that guides passivity and calms violence.

When Crane affirms in his concluding stanza that

> We danced, O Brave, we danced beyond their farms.
> In cobalt desert closures made our vows . . .
> Now is the strong prayer folded in thine arms,
> The serpent with the eagle in the boughs.

his note of pride cannot be mistaken. He has a number of reasons to feel satisfaction. He has evoked not just the Indian world but that world of the Indian as revealed through subtly overemphasizing certain aspects of poetic language. By creating symbolic landscapes that reflect the anxiety of those who behold them, he can move to a resolution in a "myth" that, if it is itself not a specific American Indian myth, evokes the process of thinking that could have led to this particular myth. That myth, as it turns out, is intimately relevant to the needs of contemporaries; it functions as a genuine bridge between the Indian and the contemporary, or more accurately, the distance separating past and present collapses in the course of the poem so that time and space no longer seem to be barriers. The strength of "The Dance" is that it offers a myth that is at once demythologized—a myth that is not forbidding but available to one and all, though no less challenging for all that. The Indian world of the past, as Crane portrays it, is hardly a place of golden perfection. The Indian, too, felt anxiety. In examining what the Indian knew, though, one may come upon a lasting truth in an essentialized form, something elemental, undeniable.

In Crane's copy of Waldo Frank's *Our America*, Alan Trachtenberg located this underlined passage on the subject of the Indian: "His magic is not, as in most religions, the tricky power of men over their gods. It lies in the power of nature herself to yield corn from irrigation, to yield meat in game. The Indian therefore does not pray to his God for direct favors. He prays for harmony between himself and the mysterious forces that surround him: of which he is one. For he has learned that from this harmony comes health."[11] The Indian chooses involvement over manipulation; he seeks to find harmony in the "forces that surround him." Though Crane changes Frank's implications, the basic idea remains; what is appealing is that the Indian resolves his difficulty himself, without invoking aid from the gods or without trying to manipulate nature through magic. He adapts to what he has.

In a sense, Crane too has adapted as best he can. There has been a guess that the quarreling couple in "The Wine Menagerie" represents an autobiographical detail, a manifestation of Crane's own childhood, but in "The Dance" it would seem even more likely that the long-standing conflict between his mother and father is reviewed again and explained as a tragic clash of two proud opposites, neither willing to grant the virtues of the other. If the reconciliation in the concluding stanzas seems somewhat abstract, and in any case a bit neat, it may be because Crane himself had no direct experience of it. Yet in that reconciliation, there is the first substantial moment of unity in the poems of *The Bridge* so far. It is a moment of wholeness and harmony which did not occur in "Proem" or in "Ave Maria" in that it promises a clear answer to discord. In a letter to Otto Kahn, Crane prefaced his commentary on "The Dance" with the statement that he was describing "the conflict between the two races in this dance." The note is puzzling because such a conflict between races is barely evident at all; Crane may have had in mind not the effort to heal the conflict between the two races but rather—what may have been to him as difficult a task—the conflict between the two sexes.

2

One good reason to follow "The Dance" with "The Harbor Dawn" is that the dream from which the poet awakens in "The Harbor Dawn" would have been revealed to him through "The Dance." The dance of the final stanzas is a positive value, a lasting insight. It is not a false value like that which had appeared so enticingly only to fade in "Cutty Sark," not a dream of intoxication and speed and spurious glitter, but a lasting dream with endless substance to it, the dream worth pursuing, the dream one can carry beyond the night into the dawn. And that is the great discovery of "The Harbor Dawn": that the star of dreams can be brought into the sunlight, that the star of loving must exist in the dry sands of the city. It is tempting, even in this poem, to lapse back into sleep, to say that only in the inner, protected reaches of the unconscious do dreams have any validity; but that is precisely what Crane overcomes in the course of this poem. This, the loveliest lyric in *The Bridge*, finds Crane turning away from the purely lyric poem he is on the verge of composing and addressing the concerns of his epic.

What dawns on Crane is that, in loving, the "deeds" of the lover are not simply heroic, chivalric activities: they are also deeds that are contracts of promise and obligation. A lover such as Crane imagines is able to include and sustain dreaminess within the self because such a person is always in the process of activating dreams, forming them into deeds. The deep value of loving another frees Crane to enter the bright new day even as he stays in touch with the dreams of the night.

Without this saving awareness—an awareness which takes shape as this poem is formed—one might as well be in a haze, half-asleep. Without the impetus of love, no one is free to articulate dreams and desires; unarticulated, unfocused, undirected, dreams without love are indistinguishable from a foggy haze. This is the situation in which Crane exists at the opening of his poem, unwilling to waken, to abandon his hazy dream world, tossed about painfully, thrown on the sands of the oncoming day only to be tugged back into the waters of the night:

> Insistently through sleep—a tide of voices—
> They meet you listening midway in your dream,
> The long, tired sounds, fog-insulated noises:
> Gongs in white surplices, beshrouded wails,
> Far strum of fog horns . . . signals dispersed in veils.

This nightmarish ebbing and flowing is exhausting—but it is understandable that Crane prefers it to the insistent beat of daily routine, a regularized throbbing from which the heart remains disconnected:

> And then a truck will lumber past the wharves
> As winch engines begin throbbing on some deck;
> Or a drunken stevedore's howl and thud below
> Comes echoing alley-upward through dim snow.

Though a fitful half-sleep may be painful because of its vagueness, it at least eludes the animal howls, the oafish puns, the mechanical beat of the daily grind.

But Crane is drawn back into half-sleep less to avoid the dull sounds of the everyday than to make them over, to incorporate them into his dreams. The poet, poised "midway" in a dream, wanting to escape from the intrusion of the city yet wishing also to take up that throbbing energy of lumbering ahead, enacts his wish in the line: "And if they take your sleep away sometimes / They give it back again." "Sometimes," poised so precisely, pivots toward both "take" and "give"; it evokes that crucial turning which allows him to begin hearing those sounds not as inimical to him but as carrying their own unique music. Yet it is only with the presence of the rising sun that he truly begins to collect himself:

> The sky,
> Cool, feathery fold, suspends, distills
> This wavering slumber. . . . Slowly—
> Immemorially the window, the half-covered chair
> Ask nothing but this sheath of pallid air.

The vast sky now becomes a "cool feathery fold," like a bed which encourages dreaming, and as the light gathers to disclose objects softly and gracefully, suspending them in a "sheath of pallid air," it is as though they are revealed with an innate simplicity that is ample enough.

In this moment of milky half-light, where things appear as if in a translucent sheath, it is as though one's inner dreams were outer, on the verge of turning real. Crane touches upon the love that is within him, a love that is capable of bringing into focus all that had so far been floating associatively. In love, cool arms murmur, close arms sing, eyes drink. All these sensations, so similar to the impossible happenings of dreams yet so vividly real, are brought together in love, in realizing the depths within another.

It is the willingness to pursue the love within him that allows the poet to bring his dreams to light. For a moment, though, this is doubtful. The frost is at the window with its clutching hands, day is approaching, the dreams of the night will melt away. Indeed, the words of the lover, set in italics, may be the words of a "waking dream." But the emphasis falls on "waking" as much as on "dream." Love has been advanced as the one possibility worth searching for. And in the final stanzas, the lover is one with the poet, imaginatively. For if the lover has special eyes—

> *eyes wide, undoubtful*
> *dark*
>   *drink the dawn—*

then this poet surely sees with those eyes. He sees in such a way as to take nourishment from the sun, not shrink from it as he had threatened to do earlier when his dreams were not in touch with his desires but simply floated about and kept him surrounded by a foggy haze.

The change is not accomplished in any obvious way; the final stanzas are as subtle as the rest of this poem, which seems so simply a description of waking to the morning but which is in truth a poem suffused with a wealth of implications. "Cyclopean towers," for instance, all too quickly suggests a one-dimensionality, a lack of depth and perspective, a flatness instead of a richness, a threat in place of a promise—all in striking contrast to the multidimensionality of *"eyes"* that *"drink the dawn":*

> The window goes blond slowly. Frostily clears.
> From Cyclopean towers across Manhattan waters
> —Two—three bright window-eyes aglitter, disk
> The sun, released—aloft with cold gulls hither.

It is the sun flickering across the "Two—three bright window-eyes" that recalls the lover's eyes. It suggests one may in fact meet responsive eyes, eyes like suns, within the very center of the city. The sun is not trapped or pinned in the narrow sheets of glass but finds its own reflection returned in the "window-eyes." As it moves across the glass, it changes the towers from one-eyed cyclops to two eyes, then three eyes, then a multitude of eyes, all blazing an answering response. And out of its stiff, frosty beginning, the stanza yields to motion. The sun is caught, contained, held a moment then lofted into the air, its energy sprung through the line break: "disk / The sun, released—aloft with cold gulls hither."

Rather than being dissipated, the fog of dreams has suffused the air, sunk into the everyday, softening the harsh outlines of things, so that the poet's dreams are no longer wandering but inviting, a part of the morning:

> The fog leans one last moment on the sill.
> Under the mistletoe of dreams, a star—
> As though to join us at some distant hill—
> Turns in the waking west and goes to sleep.

How different a conclusion this is from the morning dawn of "Cutty Sark," where the ghostly regatta appeared only to vanish. Here the star of dreams, instead of blinking out, turns invisible, a constant presence sleeping through the day, yet always there, a lasting promise. For Crane, this is an awareness new not only to *The Bridge* but to all his previous poetry. In "Faustus and Helen III" Helen vanished at dawn; the nighttime world of inner depths, of emotions unrepressed, faded away at the onset of the glare of the orderly business culture. Crane could only assert, somewhat defiantly, that there would be other nights, other Helens. In *Voyages*, too, love could not sustain itself past dawn, except as a lavish but aching memory. The loving of *Voyages* took place out in the ocean, in another world, far from the dry sands of the shore and all its conventionality; it was completely special. But in "The Harbor Dawn" Crane insists that his love lies before him, in the city, in the daylight world, in his future; love will not fade in that bright sunlight, he believes, as long as he carries with him that star of dreams, which he knows "Turns in the waking west" and always persists, as an invisible felt presence.

3

Though Eliot is actively negated all through *The Bridge*, it is in these final poems of 1926—"The Harbor Dawn" and "Van Winkle" and ultimately "The Tunnel"—that Crane most thoroughly confronts him. In "The Harbor Dawn" he takes the fog that to Eliot had appeared as a furtive creature (in the opening of "Prufrock"), like a stray dog aimlessly prodding about the city, and regards it as a beneficent presence, a link to a world of dreams that is all too easily ignored in the bright light of day. The sunlight that only appears once in the nocturnal volume *Prufrock and Other Observations* (in "La Figlia Che Piange": "Weave, weave the sunlight in your hair") is, in "The Harbor Dawn," a welcome extension of the fog which, in a friendly manner, "leans one last moment on the sill," as though lingering for a final word.

In "Van Winkle," Crane probes most deeply into his own past; unlike Eliot, whose view of the past makes it appear as hopelessly fragmented, Crane works toward an understanding that accepts the fragmentation of the past yet reveals that there can be an essential unity between past, present, and future. His affirmation is that the past should not be thought of as that which is finished or complete. It is, instead, incomplete, still to be completed in a future over which he may yet have some control.

The past throws up images not to taunt him with their perfection or with their finality but to call his attention to their incompleteness. They cry out for fulfillment, rather than mock him with their finality. Time is a continuum of which this moment, the present, is the pivotal instant.

By the end of "Van Winkle," it is remarkable how Crane has deepened and matured; like all these poems of 1926, the form of the poem is one in which Crane begins in a position which he strenuously modifies in the course of his work. His progress, in this case, is especially underscored by the shadow that comes over the opening lines when they are repeated at the close. The poem begins:

> Macadam, gun-grey as the tunny's belt,
> Leaps from Far Rockaway to Golden Gate:
> Listen! the miles a hurdy-gurdy grinds—
> Down gold arpeggios mile on mile unwinds.

And it concludes:

> Macadam, gun-grey as the tunny's belt,
> Leaps from Far Rockaway to Golden Gate . . .
> Keep hold of that nickel for car-change, Rip,—
> Have you got your *"Times"*—?
> And hurry along, Van Winkle,—it's getting late!

At the beginning, the air is full of bright possibility, and the macadam that vaults the continent is expressive of speed, of easy freedom. The poet is Adam's son, and cannot resist his playful puns: "gun-grey as the tunny's belt" has buried within it a rambunctious joke about the boxer Gene Tunney, a joke about power and speed. The poet feels himself gigantically strong, as though encompassing the continent, and the sheer oddity of the word "hurdy-gurdy" makes place-names like "Far Rockaway" and "Golden Gate" appear equally playful, inventive, childlike. At the close of the poem, however, after Crane's exploration of innocence lost and childhood spent, those same names echo ominously so that "Far Rockaway" recalls the cradle and "Golden Gate" the grave. Life is over in a blink, spent out and used up before it has begun: "it's getting late!" The bright promises of youth for a glittering future diminish into a nickel for the subway one uses to get to a job. But in this poem, the nickel is also a nick in time he has caught at the last moment, some diminished remnant of his youth. It is a nickel, he cautions himself (as a

child would be cautioned), to hold to dearly. As all that is left of the gold
of the bright morning, it is overwhelmingly precious to him. It cannot be
wasted on the hurdy-gurdy player, amusing as he is, because one can no
longer linger in childish reveries, as he had at the opening of his poem,
but must go on to be the adult who, if he is capable, will carry his childhood memories with him in a new future.

The chastened conclusion of "Van Winkle" is a long step away, then,
from its hopeful but deliberately fatuous beginning, wherein he basked
sublimely in his own lingering innocence, pleased to be able to capture
the feeling of "Times earlier," when he "hurried off to school." It is of
passing importance to note that the first two lines are all that is left of a
projected beginning to *The Bridge* composed at a much earlier, and more
innocent, time. Enclosed in a letter of February 12, 1923, to Allen Tate,
they were intended to be the opening of the whole poem:

> Macadam, gun-grey as the tunny's pelt,
> Leaps from Far Rockaway to Golden Gate,
> For first it was the road, the road only
> We heeded in joint piracy and pushed.

If this opening now strikes him as hopelessly effulgent, a childish notion, it is a mark of how far he has had to come from his earlier concept
of a long poem. It is also a clue to understanding that, at the outset of
"Van Winkle," Crane portrays himself as almost foolishly innocent. Why
recall Pisarro, or Cortes? For the exotic allure of their non-American
names? As a child (he now sees) he was in fact adult and purposeful,
looking for and cherishing heroic gestures as he hurried off to school,
tasting the coffee on his tongue. In retrospect, the poet as child seems
very adult. As an adult, the poet takes revenge, lolling on his way to
work, daydreaming and dawdling to the sounds of the hurdy-gurdy that
bring back a lost world.

It is the memory of Rip Van Winkle that reins him in and pulls him up
short—"Rip Van Winkle, bowing by the way"—for the story of Van
Winkle in effect expresses the child's hesitant belief that the transition to
adult life is impossible to make. At the same time, the tale also cautions
the child to fear daydreaming: one can sleep for twenty years and end up
as a derelict. Crane the adult recognizes his own dereliction in this figure. He feels that he has somehow slept through the transition between
child and adult, and he remains suspended, wanting to play truant from
work but too fearful of the consequences:

And Rip forgot the office hours
and he forgot the pay;
Van Winkle sweeps a tenement
way down on Avenue A.

The past can become a sleepy hollow, and one can decide not to grow up; but one pays for this by being shunted aside, consigned to a minor role in the adult world.

The opening of "Van Winkle," then, is dominated by anxieties about growing up; Rip Van Winkle, who gradually emerges as the central figure from childhood, exemplifies the split between the child and the adult, the past and the present—the gap that Crane recognizes in himself and will attempt to overcome. The movement toward healing this split begins when Crane presses beyond his youthful reveries toward memories which are genuinely dark and haunting. With "Remember, remember" and its refrain "Recall—recall," he summons an image from his past which stands simultaneously for his own present attitude toward the past. (As in "Repose of Rivers" but in a far more complex way, the images he summons up of the past contain folded within them his present stance toward the past.) Once one steps beyond pleasant daydreaming, the past is a cinder pile, dead ashes under which remains a nest of snakes, stoned under, rigidly suppressed. The "hurdy-gurdy," a playful and childlike name, reverts to the dark associations of the "grind-organ":

> The grind-organ says . . . Remember, remember
> The cinder pile at the end of the backyard
> Where we stoned the family of young
> Garter snakes under . . . And the monoplanes
> We launched—with paper wings and twisted
> Rubber bands . . .

Crane reaches into this memory with reluctance. It is not surprising, so fearsome is Crane's image of suppression, that he no sooner touches upon the memory of the stoning under than he swerves at once to an image of flight. Except that he cannot flee: the image of the stoned-under snakes from the past holds him, and it is echoed at once in the "twisted / Rubber bands" of the "monoplanes / We launched." Those snakes will not lie still. The past is not a lifeless cinder pile. And with the hesitant pursuit of "Recall—recall" the past actually starts back to life, terri-

fyingly, as the dead ash heap flickers back at his prodding to reveal
tongues of snakes, tongues of fire:

Recall—recall

the rapid tongues
That flittered from under the ash heap day
After day whenever your stick discovered
Some sunning inch of unsuspecting fibre—
It flashed back at your thrust, as clean as fire.

The past stirred to life is a stinging tongue of fire, and for a moment it is
clear how utterly lost he is, an adult pretending to be a child, a Van
Winkle pressed between then and now, split:

And Rip was slowly made aware
that he, Van Winkle, was not here
nor there. He woke and swore he'd seen Broadway
a Catskill daisy chain in May.

This singsong nursery rhyme falters and stumbles, as the rhyme of
"there" is delayed.

Out of this extreme disorientation, Crane moves to a series of distraught meditations on memory. What is it, what is memory? It strikes
like a hidden snake suddenly coming to life, yet it is oddly distant, remote and unapproachable, not simply fearful:

So memory, that strikes a rhyme out of a box,
Or splits a random smell of flowers through glass—
Is it the whip stripped from the lilac tree
One day in spring my father took to me,
Or is it the sabbatical, unconscious smile
My mother almost brought me once from church
And once only, as I recall—?

Resolving this question is of utmost importance to Crane, for the view
one takes toward memory dictates the course of one's own life. One can
choose to take memory as being the whip that stings yet suffuses the air
with the smell of lilacs, the torn branch that oddly persists in living. Yet
this definition is, while true, inadequate: it fails to include that aspect of
memory which is its incompleteness—the sense in which memory pressing itself forward into the present is not simply a surprise jack-in-the-box
or an arbitrary and whimsical association (a "random smell of flowers

through glass") but a profound expression of individual need, a sign of that which is still lost and seeking to be found. What characterizes memory is not that it is truly dead with an illusion of life about it (like the whip still scented with lilacs) but that it is truly alive with an illusion of death about it.

The past is not dead but dormant, not complete but incomplete—and what is more, it appears in the present because it represents a message undelivered, a gesture unfulfilled. The "it" that Crane had been using to ponder on memory now merges into the "it" of his mother's lost smile. Her smile, which he had thought to be lost forever, left undelivered to him one Sunday morning, is not at all absent or vanished: it is still lost, still undelivered, hovering in the air, a broken promise in need of fulfillment. As he relives this painful moment of his childhood, he becomes more insistent on the smile's presence.[12] The more this smile fades, the more emphatically it remains. If it is a betrayal, it is not like one of those clipper dreams in "Cutty Sark" which remains an impossible lure—it is a betrayal that can be reversed, if only another person can be found who will return this lost smile. Crane asserts this conviction through the increasingly dominant position of "it" and "It" and "it" and "It":

> It flickered through the snow screen, blindly
> It forsook her at the doorway, it was gone
> Before I left the window. It
> Did not return with the kiss in the hall.

The word stubbornly presses its way forward, becoming more and more prominent as the actual smile vanishes. The first "It" is barely emphasized at all, since the accent in the line falls on the first syllable in "flickered." The second "It" receives a stronger but still tremulous beat, since the trochaic substitution in the first foot of the second line is both a surprise as well as a natural continuation of the unaccented second syllable in "blindly." But the third "it" springs the rhythm of the line, a line which is itself rhythmically shaky but which gathers some of its lost impetus after the pause of the comma. And the final "It" is most noticeable. It receives a full, sure beat, and it clings to the end of the line as though never wanting to push off. In this passage, Crane is not just mimicking in rhythms his childish desperation, watching the smile fade with increasing panic: as it fades, it endures, grows even stronger, evoking a burning need for love that bridges the gap separating the child from the adult.

In "Van Winkle"—a most neglected, most important segment of *The*

Bridge—Crane looks back not only to his early life but also to the earliest versions of his long poem. The poem may contain Crane's own judgment on his first idea of what an epic poem should be: a barrage of exotic
words, all of them on the move. This now, it seems, was childish, an
evasion of the complexity of the depths within him. These depths are
brought into the open here, not simply exposed but taken up and worked
through, in a way that increasingly becomes the hallmark of these 1926
poems. Once one discovers, through self-awareness, what exactly it is
that one lacks, then one has simultaneously realized what it is that one
needs. One creates a course for the future by understanding his present
situation in terms of a past that is now viewed not as finished or final but
incomplete, in need of fulfillment. That is the essential point which
these poems develop and on which they all pivot; it is the secret of living
in the modern age, where there are no ready guideposts to action but
where one can freely turn to examine and analyze and then act upon his
own discoveries.

Less easily identifiable is the poem's firm rebuttal to Eliot (and indi-
rectly to Tate). It might have been apparent only to Tate that Crane was
finally fulfilling a promise he had made in a letter to Tate of June 12,
1922; speaking of Eliot, he said: "I have discovered a safe tangent to
strike which, if I can possibly explain the position,—goes *through* him
toward a *different goal*." Echoing images drawn from *Prufrock and Other
Observations*, Crane insists that Eliot stopped too soon, only halfway
thinking through the problems fostered by the persistence of memory.
Crane goes farther and will continue to range beyond his first influence
in his next poem, which even more directly denies the conclusions of
Eliot, "The Tunnel."

10
The Bridge in 1926 (III)

At the end of "Van Winkle," Crane prepares himself to seek, in the love of another, that lost smile he recalls from his youth. An abrupt shift intervenes if "The Tunnel" follows. But this next poem, recounting a return home from a long day—a return home in which the poet is clearly alone, obviously unrequited—is unsettling for all the right reasons: it is, first and foremost, the necessary prelude to the uniqueness of the recovery proposed in "Atlantis." Just as important, though, is the fact that the gap between the firm resolve of "Van Winkle" and the despair with which "The Tunnel" begins is a suggestion of the difficulty of sustaining or even creating a genuine relationship with another. "The Tunnel" is the acid test of Crane's ability to persevere in his beliefs, a test he very nearly fails.

"The Tunnel" is an approach to "Atlantis," the grand climax Crane has had on hand for so long (though substantially altered since 1923). The problem posed by the juxtaposition of these two poems is how can Crane, after the nadir of the subway ride, justify his glowing conclusion. Most critics have found Crane depending on the figure of the "Wop washerwoman" to help close the gap. If the subway is a modern Inferno, critics say, Crane populates it with a Persephone, who intercedes for Crane just as, say, the Virgin Mary interceded for Columbus. When Crane realizes that she endures despite the city, that she apparently intends to "bring mother eyes and hands / Back home to children and to golden hair," he finds himself renewed.[1]

Though the washerwoman, the faithful mother, may seem to be the perfect love-object for Crane (especially following the recollection of his own mother in "Van Winkle"), the episode is actually quite complicated when read in the context of the whole poem. It is significant that Crane addresses her with an "also" that includes him within her situation, enclosing both of them in a dilemma that they share:

171

> And does the daemon take you home, also,
> Wop washerwoman with the bandaged hair?
> After the corridors are swept, the cuspidors—
> The gaunt sky-barracks cleanly now, and bare,
> O Genoese, do you bring mother eyes and hands
> Back home to children and to golden hair?

It is important to recognize that these are genuine questions Crane poses, not rhetorical flourishes or projections of possibility. All is thrown into doubt. In her job, she is no more than a "Wop washerwoman" with "bandaged hair" and her duties are lower than anyone else's. Can she emerge from that humiliation to become a "Genoese," with all the proud associations with Columbus that name recalls? After exhausting herself in the "gaunt sky-barracks" has she still the extra energy to "bring mother eyes and hands / Back home"? Or will her smile, even more than his mother's, vanish long before it even reaches the doorway?

What prevents these lines from lapsing into sentimentality is that the questions relate so pressingly to Crane's own position as a poet. The force of the passage is not due to any expansive affirmation the washerwoman introduces; indeed, there is nothing expansive in the lines at all. Her presence, to the contrary, gives rise to a whole range of doubts. But Crane takes these doubts seriously: her problem is representative, even universal, and at the center of his own efforts. Must an individual live out an existence that is split in two, with work on one side, a home on the other? The passage is striking for a reason which most commentators omit in their explanations. The washerwoman, rather than acting as a Persephone or guiding spirit who helps him break away from his difficulties, actually draws attention to them and makes him acutely aware of his own dilemma. Yet critics are right in hearing an affirmative note in the passage: it is the delicacy with which Crane comes in contact with himself, with his own deepest concerns, by way of reaching out to understanding another person. It recalls the central turn in the third and fourth stanzas of "Proem." And in making this identification, however tentatively, he is pressing against the anonymity and self-isolation into which the subway setting encourages persons to fall. That makes this gesture of identification a true turning point in a poem which is a far more original and inventive work than it may at first seem.

1

Even in 1926, the idea of writing a poem critical of the subway was already somewhat hackneyed, but Crane was to give it a specific twist that actually prepared him to make a crucial turn at the very end of his poem. In other poets' versions of subway verse, for example Allen Tate's Italian sonnet of 1928, the idea is to stress the unmanageable, out of control aspects of the machine. To Tate, what is horrifying about the subway is that its immediate impact is so overwhelming that it renders one defenseless, sucked up and swept away, reduced to hysteria. Tate begins his octet:

> Dark accurate plunger down the successive hell
> Of arch on arch, where ogives burst a red
> Reverberance of hail upon the dead
> Thunder like an exploding crucible!

The subway packs Tate's poem, shouldering everything else aside in the chaos and frenzy that infects even the language which itself turns demonic. What survives, as Yvor Winters noted with approval, is the sonnet form itself, which just barely manages to control the hysteria. In the sestet, Tate confesses "I am become geometries" and condemns the subway as being that which is most adequately regarded by the "cold revery of an idiot."[2]

By contrast, Crane is uninterested in conveying first impressions. He wants to reproduce the day-by-day experience of taking the subway, rather than the special experience of helplessly trying to raise a voice to outshout it. Day by day one rides the subway defensively, on guard, not permitting the ugliness of the surroundings to penetrate his sensibility. In this respect, the subway is a paradigm for one view of the city, a view that Crane is taking at this moment of marked disillusion. The end result of his day and his evening on the town—an evening that is a hollow array of anonymous lights and empty patterns—is to "wish yourself in bed / With tabloid crime-sheets perched in easy sight." To be safe in bed, not sharing a bed, and with the violence of the city spread bitterly before him to be viewed as a jaundiced entertainment held at a safe distance— this is the sour home to which he aspires.

Deliberately submerged in himself, protective of his own self-imposed isolation, Crane addresses a "you" that is only himself; it is a part of the alienation dramatized throughout the poem, as though to move through

the city at all you must see yourself in the second-person, as a "you,"
detached and remote and thereby protected from any encroachment on
your self. There have been few modern poems which strive so steadily to
capture the air of contrived boredom that city-dwellers wear as a cloak
over themselves; it is the tone of Eliot's city poems but with its underlying defensiveness revealed. (And to his everlasting credit, Eliot accepted "The Tunnel" for publication in the *Criterion*.) Every decision
Crane makes is at odds with resolutions made earlier in the 1926 sequence. He toys, for example, with the idea of walking home, but that's
too strenuous and abruptly, almost whimsically, he drops the notion without developing it, lapsing into the security of routine:

> Or can't you quite make up your mind to ride;
> A walk is better underneath the L a brisk
> Ten blocks or so before? But you find yourself
> Preparing penguin flexions of the arms,—
> As usual you will meet the scuttle yawn:
> The subway yawns the quickest promise home.

"Scuttle yawn" is the apt characterization, "scuttle" suggesting the fast
pace of modern life, but "yawn" implying that such a pace is exhausting
and one must adopt a jaundiced attitude to survive. Others must be kept
within their own territorial space. The thing to do is protect against unexpected, unwarranted encounters, so it is essential to

> Avoid the glass doors gyring at your right,
> Where boxed alone a second, eyes take fright
> —Quite unprepared rush naked back to light.

Contrast these lines with the anticipation, at the end of "The Harbor
Dawn," when Crane saw the rising sun greet its own multiplying reflection in the "window-eyes" of the skyscrapers, as though the city were
alive with answering gazes. Crane's actions in "The Tunnel" are a disavowal of all he has learned so far in the course of his work.

On entering the subway, then, what one concentrates on, certainly
without thinking, automatically, is the dull hum in the background that
cancels out voices or reduces them to broken mutters:

> In the car
> the overtone of motion
> underground, the monotone
> of motion is the sound
> of other faces, also underground—

Of course it is not easy to remain dissociated from others, especially since the wash of voices keeps tossing up inviting strands of thought that engage the ear. In fact, Crane's deaf ear is continually penetrated by phrases and images and fragments that touch on his own, now deeply buried, concerns.[3] But he is concentrating on ignoring them, and each wave of conversation is attended to with a scornful, dismissive commentary:

> Our tongues recant like beaten weather vanes.
> This answer lives like verdigris—like
> hair beyond extinction, surcease of the bone.

Only as hair continues to grow on a corpse, so these concerns persist in his ear. A second wash of conversation, which carries images of men and women together, provokes another glare from out of the fiery wall of contempt he has built around himself: love is "A burnt match skating in a urinal."

Yet each of these dismissive phrases cuts more deeply into Crane than into the heedless voices which float around him. He must ultimately question what he is doing to himself by refusing to acknowledge what is around him. In the first of a series of major turns in the poem, he wonders whether Poe may have been haunted by a similar inability to escape into withdrawal. Are Poe's nightmare images, which fit the subway so well, efforts to repulse fearful encroachments, or are they efforts at portraying the horrors of self-imposed isolation? "Did you deny the ticket, Poe?" Crane asks. These words are crucial not because of an identity they assert between Poe and Crane—an identity farfetched and not to be pursued—but because they reveal Crane stirring, however sluggishly and morbidly, to shift out of his own isolation. He is reaching out to address himself not as an alienated "you," which is entirely self-enclosed, but by way of another person, though that other person is a dead writer whose presence is purely imaginary.

The form of "The Tunnel," however, is dominated by a series of twists, each one more ironic and perverse than the last. Each time Crane resolves to break away from his self-imposed isolation, something around him shifts and disrupts his effort. Aware that it is himself he is castigating in his isolation, aware that it is his head which is swinging from the strap, and beginning to stir back to life by way of his address to himself through Poe, he is on the verge of shattering his air of cultivated indifference. But before he can do so, the subway car reaches a stop and empties itself out, and all the inhabitants are wistfully viewed as prisoners released "somewhere above where streets / Burst suddenly in rain." Having achieved the complete self-enclosure he had sought at the beginning, he then begins to summon the energy to resist it—only to discover himself virtually abandoned in the deserted subway car. The newspapers "revolve and wing," not just echoing the white gull's wings of "Proem" but also recalling his own new longing to be free. But new things age quickly in the speedy city and are discarded to flutter helplessly in dark corners.

It is in this sudden, overwhelming emptiness that he notices the washerwoman, the other person left in the car with him. In seeing her for the first time, he regards her with an intensity of feeling that he could have better used earlier, when the car was still crowded. Now it comes too late; though he looks at her searchingly, though he forms his pressing questions, there is no recognition forthcoming, no sign, no answer. He is reaching out to another but with no response, and it seems, then, that he is more cut off than ever. The subway is a "demurring and eventful yawn" that only fosters among people an air of thorough indifference.

The episode or lack of an encounter with the washerwoman is the first time in "The Tunnel" Crane has not only ventured to acknowledge the presence of another individual (unlike Poe she is actually before him) but has addressed that other with questions of primary importance to him. When his overture arouses no answer, he will twist, with extraordinary violence, to condemn the city for its perversity; it throws up hopes only to frustrate them. In the contorted images of abortion he clearly abandons hope for any response at all:

> O cruelly to inoculate the brinking dawn
> With antennae toward worlds that glow and sink—
> To spoon us out more liquid than the dim
> Locution of the eldest star, and pack
> The conscience navelled in the plunging wind,
> Umbilical to call—and straightway die!

In the city, to be born is to die at once: to open oneself to another is to encounter straightway dismissal. A moment of tenderness or concern is swallowed up and lost.

At this the lowest point of *The Bridge*, when feeling has been reduced to "shrill ganglia / Impassioned with some song we fail to keep," the subway abruptly begins to emerge aboveground. This speedy shift has been greeted by commentators as a manifestation of a major breakthrough, a sign that events are at last turning in the poet's favor. Nothing could be less accurate. L. S. Dembo suggests that the fundamental rhythm of this part of *The Bridge* is that every death gives rise to a rebirth, every descent becomes an ascent, every Inferno has its Purgatory.[4] Crane's intention is, once again, more complex than it first appears. The abrupt shift of the subway is one more instance of the cruel twists of the machine, which is thoroughly indifferent to everyone's emotions, incapable of acting like a person. Just as the car emptied out when Crane was about to acknowledge the life in the crowd around him, now the car breaks upward just as Crane is about to bury himself. At the moment he gives up, then the subway begins to act providentially. That he follows through and so quickly changes his tune—

> And yet, like Lazarus, to feel the slope,
> The sod and billow breaking,—lifting ground,
> —A sound of waters bending astride the sky
> Unceasing with some Word that will not die . . . !

—reveals a gratitude at his release which is understandable yet craven, something akin to the gratitude the prisoner bestows upon the captor who releases him. Seizing on the routine and taking it for a portent, he is emotionally elevated. But the overall impression remains disturbing. Rather than ending on a note of exultation, the passage closes frenetically, a sudden turnaround clutched in desperate haste.

It is not this pseudo-rebirth at the subway's emergence—a rebirth that Crane severely undercuts by the pattern of perverse twists which dominates the poem—that makes "The Tunnel" so effective a counter to *The Waste Land*. Crane counters Eliot subtly by showing that the forms of writing Eliot adopts (the overheard fragment, for example, the snatch of conversation that seems to mock genuine values) are in fact by-products of the personality who is determined consciously to suppress his own feelings. The poet who descends into the Eliotic Inferno of the big city subway issues a warning to himself which he all too strictly, all too thoroughly follows: "Be minimum, then, to swim the hiving swarms." In short, Crane is in part bent on exposing the Eliotic narrator; that narrator is not, as Eliot suggests, the voice of the age, an impersonal chronicler, but a rather precise and self-willed type, spawned by the modern city which creates the wish for personal self-protection. When Crane recognizes, as he will in the coda to "The Tunnel"—the crucial transition to "Atlantis"—that he himself had willed his own fate from start to finish, and nothing about it had been preordained, then he is prepared for his final (though tragically postponed) affirmation.

In the coda to "The Tunnel," the toll taken by the subway ride is clearly in evidence. Indeed, every aspect of his journey home has amounted to a moral failure, as each effort to recover his previous resolution had been frustrated by the indifferent twists of the subway ride. Consequently, he arrives at journey's end as a man dispossessed, in disgrace. Yet it is remarkable how these final lines, while conveying the exhaustion that accompanies the poet, also ring and echo with other memories of *The Bridge*. In an image that mingles weariness with oblivious violence, "A tugboat, wheezing wreaths of steam, / Lunged past, with one galvanic blare stove up the river"—but Crane here recalls the wraiths of "The Harbor Dawn" in the "wreaths of steam," and he evokes the derelict sailor of "Cutty Sark" who, even though an apparently broken man, still "lunged up Bowery way," and he remembers the downward sucking river from a fragment entitled "Calgary Express" (which he will eventually rewrite into "The River"). The images poise hesitantly, neither dark nor light, neither negative nor positive, but balanced for either tilt. They convey Crane's exhaustion and his restlessness in that they suggest failure yet hold out still the promise of what could have been done. They prevent him from being quit of the city, even though he is on the Brooklyn side, and they keep him lingering by the waters, as though drawn to some hidden message: "I counted the echoes assembling, one after one, / Searching, thumbing the midnight on the piers."

But it is only when he seriously entertains the thought of abandoning his quest, watching his hands flounder helplessly as they "drop memory," that he is able to see that the fault is his own. In essence, the fault is that he looked to the city, expecting it to appeal to him, whereas only he holds in his hands the decisive power to accept life. The "Hand of Fire" is his own hand, no other; the test originates with himself. It is he who creates possibilities—or denies them, by choosing to box himself alone for a second, fearing the fright that could appear in the eyes of another but that could also be a prelude to a genuine encounter.

"The Tunnel" has unfolded as a series of belated recognitions, as though the speed and convenience of modern transportation outstrips the capacity of the mind to evaluate and act upon perceptions. The turn to "Atlantis" is the most important belated recognition of all: he should have walked home, across the Bridge. He should have taken at least that risk. Such a risk may well have ended (as in "Cutty Sark") in the aching frustration of a fading dream, but it might have brought him in contact with another, a contact that would have led to a walk home across the Bridge with his love hand in hand. What then is "Atlantis" if not that walk home that was not taken but that should have been taken and that will be taken someday? He stands now on the Brooklyn side of the shore, having chosen the subway over the Bridge, having chosen death over life. He has denied himself his opportunity. (There may also be a trace of an understanding here that, with his epic virtually complete, he has not in fact composed the "mystical synthesis of values in terms of our America" that he had proposed for himself.) So the poem he composes in "Atlantis" contains all that he did not do: it is the walk home that he did not take, that walk drenched in all the possibilities he looks back upon and sees he may have lost, but recovered here in a blend of memory with imagination, a fantastic creation, a dream he pledges will never fade.

2

"Atlantis" is, surely, the least-read of all Crane's poems. What makes it so unattractive is its insistent extravagance, its exhaustive ebullience. Classically, it has all the earmarks of amateur verse—it is boldly overwritten, coyly arcane, brightly uplifting. Viewed even in the context of the final version of *The Bridge* it has perhaps rebuffed more readers than it has attracted; and those it has attracted are not liable to respond to other aspects of his work.

But it is not possible to imagine a more appropriate conclusion to the 1926 sequence. In the last of a series of confident turns that characterize all the 1926 contributions to *The Bridge* Crane understands that the very unreality of "Atlantis" is essential. Here, as elsewhere, his sensitivity to the tone in his writing requires an ear tuned not to celebration but to subtlety. Columbus's opening speech in "Ave Maria" needed to be heard as bombastic, vaunting, egotistic, so he could move beyond it. The clipper dreams in "Cutty Sark" were not just the dreams of the derelict sailor reconstructed from the past but those dreams as the sailor must have known them, as utterly evanescent, impossible ever to sustain. The twin opposite landscapes in "The Dance" were each tinged with its own excess, one going to seed, the other up in smoke. For the dream in "The Harbor Dawn" to emerge powerfully at the end, Crane had to portray the hour before dawn, the misty half-sleep when one is only partially awake and shrinks back from the burden of the oncoming day, plunging back into a fitful, restless sleep, clutching to the vague dreams of the night. "Van Winkle" depended for its opening on evoking that touch of fatuity that accompanies the bright sense of recovered youth. In all these examples, the language at first never seemed as specific as it later came to be, and the reason is that only as Crane came to understand the limits of his opening position was he able to develop his poem; from the opening stanzas of "Proem," where the attention is caught by the white wings of the gull only to lead to frustration, these poems are continually composed of false starts. Understanding what it is that he lacks, Crane realizes what it is that he needs: that is the essence of these 1926 poems which rise out of nothing more and nothing less than Crane's own awareness of what he learns he must move beyond.

By the time of "Atlantis," then, we are in a position to attend to the wishfulness included in the poem, recognizing that the work is not a resolution or a synthesis but an outburst, a release of energy, a projection of an impossibly possible future. Unreal and excessive, the poetry of "Atlantis" is suffused with all the longing that has been held suspended throughout; it is the binge that has been denied—yet it is also appropriate to the circumstances.

R. W. B. Lewis wondered why this section was called "Atlantis" rather than "Cathay," then suggested that here Crane uses words that could be freely interchanged with each other: "It can thus be called Cathay or Atlantis, or by the name of any vanished city: Tyre or Troy, for example, or the Pompeii dimly suggested by the 'water-gutted lava' of 'Cutty Sark.'" [5] But the name "Atlantis" is important because it evokes a city that is not simply lost in the past, like Tyre or Troy or Pompeii, but a city as yet undiscovered in any form but which, some believe, will be rediscovered one day. Atlantis is a city fabulous in a way that other lost cities are not: though presently lost, it will someday return. It therefore stands as a parallel to human hope and desire, which also pursue that which may be recovered again. In this poem, Crane begs forgiveness for doubting the existence of a yearning that is so necessary to living.

The presence of the Bridge—as a splendid walkway arching over the city whereupon one journeys with his love—calls Crane back to the quest he had abandoned in "The Tunnel." But the poem naturally serves as a reminder that the way is not just alluring but fraught with uncertainty, open to doubt and difficulty. If the first three stanzas are relatively flowing—with each phrase stemming from the last and "on" and "Beyond" and "Onward and up" and "upward, upward" all appearing within a few lines of each other—by the fourth stanza progress becomes arduous. The eyes "pick biting way up towering looms" and peer through "smoking pyres of love and death." But if the quest is challenging it also holds out the promise of the "white, pervasive Paradigm" of "Love." In the only lines to survive nearly intact from the late drafts of 1923, the Bridge is now made to arch forward yearningly as individuals themselves reach out to one another:

> —iridescently upbourne
> Through the bright drench and fabric of our veins;
> With white escarpments swinging into light,
> Sustained in tears the cities are endowed
> And justified conclamant to the ripe fields
> Revolving through their harvests in sweet torment.

The Bridge is itself an act of searching, all-embracing and all-inclusive.

Crane must ask forgiveness, though, judging himself for lapsing from this model of all aspiration. When he says, "Thy pardon for this history, whitest flower," and begs that the idea of Atlantis (as replicated in this Bridge) will "hold thy floating singer late!" he is at once both near and distant in relation to his goal, in a way that is the peculiar hallmark of this poem. He is near in that he addresses the Bridge as though it were the lover for whom he had sought; but he is distant in that he is not speaking to an actual lover but to a projection, a symbol, that offers no response except as an appropriate conclusion to his quest.

"Atlantis" is a pledge, but it is also an oblique confession that Crane himself failed in the course of his day to discover his love. It is easy for him to renew his pledge dramatically, alone on the shore, imaginatively traversing the Bridge that he sees in the distance, elegantly reliving an alternate, ideal route home. The allure of what might have been, coupled with his own guilt at having failed to rise to the occasion at a more propitious time, suffuses his imaginary walk home with a perfection that is both a lure to the future and a chastisement for past failures. In a sense, Crane wonderfully manages to have it both ways: if there is a love for him to be met in the future, then he will walk home over the Bridge in just this way, so inspired that everything he sees will remind him of something else; but he can imagine that in its fullness as a way of castigating himself for all that he missed by taking the subway. To be fair, the poem leaves open whether Crane can, in the future, rise to the occasion. Can the failures of the past be reversed by the actions that lead to a real fu-

ture? Is there a dream that is not fading? Is it possible that masculine
and feminine, sheer antipodes of each other, can be united? The questions remain unanswered at the end, and the poem closes on a renewed
note of suspension:

> Is it Cathay,
> Now pity steeps the grass and rainbows ring
> The serpent with the eagle in the leaves . . . ?
> Whispers antiphonal in azure swing.

As a rounded, complete conclusion, as a poem of utter unification—a
fusion of the contemporary with the eternal or the machine with nature—
"Atlantis" does not succeed. But it was not intended to be that kind of
success. As a wishful projection of memory with desire, a poem both
drenched in remorse and swept with anticipation, a poem entirely aware
of its own unreality, "Atlantis" is a uniquely successful work, a poem
quite unlike most other conclusions to an epic. It confesses what other
conclusions often lead one to suspect: that the conclusion has been delivered, not earned, as a gift to the poet. Yet it is also particularly appropriate to Crane's sequence so far. It evokes a future that may be close at
hand yet remains out of reach, luring him forward continually. It does not
suggest that Crane has attained any certainty: the relationship he has
with the Bridge is a stand-in for an acknowledged absence. The Bridge
is an ideal which would prefer to have its function usurped by an actual
person. But Crane has failed to seek out that other, he has betrayed his
own resolve, and he can only recover it with a pledge and with this demonstration of the depth of his feelings. In the poem, he both affirms the
rightness of his renewed quest as well as confessing to the inadequacy of
himself and of this moment.

It is not the poem Crane set out to write; it is not even the poem that he
wanted to write. But it is a poem that acknowledges both those things
and it is a poem that makes understandable why it is the way it is, a
failure that points to success. As a splendid failure, it is an undeniable
triumph: suffused with the particular feelings of a special moment, yet
climactic and uplifting and energizing, the conclusion that he did not
earn yet could realize by understanding why he failed to earn it. No other
ending could be so appropriate for *The Bridge*.

3

These poems of *The Bridge* written in the summer of 1926 and revised in the fall and winter of 1926–27 form an illustrious sequence in their own right. A poet more confident of himself than Crane might easily have bundled them together and, pronouncing his long-overdue epic complete, moved on to newer tasks. In this form, *The Bridge* would have been a kind of urban *Voyages*, though less intense, more ample, than the six poems of love and the sea. It would have appeared as a developing narrative, a poem in process, in which the poet continually came up against examples of his own inadequacy and struggled to work beyond them.

In the sequence he fails, it is true, to find love; but to have found love would have been to compose a series of love poems instead of a cultural epic. And the 1926 *Bridge* is a cultural epic: what it accomplishes is to portray the very search for love as a quest with its own immediate rewards. To decide to undertake a quest for love is at once to counter the defects that are inherent in modern culture. The central defect is that, with its emphasis on speed, on flight, on sheer freedom, modern culture encourages persons to pursue diversionary outlets that never fulfill their true, deep needs but only temporarily assuage their longing. Modern culture seems best suited for novel celebration, false elation, illusions of progress, ephemeral intoxications. That persons are driven toward these aimless forms of release is not, Crane carefully maintains, a sign of their weakness but rather a sign that they long for change. Persons have desires, dreams, and aspirations, all of which this mobile culture frees them to pursue, but all too often the wrong inclinations are pursued, and individuals remain isolated and restless and anonymous.

These ideas are by no means unique—though it is somewhat unique to discover them held by Crane, who had at an earlier stage in his growth believed in the virtues of speed and flight. What makes the poems unique is the way Crane develops them, turning on an act of self-examination which allows the poet to shape his poem in a meaningful way even as he has no guidelines to follow. That he can accomplish this again and again, in poem after poem, illustrates that it was no temporary gift but a central understanding, certainly intuitive, that virtually created one poem after another, the next rising almost spontaneously out of its predecessor. The unity of the sequence as a whole deserves underscoring, for it is complete in a way that is rare for even the finest modern poems.

Columbus's discovery of Cathay was the realization of a dream, but he had to understand that dreams turn into nightmares if they are undertaken as expressions of power and authority and control. In "Cutty Sark" Crane recognizes an even subtler problem: that persons can be obsessed with fading dreams, holdovers from youth that remain continually alluring but serve to postpone the actual fact of living. With "Three Songs" Crane regards others who have become alienated from their own potential, largely because they contort themselves by pursuing impossible dreams. Their dreams, though as destructive as that of the derelict, are more insidious because their false pursuit of an impossible ideal is sanctioned by others, even encouraged by aspects of the culture. To break free of the contemporary view, Crane shifts ground to the past of "The Dance" and there finds confirmed what he had suspected in "Three Songs": that it is destructive for the masculine and the feminine to be apart, creative for them to be together. This confirmation allows him, in "The Harbor Dawn," to waken with a new sense of promise, a belief that one can carry forward his inner feelings to the outer world. This is further developed in "Van Winkle" through his conviction that the past is not finished but incomplete, awaiting fulfillment in a new future. But the difficulty of an oppressive custom hangs over the poet in "The Tunnel," and it is only after failing to live up to his own high standards that Crane, in the final poem, recovers his original impetus.

This version of *The Bridge*—arranged in a format that follows the likely order in which the poems actually made themselves appear— would have been a breathtaking achievement. At its center would be the confirmation of "The Dance," but a confirmation approached carefully through the disquieting analysis of "Three Songs." "The Dance" in turn would give rise to the waking dream of "The Harbor Dawn" which would then shift the burden to Crane himself, now charged with enacting his own realizations. The first half of the sequence, up to "The Dance," would have been exploratory, groping, and tentative, as the dimensions of the problem of modern culture are gradually revealed; the second half would represent the actual difficulty of undertaking the quest, a difficulty not resolved but acknowledged with impressive honesty in "The Tunnel" and in "Atlantis."

Not only is the 1926 sequence an impressive poem in its own right, it is free of the confusion created by Crane's own assemblage of his poems, an order established as early as spring 1927. In the 1927 assemblage, which is identical to the published version except for poems added later in 1927 and 1929, "The Harbor Dawn" follows "Ave Maria." The dream glimpsed in "The Harbor Dawn" is not, then, the dream of "The Dance" but the revelations of Columbus. It is a peculiar pairing. "Ave Maria" charges the poet to be careful of greed and egotism, but this never appears as a problem to the poet waking in bed and recalling an imaginary lover. With this juxtaposition, it becomes plausible to focus on the relation between Columbus and the Virgin Mary, disrupting the true course of "Ave Maria" and spiritualizing the love in "The Harbor Dawn."

If "Cutty Sark" follows "Ave Maria," as it had in the course of composition, then Crane, contrasting Columbus and the derelict sailor, is in a position to judge the inadequacy of the old sailor's dreams. But in 1927, "Cutty Sark" is placed after the long journey back into the past that is Crane's new ambitious version of "Powhatan's Daughter." The result encourages one to think that "Cutty Sark" represents an example of the aging of a once youthful country. We are witness to the spectacle of an old man, lost in memories that point to a glorious past. The implication becomes that the country has fatally tended to set aside its youthful dreams—a conclusion quite the opposite of the 1926 poem, which maintains that by clinging to youthful dreams one postpones actual living.

The 1926 sequence places an unmistakable emphasis on what people can do for themselves: the poet, in "Van Winkle," can make over the past if he searches for a future that will deliver the smile that is not forgotten but only lost. When he shifts to "The Tunnel," then, our attention is already focused on his actions as an individual, and it becomes readily apparent that, entering the subway, he is deliberately suppressing his best self. In 1927, Crane placed "Three Songs" before "The Tunnel" (and in 1929 he added "Quaker Hill" as a transition); "Three Songs," grouped in a portion of the poem along with "Cutty Sark" in which the setting is the present, suggests at once that there may be something debased as a characteristic of contemporary life. As a result, entering "The Tunnel" we are prepared to expect numbness as an overall cultural condition, not a choice that, as in 1926, an individual may make. Moreover, in 1926, with "Van Winkle," Crane remains intent upon his search for love, and "The Tunnel" becomes an interlude in which he loses his way only to recover it in "Atlantis." But if "The Tunnel" portrays an overwhelming cultural condition, as it would appear to do in the 1927 assemblage, then the sudden enthusiasm of "Atlantis" would seem truly unearned, a surprise, an uncalled-for reversal of the long despair building since "Cutty Sark."

By 1927, Crane had devised an arrangement for his work that was re-markably cumbersome; the poems placed side by side not only did not shed light on each other, they actually illuminate eccentric aspects of themselves. They emphasize what should be in the background, and they minimize what should be in the foreground. If the 1926 *Bridge* was a breathtaking achievement, it was also a delicate accomplishment; in-deed, each poem rises or falls depending on Crane's ear for language, his ability to catch the falseness or excess or strain in his opening words. Perhaps because of the distortion brought about by his 1927 assemblage, he loses this delicacy of tone in his later additions to *The Bridge*. Each of the 1926 poems flowed wonderfully out of its predecessor and toward its successor. But once Crane pulled out of that flow, he lost those subtle interactions that kept yielding him so many new insights.

11

From "Calgary Express"
to "The River"

Crane never seems to have entertained the possibility that, by late 1926, his long poem was virtually complete. Quite the contrary, he considered those new poems which were appearing so unpremeditatedly as a happy bonus, an offshoot of that historical panorama which made up his overall scheme for *The Bridge*. He never acknowledged these poems as the radical breakthroughs they were, breakthroughs that thoroughly changed the rules of the game he had set out for himself. He had intended to write a conventional epic with an unconventional ending: a panorama of American history that concluded with a poem, the "Finale" of 1923, that somehow fused together time and space. What he had written so far, however, was in the line of a personal epic or a lyrical epic, a self-analytical "Song of Myself" in an urban setting, as composed by a Rimbaud who had matured.

One reason Crane could remain so insensitive to what he had accomplished was his own blinding ambition. He so relished the idea of writing a lengthy poem (especially after so many years of putting it off)—a poem that would include in it one section, "Powhatan's Daughter," that was itself as long as the five parts of *The Waste Land*—that he could not resist the temptation of adding as many embellishments to the original frame as possible. His glee is unmistakable when, halfway through his weeks of creativity on the Isle of Pines, he writes to Waldo Frank (August 12, 1926): "*The Bridge* is half again as long as *The Wasteland*,—and it's only half finished!"

In an outline sent to Yvor Winters early in 1927, he unveiled his latest version of his project, one which integrated the new, unplanned material with that which had been planned from the start. In this outline, which closely resembles the final, published arrangement of the sequence, he

187

aimed at a compromise. ("Those marked # are complete," he informed
Winters.)[1]

Projected Plan of THE BRIDGE

Dedication—to Brooklyn Bridge
1— Ave Maria
2— *Powhatan's Daughter*
    # (1) The Harbor Dawn
    # (2) Van Winkle
        (3) The River
    # (4) The Dance
        (5) Indiana
3— Cape Hatteras
4— Cutty Sark
5— The Mango Tree—may not use this
6— Three Songs
7— The Calgary Express
8— 1920 Whistles—ditto
9— The Tunnel
10— Atlantis

He has returned to his original framework, greatly expanded. Of the six
poems sketched out for the benefit of his patron in March 1926—"Co-
lumbus," "Pokahantus," "Whitman," "John Brown," "Subway," and
"The Bridge"—the first two and the last two are completed and in place.
"Columbus" and "Pokahantus" have become "Ave Maria" and "The
Dance" (a segment in the newly expanded "Powhatan's Daughter");
"Subway" and "The Bridge" have become "The Tunnel" and "Atlantis."
In between, however, lie two poems promised but as yet undelivered:
"Whitman," now retitled "Cape Hatteras," and "John Brown," now re-
titled "Calgary Express."[2] The new, unplanned poems appear to have
been distributed at random through the sequence, though always with an
eye toward preserving a semblance of the chronological framework.

A second look, however, suggests that the distribution might not be
entirely random. This compromise arrangement, while organized to
bring the burgeoning sequence back in line with the historical framework, may also have been designed actually to encourage further contributions to the long poem. It is, after all, a strange integration—with
glaring gaps in it. Crane may have thought to scatter his completed
poems strategically, using them to create more gaps which he then must
begin to close. A projected poem appears between "Van Winkle" and

"The Dance." Two projected poems are needed to cross from "The Dance" to "Cutty Sark." Two more new poems are to be written before arriving at "The Tunnel." It is possible, of course, that this new outline simply reveals him in the act of postponing the difficult work of integration, but a March 1927 letter to Yvor Winters suggests that he was more likely to be prodding himself into expanding his already lengthy poem.

In early 1927, he was still close to his positive experience on the Isle of Pines when so much surprising new writing had suddenly appeared. To set before himself a framework full of suggestive gaps was, perhaps, to invite the recurrence of a comparable flurry of new writing. In a letter to Winters, written just before taking up work on the part of *The Bridge* that would become "The River," he displays a wary attitude toward organizing and planning:

> It's impossible to imagine without undertaking a like problem oneself—what endless problems arise in carrying forward the conception of a scheme like The Bridge. It takes more than ordinary logic, of course, to fuse all the multitudinous aspects of such a theme—I carried the embryonic idea of the poem about with me for six years before I ever wrote a line. Then there was a sudden impetus, the results of which you have seen almost entirely. I am beginning to think that it may be six more years before the materials for the rest of the poem shall have reached a sufficiently mature organization to be ready for paper. Logic or no logic, I can never do anything that is worth while without the assent of my intuitions. The logical progression of The Bridge is well in my mind. But one has to fight even that! At least one has to be ready to doubt its validity thoroughly on the slightest whispering approach of what I call "temperature"—the condition for organic fusion of experience, logical or no. . . . There seems to be really no convincing modus operandi but what you might call alert blindness.[3]

Crane writes of his framework not as though it were a support but rather as a suggestive barrier, existing chiefly to be surmounted. The poet must be prepared to let his materials ripen, at which point his materials then choose him. Though the logical progression of the poems is worked out, "one has to fight even that."

Judging from this letter, Crane was capable of placing his poems in an order designed to be a temporary, and provocative, expedient. Certainly he speaks as though the entire arrangement could all change overnight, dramatically, with an onslaught of new poetry. But when no new outburst emerged, when lightning refused to strike twice, when the only new work was revising old work, then the temporary order became a fixture; and he had to scramble to fill the gaps as best he could.

1

"The River" is a product of his struggle to take the gaps in his long poem and fill them with writing that drastically expands the surface of his epic but adds nothing to its scope. As it stood in 1926, *The Bridge* was—from the perspective of the conventional epic—quite a curious, perhaps even alarming, performance. It was populated by a derelict sailor, a burlesque dancer, a secretary, two Indians, Rip Van Winkle, and a washerwoman. There was more to do with the sea and sailing than with the machine. Apart from the passage on Columbus, the historical references were fragmentary and negligible: clipper ships, an Indian myth (which had been invented), and snippets from a schoolboy's text-book. The opportunity, then, to write a new poem, at a crucial point in "Powhatan's Daughter," offered itself as a chance to introduce a touch of the panoramic, so plainly absent from much of the sequence so far, and to take note, at long last, of the influence of the machine.

If these challenges were not ambitious enough, Crane is also con-cerned with another problem. He has on hand seven, possibly eight, quatrains originally composed in the summer of 1926 for "Calgary Ex-press," and it now seems reasonable to employ them as the conclusion to "The River."[4] "Calgary Express," formerly entitled "John Brown," was to have taken place on a Pullman sleeper: "The main theme is the story of John Brown," Crane wrote, possibly in the spring of 1926, "which pre-dominates over the interwoven 'personal, biographical details' as it runs through the mind of a Negro porter, shining shoes and humming to him-self. In a way it takes in the whole racial history of America."[5] Sometime in early 1927, perhaps at the same time he realized what an odd group of characters he had assembled so far for his national epic, he abandoned the idea of portraying "the whole racial history of America." In the final assemblage of "The River," all racial history (with the possible exception of a passing glance at the white man and the Indian) has been thoroughly expunged. It is possible that Crane abandoned the ambitions of "Calgary Express" because he felt his own experience of racial tension was too superficial to do justice to the subject. Yet that objection, which has even wider application to his experience with Indians (he used to report that the name "Maquokeeta" had been given to him by a Manhattan taxi driver)[6] did not prevent him from writing "The Dance." The more likely explanation is that he shied away from the sentiments in "Calgary Express." In 1926, they were next to revolutionary (mild though they now seem), and they are discernible still even in the fragment of "Calgary Express" which was taken over whole to fit the end of "The River."

All that is left of "Calgary Express" (and perhaps all that was ever written) appears as the last eight quatrains in "The River." Judging from that fragment, what can be told about the unfinished poem? In Crane's explanatory outline, he had the porter meditating while "humming to himself." Presumably, toward the end of his poem, he was to break into a spiritual, a spiritual that would somehow unite the strands of the porter's own "personal, biographical details" with the porter's memory of John Brown. And in fact the quatrains that end "The River" are noteworthy for their stately rhythms and frequent rhymes as though they were intended to reproduce the sonority of a spiritual. The outline also mentions that the poem was to take in "the whole racial history of America," and these quatrains also allow for that possibility, though it requires some reconsideration before that is evident.

As the quatrains bear out (when viewed from the perspective of the unfinished "Calgary Express" rather than "The River"), the whole racial history of America is a history of thwarted progress. But what Crane offers as a critical view of the sorry relation between the races is tactfully (or perhaps shrewdly) masked by appearing in the guise of an innocent meditation on the course of the Mississippi River. Needless to say, the idea that the porter must speak in a code which only the initiated can hear, and which sounds like innocent chatter to everyone else, itself indicates Crane's familiarity with certain aspects of living as a member of an oppressed minority. On a superficial level, the lyrics of the porter's "spiritual" simply evoke the Mississippi River as the natural route homeward; in addition, the termination of the river is both the Southland, from which the black man migrated, as well as the promised land. As the river flows southward it both recounts the progress of the porter and draws him to his reward, the gates of heaven, the true land of promise with its fine hosannas. On its surface, the fragment appears as innocent and even beguiling, in keeping with stereotyped ideas of porters—the waywardness of black folks, their musical talents, their belief in a Promised Land, and so forth.

The river, though, carries another tune, one right below its surface, a tune an alert, sophisticated reader would quickly overhear. In that other tune, the porter begins by cautioning himself to submit to the quiet, subdued flow of the river. Though he is one of the "born pioneers in time's despite, / Grimed tributaries to an ancient flow," he realizes that there is "no frontier" for him and advises himself to "drift in stillness, as from Jordan's brow." Yet such a deliberate act of submission, the porter also recognizes, is a postponement of living, even a capitulation to despair. The river is slow because "loth to take more tribute," as though reluctant to bear more freight, swollen enough as it is with those who have already submitted to it. To give way to the manner of the river, to drift in stillness, is to learn that you have spent your dream and gained nothing. Your return downstream to the Southland indicates, then, your lack of progress:

> The River, spreading, flows—and spends your dream.
> What are you, lost within this tideless spell?
> You are your father's father, and the stream—
> A liquid theme that floating niggers swell.

Superficially, this stanza is no more than a clever interpolation of stereotyped images: black folks are irresponsible, always spending the little they have, then wandering lost as their fathers had before them; fortunately, their talent for minstrelsy is sufficient to cheer them in their despondent state. From another angle, however, the stanza is bitterly blunt: the dream of progress, the promise of emancipation, is forgone once one prostrates oneself, submitting to the muteness of the river, "sliding prone / Like one whose eyes were buried long ago." "You are your father's father" then becomes a dolorous gauge of how little progress has occurred. And "nigger" is no longer a mere phrase from the vernacular: it retains its edge of contempt, for by submitting you become no more than a "floating nigger," a victim with no cause, no rights, no future.

Crane continues in this double vein, always from one angle simply describing the Mississippi River in terms of a spiritual, but from another angle revealing the angry bitterness of a race that has been displaced, its promises broken. If the river, in the next stanza, is presented as avaricious, as drinking "the farthest dale," remorselessly pulling mud and clay and roots in its wake, this is on the one hand simply a description of the actual Mississippi. But consider the same description from the vantage point of the porter, and the river then appears to be undergoing a significant change. Up till now, the river had been an emblem of submission; it invited others to submit to its flow silently. Now, however, so swollen is it with submissions, with the bodies of floating niggers, that it begins to move according to the will of the mass of persons who have merged with it. The coherence of the black race as a whole, moving together, at some point passes beyond mere submissiveness and becomes a force in its own, a unified power that is accumulating and increasing in strength. As this river gains momentum, then, it masses together because of these numbers of persons:

> O quarrying passion, undertowed sunlight!
> The basalt surface drags a jungle grace
> Ochreous and lynx-barred in lengthening might;
> Patience! and you shall reach the biding place!

> Over De Soto's bones the freighted floors
> Throb past the City storied of three thrones.
> Down two more turns the Mississippi pours
> (Anon tall ironsides up from salt lagoons).

These stanzas reveal a whole new meaning to the initiate. Superficially, the lines are just what they have been praised for being by critics who have admired them because they seem a rare instance in which Crane is simply, if lushly, descriptive: they are not weighed down with thinking, they are simply exotic descriptions of the Mississippi with a few historical references tossed in for local color. A second look, though, discloses a host of multihued black, brown, and sepia faces moving together in a "jungle grace." The "Ochreous and lynx-barred" colors are not simply a play of sunlight imagined below "The basalt surface": these are clues to identify the color of the faces as they assemble to move together. Sunlight is "undertowed" and the "Quarrying passion" is repressed; but the drawing-under and the repression have the effect of concentrating, of building with energy in a "lengthening might." When the river gains speed, disturbing the bones of that imperial conqueror De Soto, disrupting "the City storied of three thrones" (with "thrones" an emblem of obedience), the sense is of a strengthening force no longer able to be constrained, literally heaving its way up out from within the oppressive weight of a long history of exploitation. (Perhaps Williams was correct when, after reading the passage, he felt that Crane had borrowed from his "Destruction of Tenochtitlan.")[7] "Tall ironsides"—a warship—is ominously released from the mud, later ("Anon") to emerge on the surface.

The conclusion of the fragment is no less unsettling to those who can hear the note of prophecy in the porter's apparently innocent descriptions. When the river reaches its terminus, its speed and strength enormously increased, it quite naturally rushes to break free of any constrictions. "And flows within itself, heaps itself free" is, of course, a description of the river water backing up and spreading out across the delta. But in the underground context of the poem, it is also the portrayal of a revolutionary urge to break free of constraint, to escape from bondage. "Poised wholly on its dream, a mustard glow / Tortured by history, its one will —flow!" From the porter's perspective, this image of the river carries a distinct significance. Underneath his superficial air of subservience, beneath his guise of a harmless drifter who is bemused by spirituals and possesses a childlike innocence and waywardness, the black man fervently retains all his old dreams of emancipation. And he is still "Poised wholly" on a dream, and, though "Tortured" by a history of exploitation and repression, he has an unbroken will to be free. To suppress his dream only adds to its strength, increasing the likelihood that the moment must soon arrive when the bondage is too great to be endured. At the moment, the river meets "No embrace . . . but the stinging sea," and it spreads back as though it had met the master's whip. But "The Passion" remains to spread outward, in "wide tongues, choked and slow."

Had it been completed, "Calgary Express" could have found a niche in the 1926 *Bridge* between "Three Songs" and "The Dance." (Crane may have written it at the time he was composing both these poems.)[8] Since the poem would have begun, according to Crane's note, with a porter alternately blending the story of John Brown with memories of his sweetheart, it would emerge naturally enough from the background of womanless men and manless women in "Three Songs." The porter's transient occupation separates him from his sweetheart, yet in 1926 his employment is among the very best for which a black man dare hope. The black man too has his dream, and to frustrate a dream is to risk the potential explosion hinted at in the conclusion. To frustrate a dream is to court violence, and from this point Crane could move toward the presentation of Maquokeeta and Pocahontas, lovers separated from one another with a resulting confusion. Indeed, the theme of the conflict between the races, which Crane stated he had presented in "The Dance" but which hardly seems in evidence, would have been more prominent if "The Dance" had been preceded by a complete version of "Calgary Express."[9]

The Indian culture has nearly been eradicated from the present. Per-

haps a similar ominous fate lies in store for black Americans? But the
apocalyptic ending of "Calgary Express" is avoided in "The Dance" because the two lovers are united, if only imaginatively, and the distance
between them is overcome. Is the truly daring suggestion in "Calgary
Express" the statement that a similar marriage must extend between the
races? That solution would have been familiar to Crane from Eugene
O'Neill's *All God's Chillun Got Wings* (1924), a play he had attended on
its opening night and to which he later brought friends visiting from
Cleveland.[10] In 1926, that solution would have been truly provocative
indeed.

2

Yvor Winters called the section in "The River" beginning "And Pullman breakfasters glide glistening steel" all the way to the conclusion
(which includes the fragment from "Calgary Express") "the one deeply
impressive passage of any length in *The Bridge*," and he added that it,
"along with a few earlier poems, is probably the best writing in Crane."[11]
Allen Tate said, "'The River' has some blemishes toward the end, but by
and large it is a masterpiece of order and style; it alone is enough to
place Crane in the first rank of American poets, living or dead."[12] This
lavish praise from two of Crane's most stringent critics is a testament
to his success at completely burying the suggestive crosscurrents of
"Calgary Express." Winters, who made a practice of excerpting only segments of the poetry for praise, in this case accepted both old and new
writing as equally flawless, and Tate also considered the poem as a fundamentally whole work. How did Crane accomplish the almost impossible task of integrating the "Calgary Express" fragment into a poem that
had no mention of a porter, much less the racial history of America?

"The River" shows little evidence of that "temperature" that indicated
the "organic fusion of experience" so prized by Crane and perhaps on
display in the "Calgary Express" fragment. But it is an excellent example of Crane making intelligent, if uninspired, decisions while composing a poem. Intellectually, it is a satisfying work, with loose ends
quite remarkably tied together. To recycle the "Calgary Express" fragment, Crane approached it by imagining two distinct groups of individuals, each of which gains a benefit by combining with the other. The general form behind the new additions that turn "Calgary Express" into
"The River" is similar to the quasi dialectic of "The Dance" in which

certain persons are weak by themselves but strong when united with opposites.[13] The passengers on the streamliner make up one group. They
move rapidly and securely to their destinations, and they are all firm forward motion. But they have no awareness of what they pass through as
they move, no appreciation of what lies beyond their Pullman window
frames. It is a furtive blur, a flashing scene, like twisting a radio dial:
"brooks connecting ears / and no more sermons windows flashing roar /
breathtaking—as you like it . . . eh?" The tramps abroad on the land
make up the other group. Hopping the slow freight, they have no forward
direction but are always being shunted aside for the streamliners. Yet
"They know a body under the wide rain." They appreciate the beauty of
the continent, for they "take their liquor slow" and can be intoxicated by
the scenery. Though both the passengers and the tramps are restless—
and to that extent resemble pioneers—neither group by itself is entirely
attractive. Each can benefit from the example of the other. The passengers speed west effortlessly, ignorant of the land over which they
glide; the tramps dawdle aimlessly, proceeding nowhere in particular.
The passengers need to take it easy; the tramps need some positive
direction.

Crane reserves most of his attention for the tramps for a variety of reasons, one of which is his general inclination throughout *The Bridge* to
identify with those who are overlooked, neglected, and ignored. They
also pick up where "Van Winkle" left off, in an atmosphere of youth prolonged, with unfortunate results. And they provide him with an aspect of
that which had, in "Calgary Express," moved him as the plight of the
black man: the sense of human life wasted. This waste, furthermore, is
similar to the lost time of his own wandering existence, and it is especially pertinent to him now, anxious as he is to complete *The Bridge* and
having nothing but difficulty in doing so. Some of his most effective, and
tenderest, passages center on the tramps who are simply killing time,
hopelessly rambling without the strength of character to pull their lives
together:

> "There's no place like Booneville though, Buddy,"
> One said, excising a last burr from his vest,
> "—For early trouting." Then peering in the can,
> "—But I kept on the tracks." Possessed, resigned,
> He trod the fire down pensively and grinned,
> Spreading dry shingles of a beard. . . .

The tramp evaluates Booneville while "excising a last burr from his vest," shading his words with a gesture of precision to emphasize the care behind his pronouncement. Then suddenly baffled, he peers into the dead end of his life and admits, "But I kept on the tracks." Keeping on the tracks is ambiguous: it implies both following a trail as well as conforming to a certain orderliness. The wandering existence has its own kind of easy conformity at the same time as it preserves a demanding search that drives from within. As he treads the fire down "pensively" it seems he is thinking of fires within himself that he has suppressed.

Later, however, Crane displays a measure of contempt for the tramps. This change in attitude is a rather important step, for beyond its somewhat programmatic quasi dialectic of opposites in need of combination "The River" is unified, oddly enough, by a series of incidents that are designed to be disquieting, and each of which seems aimed at startling (and ultimately frightening) the reader, as well as the poet, out of a specious sense of ease and relaxation. As a child, Crane recalls spying on the tramps outside his father's factory and reacting with mixed emotions; as an adult, he now arouses his childish fear of them precisely to warn himself away from the attractions of their wandering, unfocused existence. They reflect all too clearly his own inability, at this point in his life, to marshal his strength; they remain as Van Winkles who have not yet awakened, "Holding to childhood like some termless play . . ."

> hopping the slow freight
> —Memphis to Tallahassee—riding the rods
> Blind fists of nothing, humpty-dumpty clods.

On the other hand, it is clear that he remains drawn to them. They "touch something like a key perhaps," intimate as they are with the body of the continent.

In meditating on both what is wrong and what is right with the tramps, Crane is imitating his exploratory methods of 1926, but in a way that is markedly less intuitive, notably more cumbersome. But his meditations eventually allow him to confront his own painful sense of constriction, for the capacious wandering of the tramps emphasizes, by contrast, his own painful fixity. Trying to stretch "past the circuit of the lamp's thin flame," he longs to emulate those locomotives whose whistles probing through the night, "sounding the long blizzards out," move forward in a tactile fashion, nosing through the dark like genuine pioneers. He ends in dismay, however, when the whistles move away from him, dying on the wind, like "Papooses crying on the wind's long mane" who "Screamed redskin dynasties that fled the brain, /—Dead echoes!" Like the tramps, left behind by the "20th Century," Crane is "still hungry on the tracks," but unlike them he is not content simply to be left "ploddingly / watching the tail lights wizen and converge" as he is abandoned. He insists on new, forceful movement; and in this poem, it seems he can best goad himself into moving by frightening himself. In the passage focusing on the old gods of the rain, he prods himself with a fearful image of burial. Instead of conceiving of the Indian as still alive, howling in the corridors of the wind—an option he seems on the verge of taking—he images forth a nation that has been buried, utterly forgotten. In a claustrophobic sequence of events, he pictures a most elaborate method by which the old Indian gods of the rain lie deeply buried below "Iron Mountain," barely kept alive with kernels of corn brought to them by eyeless fish who have received the kernels from "querulous crows." It is baffling, this sudden emphasis on a hierarchy of crows and eyeless fish and rain gods—so bizarre that it surely must originate in some actual Indian myth, its significance now lost to us. But it need not be that: the elaborate rite surely reflects the poet's sense of the elaborate efforts he must undergo, all for a mere kernel. Trapped "within the circuit of the lamp's thin flame," he subsists mainly on glimpses and guesses and echoes, on the names of Indian tribes emblazoned on Pullman cars, or the Indian place-names caught up in slogans displayed on boxcars: Chesapeake & Ohio, Milwaukee Road, Chicago Northwestern.[14] In brief, the gods of the rain passage impresses upon him how thoroughly he is buried, how very little he has with which to work.

Out of this excruciating, narrow suffocation, Crane simply breaks away, goaded into action:

> Such pilferings make up their timeless eatage,
> Propitiate them for their timber torn
> By iron, iron—always the iron dealt cleavage!
> They doze now, below axe and powder horn.
>
> And Pullman breakfasters glide glistening steel
> From tunnel into field—iron strides the dew—
> Straddles a hill, a dance of wheel on wheel.

Spurred by nothing more but nothing less than an overwhelming sense of his own unbearable constriction, he bursts from the tunnel into light and air, and his entire poem begins to move with the strength and purpose of an express that negotiates the land, striding and straddling the body of the continent by moving in relation to it.

The riders on this train merge the qualities of the passengers and the tramps. They move forward purposefully but also aware of the very land that surrounds them. They are urged into throwing open the windows that had previously barred them from the physical experience of the land, and they are asked to stretch forward in a gesture of sheer sensual enjoyment:

> And if it's summer and the sun's in dusk
> Maybe the breeze will lift the river's musk
> —As though the waters breathed that you might know
> *Memphis Johnny, Steamboat Bill, Missouri Joe.*
> Oh, lean from the window if the train slows down
> As though you touched hands with some ancient clown.

The gift that Crane would bestow in "The River" is a sense of one's own mortality that is so pressing—as in the burial images in the gods of the rain passage—that one wishes to live each moment as though it were utterly radiant and precious. To awaken to the inevitability of one's death, to smell the musk of the river, to sense all that has passed before—all this is a spur to make one keenly aware of the life of the moment, the life at hand. Not even those who might resist, who might prefer their complacency, are left free from the transforming awareness that is animating Crane. He addresses "Sheriff, Brakeman and Authority" as "you, too," who "feed the River timelessly." The river of time devours all: "Few evade full measure of their fate"—though some do:

> I could believe he joked at heaven's gate—
> Dan Midland—jolted from the cold brake-beam.

Dan Midland, a mythical hobo, can retain his aplomb perhaps because he knew so clearly that riding the rods would someday bring him a quick final end. Knowing that, he enjoyed each moment of living; death can be cheated only if its eternal presence is used as a goad to living each moment as vitally as possible.

It is at this point that Crane is able to turn to the quatrains he had composed for "Calgary Express" and incorporate them into a singularly new context. The river appearing in them has become not just the Mississippi but the river of time. At first, time passes in a slow and stately manner, measured and dignified; the "born pioneers in time's despite" are the riders who have been awakened by Crane to a sense of time passing, so that each moment is precious, never to be repeated again. For when one is aware that he is drifting down a river of time, he is also aware that the river ends in "No embrace . . . but the stinging sea." The river of time leads to death. And the closer the river draws to the sea, the more it gathers momentum and the faster one's life goes by; caught up in that unceasing downward flow, time passes more rapidly as one ages. And with that sense of time passing ever more rapidly, one must realize that his dreams are in jeopardy. If one has postponed his dreams again and again while living, then one discovers those dreams again when one is on the edge of death. They now have a forcefulness that grows directly out of the fact that they have been realized too late: "The River lifts itself from its long bed, // Poised wholly on its dream."

Here is another frightening image, like others in "The River," an image of time as a river passing more rapidly each moment till a life is over and has emptied into the anonymous sea, with all its dreams unrealized. By developing this fearful overview of a life finished before it has begun, Crane would spur us into action, pressing us to take up those dreams we now have, acting upon them with an urgency and forcefulness that comes out of recognizing our mortality. In these quatrains as written for "Calgary Express," the black man, submitting to postures of deference, wasted his life and spent his dream, but as he grew more submissive he also grew more frustrated, and as his river rushed to the sea, it increased in strength and power until it was on the verge of breaking free. In the exact same quatrains which now have been shifted to "The River," everyone tends fatally to drift, to submit themselves to time, to waste their lives, as they are swept along to an inevitable death—at which point it is realized, too late, that their dreams are still unfulfilled. In "The River," the intricate double meanings of "Calgary Express" are completely lost or persist only as odd allusions; "De Soto," for example, only appears as a reminder that the river of time does not discriminate between the great and the obscure: time the devourer devours us all.

Knowing the "Calgary Express" fragment and guessing at its possible evolution, one can only regret that Crane lost sight of his original objectives. As an act of surgery, "The River" transforms a bold piece of virtuoso writing into a somewhat vague travelogue. The powerful pressing motion of the quatrains still is present, but the intricate allusions have all been lost; as a result, the final passage seems impressive but without a specific subject. The passage has indeed helped to maintain the image of Crane as a poet who could write ravishingly about nothing at all.[15] The "Calgary Express" fragment reveals the true Crane, the poet who could display a rare ability to capture the feelings as they were in conflict with one another.

His effort, at this late point in his epic, to inject history and the machine into his long poem must also be judged as less than successful. If he was enamored of ships and sailing, he displayed no comparable attachment to trains and travel (though he does reveal an impressive vocabulary of railroad slang).[16] But the lure of the tramp's life is never as attractive as the youthful visions of clipper ships in "Cutty Sark." His notion that the streamliner encourages a certain isolation is more convincingly presented in the subway demon of "The Tunnel." And the historical references remain almost exclusively in the realm of folk history.

The most impressive aspect of "The River" is perhaps Crane's indication that one must take courage from meditating on one's mortality. Tramps and passengers are held together by this overriding idea: what is slow and ambling in Crane is goaded into action by this awareness of time passing, and what is hasty and urgent in him is opened to an awareness of what there is in the present, to be savored in the moment. Intellectually, the introduction of the river of time in which all must perish resolves the dichotomy between the opposites developed in the poem. But the river of time is the most personal element in the poem also, the sense in which this poem, like early works of The Bridge, is addressed to Crane himself. One must be prepared to confront that which is fearful; out of that confrontation, one will receive a new energy. Out of his own sense of time wasted, out of his own stalling over the concluding portions of The Bridge, he realized this poem, a strange mixture of the scarifying and the sentimental that is honorable enough work but not Crane at his finest.

12
The Late Poems (I):
The "Carib Suite"

In the summer of 1927, around the time "The River" was being completed, Crane began arranging a group of short poems, all of which centered on his days in the Caribbean, into what he termed a "Carib Suite." These poems, posthumously collected—along with other, unrelated work—as *Key West: An Island Sheaf* (in the 1933 *Collected Poems*), have proved to be a puzzle. They appear to be quite uncharacteristic of Crane. In these Caribbean poems, there are no expressions of love, and no poems that end in an ecstasy of celebration; there are no poems of city life and no poems focusing on the machine. Moreover, their language is noteworthy for its clarity and directness. Usually four or five quatrains at their longest, in blank verse, often in rhyme, the overall impression these poems convey is of a modesty rarely associated with Crane's work.

Just because the Caribbean poems are so untypical, the tendency has been to read them as meaningful precisely because of their untypicality. The single critic who has sought to perceive them as a unified group, M. D. Uroff, argues that they record an especially unhappy moment in Crane's writing career. They are the register of a poet who is unable to create, who is locked in stasis, and they are dominated, almost overwhelmingly, by a sense of painful paralysis. Crane's sensibility, Uroff suggests, was immediately inclined to imbue the mechanical world with vitality, to render the inanimate cityscape as surging with life. Paradoxically, when he is taken to the real country, when he is brought face to face with a landscape teeming with life, he is rendered mute and dumb. There is nothing to transform; the role of the poet has been usurped by a monstrous Nature. As a result, the poems can only be peculiarly static since the poet is unable to participate in the life around him. In Uroff's view, the plain language is simply flat and empty: this is the anti-poetry of *White Buildings* and *The Bridge*.[1]

Several nagging questions remain, however, even after Uroff's pioneering interpretation. For example, several of these poems were written originally in the summer of 1926; how could Crane move back and forth from *The Bridge* to *Key West?* Uroff suggests this was a pendulum movement, akin to a manic-depressive cycle, in which he composed his epic in moods of elation and his lyrics in moods of despair. But the 1926 *Bridge* is not a poem of sheer elation, however elated Crane may have been at the prospect of actually composing it: it is predominantly thoughtful, analytical, exploratory. It may be perhaps that the Caribbean poems are not the product of dark despair, though they certainly remain strikingly somber. Is it likely that Crane would suddenly abandon his favorite themes, the necessity to love, the beauty of charity, the need for accepting the individuality of others? Has he set aside the intricacy of his previous work, or is it taking on a new form?

These Caribbean poems are even more unified as a group than Uroff maintains; taken together, in fact, they comprise a brief sequence, a miniature epic, very much in keeping with Crane's attitudes at the time. They are not so much poems that are simply descriptive of the tropics— which would, as Uroff acknowledges, make them quite unusual performances for Crane—as they are poems with a sure but subtle moral intelligence working through them, investing incidents and episodes with an unusual gravity. A description of a palm tree resonates with moral implications: Crane is often describing types, human types, but in an oblique way, in the guise of describing a landscape (as in "The Dance") and without calling attention to his own presence. But the reason the poet prefers not to be more fully involved is that the situations he is presenting are so morally unattractive that he prefers to remain outside them. (Eventually, in a sequence of these works which he himself arranged, he is finally drawn in and castigates himself for his own former lack of involvement.) These are, to be sure, minor works—there are no undiscovered masterpieces hidden among them. But they are all profoundly intelligent poems which suffer if readers approach them expecting to be met with the thunder and lightning of visionary poetry. As in his *White Buildings* lyrics, Crane is more sophisticated than his critics have been prepared to credit; all the poems repay close attention and a handful—"The Idiot," "Royal Palm," "The Air Plant"—are substantial achievements.

1

Though many of these Caribbean poems were written, at least in their
first form, along with the poetry of the 1926 *Bridge*, it is most likely that
they were brought to their final form in the summer of 1927, when Crane
had actually lost much of his impetus to write. *The Bridge* was not ad-
vancing, and his decision to arrange a "Carib Suite" may have been in
part a strategy to revive his flagging interest in the epic. In taking up the
Caribbean poems, he would be reflecting back on that tropical scene out
of which so many new poems had unexpectedly flowered; since he was as
stymied in the summer of 1927 as he had felt himself to be in the summer
of 1926, his return to the Caribbean setting may have been in hopes of
effecting a turnaround as dramatic as that which had redeemed him the
year before. If he emphasizes, in many poems, a certain bleakness in
the tropics, it may be with the expectation of breaking away from it.

Though Crane had referred to certain of the individual poems in correspondence from the summer of 1926, he first discusses the idea of a suite
in a July 18, 1927, letter to Yvor Winters.[2] There will be six poems all
together (in this order): "O Carib Isle!," "Island Quarry," "The Air
Plant," "Royal Palm," "The Idiot," and "Eternity." The last two are still
to be written, and "Eternity" will conclude the suite with a "description
of the ruins" left in the aftermath of a hurricane. As things were to turn
out, the final poem would not be a description of the ruins left but of the
very hurricane experience itself ("The Hurricane"), even though at some
time he had written such a description and even titled it "Eternity." The
substitution of the storm for its ruins may have been in line with his desire for a return to the sweeping storm of new poetry. In October 1926, a
hurricane had in fact arrived on the Isle of Pines, reducing his quarters
to rubble and effectively interrupting work on *The Bridge*. At least once
he spoke of this storm as though he had called it up out of the poem he
had completed before beginning *The Bridge*; referring with familiar contempt to Harriet Monroe, editor of *Poetry*, he wrote to Yvor Winters that
"Aunt Harriet has just taken 'O Carib Isle,' a rather violent lyric urging
the hurricane on the Isle of Pines, which, of course, *came*."[3] In his own
mind, to rouse the hurricane again would be equivalent to the creative
frenzy that had initiated *The Bridge*. The way back to his epic could be
reached by a detour through the "Carib Suite."

The hurricane which finally manifested itself in his suite, however,
resembled more closely the hurricane that had interrupted his writing

than the storm that originated it. The suite did not give rise to a sustained burst of new poetry, either for itself or for *The Bridge*. For a brief time, the suite began to expand just as the epic had in 1926. After producing an unanticipated new poem almost overnight, "The Mermen," Crane believed he was on the verge of serendipitous days. Mailing an early version off to Winters, he pointed to the epigraph of the poem: "The coincidence of the quotation is scarcely credible: after writing the last line I dipped into *Lear*, and, believe me or no—that's the first line I saw!"[4] But "The Mermen" is a strange, unpolished poem, a cryptic fragment of a piece, and its epigraph sheds little light on its purpose. Winters evidently threw cold water on the project when he wrote back that this new verse was no better than the pieces "just grabbed up for anthologies."[5] The creative outburst halted soon after, and Crane eventually parcelled the poems out, some to appear in scattered issues of *The Dial* ("The Air Plant," "The Mermen"), a few to remain unpublished except posthumously ("Key West," "Imperator Victus"), and one group to appear in *transition* (under the title "East of Yucatan") in a form closest to the planned suite: early versions of "Island Quarry," "Royal Palm," "Bacardi Spreads the Eagle's Wings," "The Idiot," and "The Hurricane."

Even in the truncated form of "East of Yucatan," with only five of the dozen or so poems represented, Crane found an arrangement that highlights the connections among his poems, showing each one off to its best advantage. Though the poems could appear to be simply bleak or merely descriptive if approached as separate poems or found among the stray verse gathered in section three of the *Collected Poems* (1933), when taken together they form a suite that is designed to be provocative and unsettling, a suite in which the poet is put off from involvement. It is not that the poems confess to the poet's incapacity for involvement: it is rather that the subjects of the poems cast such a bad light that it is almost impossible to wish for involvement. In "Three Songs" he had looked askance at various types of the contemporary, but he wrote of them from inside, sympathetically, in such a way as the subjects of the poems themselves might understand. The mariner, the men in the Winter Garden, and Mary are all desperate for a meaningful change whether they admit or deny the fact. But the subjects of the Caribbean poems lack any such urgency; they are lost, but they lack a way out of their dilemma—some, indeed, are even satisfied with their present position. The only exception occurs in "The Idiot," the one poem in which the poet himself appears and learns that, because of his own lack of involvement, he may be as deplorable as those he has been exposing. But that one gesture of expiation is not enough to redeem what is an entirely fallen world; it is too little too late, and the sequence, instead of concluding in a burst of energy, ends with the Day of Wrath, the hour of judgment, a terrifying display which threatens to obliterate one and all. Such dismissive force seems to be all that the poet and his subjects are felt to deserve.

2

The first of the "East of Yucatan" poems, "Island Quarry," portrays a narrator whose decision to be strong is exposed as a form of weakness. As a cautionary fable designed to stir doubts and raise questions, the poem provides an excellent introduction to the group. On an island, two roads diverge. One is a "turning" "around the roots of a mountain," the other is a "straight road" that seems "to play below the stone." The other road, the road that does not turn but goes on into stone, is dominated by a

> fierce
> Profile of marble spiked with yonder
> Palms against the sunset's towering sea, and maybe
> Against mankind.

The speaker is attracted to that "straight road" which leads into a world of hard edges and stony certainties; it leads to a marble quarry where men saw marble "only into / Flat prison slabs," "square sheets" (rather than sculpting it in expressive designs).[6] And if that road is dominated by a "fierce / Profile" "spiked . . . against the sunset's towering sea"— as though it offered a refuge—it is also "Against mankind." It is a road in which one may win protection but at the expense of cutting himself off from others.

The alternate road, however, that goes "around the roots of the mountain," is a fragile path. When the speaker considers it, he stammers. At special moments "In dusk" it appears to be bathed in an inviting air of softness, but this may be an illusion. And so the speaker chooses against that pliant way, the alternate path:

> —It is at times as though the eyes burned hard and glad
> And did not take the goat path quivering to the right,

Wide of the mountain—thence to tears and sleep—
But went on into marble that did not weep.

He is, however, not very persuasive as to the propriety of his choice,
even though the alternative he appears to reject has been reduced even
further to a "goat path quivering to the right." That overgrown path leads
"to the right," possibly the correct choice; but he has had enough of vulnerability, and he is drawn instead to the prison slabs of stone, the firm
"marble that does not weep," that is inexpressive.

And yet there is nothing very stony or assertive about the poem as a
whole. If anything, a stonelike numbness runs through it, but it is interrupted by a vague sense of insecurity. The rhythm of the final line is
especially uncertain: "But went on into marble that does not weep." This
line recalls that the poem throughout shifts laxly between iambic lines
resembling firm blank verse and anapestic lines that are sluggishly conversational. One inclination is to read the last line as blank verse, prepared by the iambic feet in the preceding line. But the emphasis falls on
awkward places, on the first syllable in "into" and on "that." The line
wants to break from its metrical bond into a conversational flow, with
anapestic rhythms falling on "on," the first syllable of "marble" and
"not." But that turns awkward too. The two counter-rhythms exist uneasily
together, in a divided poem. Under the loose conversational rhythm there
remains the taut iambic rhythm, so that the lines waver uncertainly, as
though no decision were made at all. The speaker is stuck without a resolution. He is in the middle of the way and, though he would like to
choose, he simply hangs there, without a sure sense of where to turn.

Framed by the broken parable of "Island Quarry," the other poems appear as written by a poet who is drawn toward the tough stance but who is
hesitant to adopt it, knowing it is "against mankind." If this is true of the
poet, however, the subjects in his poems have no such recalcitrance:
they have made their choice. At first glance, "Royal Palm," the next
poem in "East of Yucatan," seems to be an exception, for the poem offers
itself as nothing more than a picturesque illustration of a palm tree, an
ornament. But it is not the poem that is the ornament, it is the palm tree;
what the poem suggests is that the palm tree, by endorsing its regal status as above all, betrays an obligation. As Uroff notes, the palm offers no
genuine relief from the sun.[7] Its "charities" are neither practical nor
useful; they are "more-than-regal" and amount to the idea that its "Green
rustlings" and "whispered light" "Drift coolly" and provide an illusion of

relief from the sun. By soaring so effortlessly in the air, it invites others
to soar with it; but only it can soar and the invitation is false. It tenders
no saving shadow, no escape from the "noontide's blazed asperities."

The true effect of the Royal Palm is to make others even more aware of
that which it soars away from:

> Forever fruitless, and beyond that yield
> Of sweat the jungle presses with hot love
> And tendril till our deathward breath is sealed—
> It grazes the horizon, launched above
>
> Mortality—ascending . . .

The Royal Palm invites appreciation, but it leaves behind those who
view it. They remain in the pressing jungle while the palm is launched
"above // Mortality." Crane stresses an identical point more subtly in the
lines, "Unshackled, casual of its azured height / As though it soared
suchwise through heaven too." "Suchwise" is the word that catches the
attention; rhythmically, it is a trochaic substitution which gives the
otherwise iambic line a lilting edge. As diction, however, it is a word the
ordinariness of which stands out from the elevated vocabulary of "as-
cending emerald-bright" and "casual of its azured height." We are reminded, firmly but gently, with aristocratic deference, that we do not
soar accompanying the Royal Palm in the bower of heaven; we only soar
"suchwise."

The Royal Palm remains aloof, "Uneaten of the earth or aught earth
holds." True, the tree does possess a "grey trunk, that's elephantine,"
but this is the closest to a specific physical description that the poem
provides or the Royal Palm offers. And rhythmically, this line is the most
anxious of all in the poem: "And the grey trunk, that's elephantine, rear."
It can be scanned, with an emphasis on "grey trunk," "rear" and the first
and fourth syllables of "elephantine," as a spondee, an iamb, and a
spondee—but that scansion is such a disheveled collection of rhythms it
is tantamount to admitting that all order has temporarily collapsed. The
casual syntax ("that's elephantine"), which occurs at no other point in
the poem, accompanies a prosaic and conversational rhythm, which also
occurs at no other point in the poem. This line excepted, "Royal Palm"
is written in an elevated diction, with a formal syntax, in rhymed blank
verse of four quatrains. The point may be that the Royal Palm disdains
its own earthly body, its trunk, which is closest to the jungle; even to

mention that it associates with the earth is disruptive, and it soars straightaway from even that thought. Its next line, incidentally, recovers the composure of blank verse: "its frondings sighing in aetherial folds." Everything about the palm swings away from the earthy, the sweaty, the common, and toward "aetherial folds."

On the one hand, "Royal Palm" simply describes a Royal Palm; on the other hand, the Royal Palm is presented as aloof, remote, untouchable. One cannot approach it for anything more than a quick description; it disdains contact with the actual. The poem is something of a tour de force, then, as it conveys a patronizing aloofness through the format of a description that is all the aloof object allows.

Crane sent a copy of the "East of Yucatan" poems to Waldo Frank and mentioned in passing, "There is another poem, 'The Air Plant,' properly belonging to this series, which ought to be out soon in *The Dial*."[8] "The Air Plant" would have discreetly illuminated "Royal Palm"; it pretends, also, to be a straight description but it too is loaded with implications. At first appearance, the air plant is an enterprising bit of vegetation which "thrives on saline nothingness," flourishing where nothing else will grow. And it is lively and animated, "A bird almost—of almost bird alarms." But this first stanza, as is typical of Crane, is liable to extreme modification; the poem gets underway, past first impressions, in the second stanza, when the verb "Is" redirects the attention. The air plant begins to appear as the repugnant thing it is. Even the lizard's throat, disgusting as it seems, is not nearly so repellent; the air plant

> Is pulmonary to the wind that jars
> Its tentacles horrific in their lurch.
> The lizard's throat, held bloated for a fly,
> Balloons but warily from this throbbing perch.

When the wind comes up, this plant (which had seemed to be merely enterprising) turns out to be hideously pliant, malleable, amenable. It can adopt even the gestures of a bird. It goes along without any resistance, complaisant in the extreme. Even the lizard, itself an untrustworthy creature disgustingly poised to trap a fly, must eye it "warily" as though "this throbbing perch" were easily capable of turning and swallowing it.

In a third stanza, Crane contrasts it to the cactus which at least bleeds when "stricken off the stalk." But the air plant, by opting to be complaisant, is invulnerable: it has nothing to defend—it is bloodless, shad-

owless, entirely disengaged. It simply goes along, bending to whatever
wind, mimicking "the air's thin talk," a "Ventriloquist of the Blue." So
reprehensible is it that it evokes a melodramatic image of encroaching
disaster: "beachward creeps the shark-swept Spanish Main." And the
hurricane itself is the plant's "apotheosis" not just because of its intense
concentration of wind but because it obliterates all in its path and the air
plant asks to be obliterated. The hurricane in the final poem represents
that Day of Wrath when all those who lacked the courage to speak out
against the drift of things will be called to account.

3

One of the first poems Crane wrote after he had decided to organize his
Caribbean poems into a suite was "The Mermen." Though the poem is
surely one of his most gnomic bits of verse, a plausible reading of it
emerges from the sequence (even though it appeared not in the sequence
but as a separate poem in *The Dial*). It is a dramatic monologue designed
to expose the sorry attitude of the speaker, an American or perhaps British imperialist in the West Indies. The speaker bemoans the fact that
there is nothing paradisal in this paradise, at least at present, and he
longs for the days when his predecessors in imperialism, the Spaniards,
occupied the area.

The poem hinges on an ambiguity concerning the identity of "The
Cross." At first it appears to be the emblem of Christian charity, the symbol of the civilizing influence the Spaniards thought to introduce to the
barbaric natives: "The Cross alone has flown the wave." But since "the
Cross sank," since the Spaniards furled their sails, "much that's warped
and cracked / Has followed in its name." This sentiment is true enough,
but the speaker is recognizably part of the problem rather than part of
any solution. He has nothing but contempt for the West Indies in their
present state. It is, to him, a place where "Buddhas and engines serve us
undersea": natives (or "Buddhas," presumably a contemptuous nick-
name) and machinery are treated alike as servants—though why anyone
would choose to dwell in the Caribbean is a mystery to the speaker. He
thinks of it as a hell (and we realize that he must make life a hell for the
natives).

As the speaker displays his contempt, it is evident that "The Cross"
he has in mind is not the church of Christian charity but a church
of stern, repressive measures. Nowadays one must sack hell of every

ingenuity to get natives to function at all; but back in the good old days, "Oh—"

> Gallows and guillotines to hail the sun
> And smoking racks for penance when day's done!

It was easier to keep the natives in line. They knew respect. Those were the paradisal days. The speaker contemplates that past with a relish which Crane, as poet distinct from the speaker, eagerly bares in all its repugnance. The poem attains an ironic pitch in its last lines:

> Leave us, you idols of futurity—alone,
> Here where we finger moidores of spent grace
> And ponder the bright stains that starred this Throne
>
> —This Cross, agleam still with a human face!

The speaker fingers "moidores," Portuguese coins of elegant beauty, the "bright stains" of which can only recall stains of native blood, tainting the wealth of the Indies. To the speaker, however, the stains are bright because harshness and repression are appealing. To the reader, the incident comes as a disgusting revelation: those gold coins are the real "Cross" on which the natives are sacrificed; they recall that past when the island was a source of wealth, worth plundering. There is not much of that now; the islands have been exhausted. And the "human face" that still gleams from the gold coin, the face perched on the "Throne" starred with "bright stains," is now viewed by the reader in multiple perspectives. To the natives, that face is the very face of the white man: a cold, unyielding, chiseled countenance. To the speaker, the coin is to be savored because it recalls the stern, virtuous days of the imperialist past. In the epigraph to the poem, a cryptic quote from *King Lear*, Lear imperiously banishes Kent from his homeland in a naked show of power. As Lear to Kent, so the speaker to the natives; and we are to react to the speaker with the same dismay and revulsion that Lear's act provokes. Though complicated, twisted, and compressed, "The Mermen" is not unintelligible, though it is by no means a particularly effective piece.

At this point, Crane could have inserted an additional poem without disrupting his general theme. In "Imperator Victus" the "Big guns" of an imperial Navy demonstrate that America is now in charge; the "King of Spain" is "That defunct boss." (The Spanish-American War, of course, was less than thirty years old when the poem was written, well within the memories of most people in the West Indies.) The message delivered by

the guns is for the instruction of the natives—a show of power to remind
them of their place (which is that they no longer have a place). The natives are quick to indicate, in a fawning Pidgin English, that the message
has been heard loud and clear: "Big guns again / No speakee well / But
plain." Crane's sensitivity toward language suggests that the point of including such Pidgin English is to remind us that the tourists, the Americans, and the U.S. Navy make no effort to understand the native language (and, therefore, the native point of view). The interlopers, not
speaking the native tongue, resort to force to make themselves understood "Plain." The natives, getting the message, translate it into appropriately brutal terms, speaking in the pidgin talk. And of course the reason the natives pick up the idea so rapidly is that there is a fundamental
identity between the Spanish and the American imperialists. The guns
clearly "tell / The Spanish Main // The Dollar from the Cross." Worship
of the Cross has simply been replaced by worship of the Dollar.

Both "The Mermen" and "Imperator Victus" have affinities with a
forthright brief poem which Crane did include in "East of Yucatan."
"Bacardi Spreads the Eagle's Wings" is an anecdote that we overhear
told by a tourist; the anecdote and the tourist's attitude strikingly under-
score the ugly sense of superiority white men display to the natives.
There is not a moment's concern for the plight of those "Native high-
steppers"—they are the victims of what the tourist holds to be an amusing joke, and they are the butt of an ugly racial remark. The possibility
that the stranded natives might have faced danger is brushed away, and
it never occurs to the speaker to sympathize with their joy at actually
owning their own launch, however frail it might have been.

It is likely the case that the natives had been swindled in their pur-
chase, sold an inferior and dangerous craft. Especially when approaching this poem by way of "The Mermen" and "Imperator Victus," it is
evident that "Bacardi" impels us toward imagining the natives as persons,
with a neglected (and invisible) culture all their own, clearly warped by
long eras of foreign rule. The poem, minor as it is, is not without its
impact, and it prepares us to acknowledge the importance in "The
Idiot," the next poem, of taking the initiative to break away from stereotyped perceptions.

Before turning to that poem, however, it is appropriate to comment on
"Key West," an unpublished (and possibly unfinished)[9] work which
could have served as an introduction to the entire sequence. Crane believed that "O Carib Isle!" properly belonged at the start of his suite; he

included it in his initial outline of the series to Winters and he mentioned it again in his letter to Frank. The fact that it had been previously
published in *transition* may have governed his decision to submit "East
of Yucatan" to that journal. The poem would have been appropriate, especially in its final version. The hardened shell the poet forms about
himself, eviscerating his own sensitivity, is comparable to the tough indifference displayed by many in various ways through the suite. With
"O Carib Isle!" the sequence would have drawn closer attention to the
difficulty of maintaining sensitivity toward other persons while in the
tropics. "Key West" would have been less imposing as a prelude, but it
is a poem that demonstrates a fear of vulnerability and that would hint at
why a shell of invulnerability would be so prized. In this poem, the poet
lacks any supporting faith; he has lost the sort of ebullience and confidence he had demonstrated earlier in "Repose of Rivers." Underneath
"skies impartial" he is left to himself, on a "single march" that could
lead "To heaven or hades"—or to nowhere. Instead of moving toward
either extreme, he plods to "an equally frugal noon," lapsing into dead
center.

On the one hand, he rejects the "dead conclusion" that so many "millions" follow. He recognizes that their "confusion" ("doubly mocked,"
once by themselves and once by him) leads only into "apish nightmares"
in which the modern city is "steel-strung stone," a labyrinth of steel resembling a graveyard of vaults. But on the other hand, he cannot discover the true "gold" that would counteract this deadliness, and he is
baffled at its absence:

> O steel and stone! But gold was, scarcity before.
> And here is water, and a little wind. . . .
> There is no breath of friends and no more shore
> Where gold has not been sold and conscience tinned.

The true gold is the "breath of friends," which does not exist here, and
he writhes in despair; what he has yet to recognize, of course, is that
there is a life around him on the island to which he can be alert and
responsive. A supportive faith, that is, is created by persons capable of
reaching out to others.

"The Idiot" is the single poem in the sequence in which the poet
makes an appearance as other than an onlooker, and he begins it, in a
way appropriate to the sequence, by noting his own inclination to evade
the individual at the center of his poem: "Sheer over to the side," he

instructs himself as he dodges the idiot boy. Yet there is nothing discreet or merciful in this act of avoidance; he swerves away in order to spy on this pitiful creature. "For see," he continues, "That's why those children laughed / In such infernal circles," as the boy is shown to be "Fumbling his sex," "daft / With squint lanterns in his head." Confronting the idiot boy is to be avoided, at the same time as Crane remains free to detail the boy's outrageous adventures. In this respect, the opening of this poem cannot but serve as a reminder that Crane has been regularly reporting on a number of episodes, in his previous poems, from which he has drawn back in condemnation; he is somewhat like a spy who is fascinated by that which repulses him, but he has himself remained aloof, apart, and disengaged.

"The Idiot" upsets his poise, though the incident which brings him up short is stumbled onto accidentally, not encouraged by him:

> I hurried by. But back from the hot shore
> Passed him again . . . He was alone, agape;
>
> One hand dealt out a kite string, a tin can
> The other tilted, peeled and clamped to eye.
> That kite aloft—you should have watched him scan
> Its course, though he'd clamped midnight to noon sky!

Crane had written of this particular incident earlier, in an unpublished prose poem "Lenses":

> And the idiot boy by the road, with carbonated eyes, laughing or extending a phallus through the grating,—talking to a kite high in the afternoon, or in the twilight scanning pebbles among cinders in the road through a twice-opened tomato can.

"Lenses" could be autobiography; it tells a different story than "The Idiot," in which details have been compressed to make a point. Of this change, M. D. Uroff comments: "But his poem is darker than the actual experience. In real life, the tin-can telescope had been opened at both ends; in the poem there is only one 'peeled end' which is clapped to his eye, leaving no exit to the world or human community. Once again Crane depicts a moment of stasis. The lone boy stands still and the poet observes him from a distance; there is no movement toward human contact between them, no movement of love to draw them together."[10]

This is not quite on the mark; here as elsewhere in the Caribbean poems Crane is subtle, not static, and he has altered the incident not simply to darken it but to shed light on certain moral implications. In the poem, the action of the idiot, peering in his useless telescope, ultimately causes Crane to realize his mistreatment, and it becomes the basis for Crane's own chastisement of himself at the end of the poem. The idiot, no doubt in emulation of adults he has seen, plays with a homemade telescope which actually blocks out all sight. If at first this seems pathetic, a second thought reveals that he must be aware that he can see nothing, that he is thoroughly blinded. Yet he is undisturbed, peering into darkness, not because he is a fool but because he has learned that to look and to be utterly blind is one of the characteristics of being an adult; after all, the adults he has observed are—unlike the children who taunt him openly—utterly blind to him. They sheer over to the side and do not speak. For him to play at being an adult, then, is, as far as he is concerned, to accept an absolute blindness to the things about him.

This episode is a revelation to Crane. Not only does it make him aware that the idiot has been observing others all along, and that the evasive tactics of adults have not gone unnoticed, it also makes him aware that the idiot has tried to emulate the behavior of the adults. And of course the idiot's emulation strikingly reveals the extent of the irresponsibility of the adults. It is a brief moment of contact with another, the only such moment in the group of poems, and it causes distinct reverberations. In his other Caribbean poetry, Crane has been standing aside and looking askance at others, judging them for their weaknesses, for their tendency toward aloofness or their willingness to be complaisant. Is the poet, too, guilty of casting a bad light by his own detachment? Is he no better than the subjects of his poems, no better than the way he distantly responds to others, as a faraway spy?

Whether or not these questions resound through the other poems in the suite, they are felt as a presence in the ending of "The Idiot." Crane hears the voice of the idiot singing, innocently praising God, and he appreciates it because it lifts past all barriers—though at the same time it reminds him of his own fallen state, his own moral failure:

> And since, through these barricades of green,
> A *Dios Gracias, grac*—I've heard his song
> Above all reason lifting, halt serene—
> My trespass vision shrinks to face his wrong.

The earlier version in *transition* was less pointed; the last line read: "Uncancelled as the stars that sum no wrong."[11] This was perhaps a bit too beguiling. The final version is preferable because it blends the song of innocence with the sting of experience in the poet's mind. "His wrong" is not just the idiot boy's "wrong," not just the handicap he labors under, but the wrong done to the boy by the poet through his failure to acknowledge him earlier. Crane frequently claimed William Blake as one of his mentors, and with "The Idiot" he composes a work which is a worthy successor to any of Blake's songs of innocence and experience. Of all the "Carib Suite" poems, it is the subtlest, and its reversal in mid-course, its pivotting on the poet's sudden understanding of his own error, brings it closest to the poems of the 1926 *Bridge*.

If all recognized their wrong, if "his wrong" was always the wrong I do to him and not the wrong he labors under according to my perception, then there would be no need for what now appears as the inevitable conclusion to "East of Yucatan": the Day of Judgment, the hour of wrath, the hurricane of destruction which wipes all away and which may be all that the Caribbean subjects, including the poet, deserve. In this storm, no one is safe any longer: "Nor Lord, may worm outdeep // Thy drum's gambade, its plunge abscond!" What is the origin of this sudden apocalypse? Human values have been forgotten, as the sequence has dramatically, if subtly, demonstrated. The scriptures, those words that invoke human charity, have been regarded by the subjects as no matter for concern. And therefore the scriptures are now torn from the stone on which they should have been permanently engraved and are loosed with a vengeance on the wind:

> Ay! Scripture flee'th stone!
> Milk-bright, Thy chisel wind
>
> Rescindeth flesh from bone
> To quivering whittling thinned—

As a storm that swirls up in response to the various displays of inhumanity throughout the Caribbean poems, "The Hurricane" is an appropriate conclusion. Apocalyptic without being celebratory, it is in keeping with the oblique tone of the sequence. If the milk of human kindness is suppressed, it will eventually burst out but curdled to a fury. The forgotten scriptures will now be engraved, with "whittling," on the hearts of those who survive, if there are any. The "Milk-bright chisel wind" will render them unforgettable.

"The Hurricane," odd as it is, becomes a fitting conclusion to "East of Yucatan" and the "Carib Suite" in general; it is not the moment of joyous, creative frenzy Crane may have set out to evoke, but it is the proper last word for the subjects in these poems. The poems are dark, but they are not simply admissions of despair or stasis or collapse. The sequence probes various forms of moral evasion in writing that is sometimes direct, sometimes gnarled, sometimes hesitant, but altogether surprisingly supple. The Caribbean poems, especially when read together, rescued from their haphazard assemblage in the posthumous *Key West* collection, are efforts to write serious poetry in a short form. Crane rarely limited himself so severely, and he may have been hoping, as Winters implied, to perfect a style that was more suitable to publication in anthologies and in journals. If these poems were an experiment in writing clearly and descriptively without sacrificing subtlety, many of them achieved that goal to a surprising degree; they offer a tantalizing glimpse of what Crane might have gone on to write had he lived longer, under more auspicious circumstances.

13

Later Additions to *The Bridge*

What did Crane hope to accomplish when, in 1929, he composed three additional poems to round out his work on *The Bridge?* These three poems became at once, and have still remained, without question the most controversial sections of the sequence. "Indiana" moved Winters and Tate to judgments that border on invective.[1] To this day the poem is still regarded as an embarrassment. "Quaker Hill" has both supporters and detractors, but a majority of critics agree that its undisguised bitterness is strikingly at odds with the rest of the poems. And "Cape Hatteras" has provoked commentary ranging from sheer disparagement to unmitigated praise, usually in exact proportion to the commentator's regard for Whitman, who is himself still so provocative a figure.[2]

Crane did not have to compose this additional work. He had a standing offer from Harry and Caresse Crosby, founders of the prestigious Black Sun Press (Paris), to print his poems just as they were, even if he felt they were incomplete. But in a letter to Isidor Schneider of May 1, 1929, he was anything but enthusiastic about such an arrangement:

> If it eventuates that I have the wit or inspiration to add to it later—such additions can be incorporated in some later edition. I've alternated between embarrassment and indifference for so long that when the Crosbys urged me to let them have it, declaring that it reads well enough as it is, I gave in. Malcolm advised as much before I left America, so I feel there may be some justification. The poems, arranged as you may remember, do have a certain progression I think. And maybe the gaps are more evident to me than others. . . . Indeed, they must be.

Though he has good news to announce, he appears both apologetic and anxious, and more than a little uncertain about the wisdom of his decision. So it is not surprising to learn that a few weeks after this letter, he is at work on new sections of *The Bridge*, despite the willingness of the Crosbys to sponsor a second edition.

Once Crane began to consider adding new sections, his overall anxiety over the incomplete *Bridge* surfaced in several ways. He was unsure, for example, about the narrative line. One of the first additions he made to the sequence was not a new poem but the series of elliptical gloss notes which accompany poems in the first half of *The Bridge*, then abruptly drop out of sight. Written in a dense, quasi-poetic prose, they verge uneasily between prose commentary and the somewhat affected quotations that precede each section. Judging from these notes, Crane wanted the five sections of "Powhatan's Daughter" to appear as the poet's own version of Columbus's quest. As Columbus discovered the body of America, so the poet does too, imaginatively, in the figure of Pocahontas. To assert this overview, Crane must skim the surface of his poetry, minimizing some of its salient features. To identify memory in "Van Winkle" as "time's truant," for example, is to downplay all the disturbing aspects of memory that, in 1926, he had struggled with so tormentedly. The effort to highlight a narrative line that supposedly reveals a connection between Columbus and the poet is the first ominous indication that the final additions to *The Bridge* will too readily reflect Crane's own anxious tendency to conventionalize his own work.

Further evidence of his increasing concern with the problem of a narrative line goes back to 1927, in a letter written to his patron after "The River" had been completed. Here he is at pains to steer Otto Kahn away from any thought that the poems, arranged in the sequence of their final, published version, do not follow after one another; indeed, he talks of little else in his commentary except linkages. The hazy fog that begins "The Harbor Dawn" is an "admirable transition" between the centuries that separate the poet and Columbus. Since the poems in "Powhatan's Daughter" deal with the five ages of man (Crane says), in "Van Winkle" the poet thinks of his youth and "the 'childhood' of the continental conquest." In "The River" the subway of "Van Winkle" turns into an express train, which eventually leads away from the urban setting and transports the reader "into interior after interior, finally to the great River." In "The Dance" the poet enters the Indian world, and "Indiana" is to be "a lyrical summary of the period of conquest" (at this time, the poem was still unwritten). In offering this commentary, Crane presents his poems as though they could be read as a novel, as a narrative tale. To know such linkages underlie the poems is of dubious value to the reader because Crane's odd perspective places a distorting emphasis on the beginnings and endings: instead of being allowed to open and develop and conclude in the exploratory way in which they were written, the poems are forced to take a place in a conventional frame. Even worse, Crane's defense of his work encourages the notion that all connections among his poems are as contrived and arbitrary as the ones he emphasizes here.[3]

It may be, of course, that in addressing himself to his patron, Crane was hampered by the sense that he must speak down; it would be prudent, therefore, for him to point out the simpler problems that might discourage the untutored reader. But in 1930, after *The Bridge* had been published, he offered extracts from this letter to Eda Lou Walton, then teaching a course in contemporary poetry that included *The Bridge*, and he had further plans to elaborate the letter "into a more or less formalized essay" for Paul Rosenfeld.[4] (Perhaps on the strength of this remark, the letter itself was published in the *Hound & Horn* for July-September 1934, and it seems to have formed a basis for the harsh appraisal of Blackmur in his 1935 essay.)[5]

By the fall of 1927, when this letter was written, the likelihood was that Crane had lost confidence in his own writing. Looking back on those portions of *The Bridge* he had written in 1926, he must have often wondered what his achievement amounted to. He had, after all, initially proposed a panoramic history of America, with heroes and heroines abounding, and he had marshaled all his poems, even the new ones, into a sequence which remained somewhat chronological. But here, despite all those efforts, was a quirky, personal poem populated by oddballs and misfits; the role his parents played in this poem, for example, could have struck him as typical of how far he had let himself be led astray. His two parents appeared in a most disturbing light: one administered a whipping, and the other withheld affection at a crucial moment. Furthermore, the setting of the poem remained resolutely within the boundaries of the modern city; and when the scene temporarily changed, it tended to stray out toward the open sea, just as though Crane were unwilling to focus on American history. Where were the impressive events of American history, the great battles, the great inventions, the great conquests? And where were the contemporary problems, the issues debated by intellectuals? Where was, as a matter of fact, the machine?

It is evident from "The River" that Crane was, as early as the spring of 1927, concerned over these omissions and convinced of the importance of rectifying them. He turned away from the revolutionary sentiments in the "Calgary Express" fragment to compose a more general poem with relevance for everyone. That change of heart is significant: instead of trusting that his audience would show interest in the plight of a disadvantaged group, he provides his audience with a poem that insists he has something to offer them. If he brings into his poem more shady characters—tramps—he balances them with the elegance and prestige and novelty of the 20th Century Limited. The terrain of "The River" expands enormously: not only do we actually leave New York City right from the start (almost assertively, as though Crane has to put himself on the train in order to change his scenery) but we journey westward to the upper Mississippi Valley, then roll down the river to New Orleans. In the meantime, through the recollections of the tramps, we are afforded glimpses of "The last bear, shot drinking in the Dakotas," references to "Cheyenne and Kalamazoo," a nod to "Booneville," a side excursion to the "Ozarks, domed by Iron Mountain," a memory of cannery-works in Akron, a glimpse of Cairo, Illinois, and a "half-hour's wait at Siskiyou."[6] Folk heroes are scattered about: Casey Jones, Memphis Johnny, Steamboat Bill, Dan Midland. There are favorite songs like "Deep River" and "My Old Kentucky Home." Instead of fearsome fathers and frowning mothers, Aunt Sally Simpson smiles. The poem, in fact, seems to depend on the traditional American prejudice against the evils of the modern city: in the country, we recover a slower life-style, more cordial, more appealing than the aggressive scurry of the bustling city. (Crane's idea in 1926, of course, had been that the challenge was to soar in the city rather than flee from it.) But "The River" seems to take a bead on easy targets: Crane's irony in the opening lines is directed against that perennial object of derision, the advertising slogan. Yet "The River" is itself as self-consciously up to date as the latest commercial: it makes mention of radio, the telegraph, the Mazda light, and the streamliner.

It seems plain that "The River" was designed as a popular poem in the vein of Carl Sandburg or Sherwood Anderson. It is packed with folksy images and current references, and it tends to play the city off against the country. In fact, his father wrote back after receiving "The River" (the only portion of the poem Crane seems to have sent him): "the enclosure was, I believe, the best I have seen of your work," adding with a good deal of the shrewd businessman's intelligence: "Something of this nature, in my humble opinion, would sell better than other things I have seen; it does not leave quite so much to the imagination."[7] This rare en-

dorsement alone is enough to indicate that Crane had modulated his
work in a proper fashion.

This appeal, needless to say, was conspicuously absent from the 1926
poems. The pop-tune lyrics of "Virginia," for example, are hollow stuff
that convey their own essential dishonesty. The colloquial conversation
interspersed in "The Tunnel" is painful to hear, not affable; in a mocking
fashion, it recalls him to hopes that he would, at this dramatic point in
his sequence, have preferred remain dormant. The "nickel-in-the-slot
pianola" of "Cutty Sark" spins out a tune that increasingly calls in question the heroic reveries of the derelict sailor. In short, the 1926 poems
are as bold as *The Waste Land* in appropriating images and diction, fragments of conversation and snatches of song, not customarily associated
with nonsatiric poetry. What is disheartening in "The River" is that
Crane often presents an ornamental detail as though it were sufficient in
itself:

> Strange bird-wit, like the elemental gist
> Of unwalled winds they offer, singing low
> *My Old Kentucky Home*, and *Casey Jones*,
> *Some Sunny Day*. I heard a road-gang chanting so.
> And afterwards, who had a colt's eyes—one said,
> "Jesus! I remember watermelon days!" and sped
> High in a cloud of merriment, recalled
> "—And when my Aunt Sally Simpson smiled," he drawled—
> "It was almost Louisiana, long ago."

In "The River," we are meant to approve wholeheartedly of the sweep
and grandeur of the poem as it ranges across the continent, lighting
on attractive details; but in "Ave Maria" the glorious reverie in which
Columbus recalls his first sight of the new world was not just a stunning
moment in its own right, it portrayed also the troublesome pride in which
Columbus revelled. There is a double-edged quality, an intricacy, in the
1926 poems—evident clearly enough in even the "Calgary Express"
fragment—that is beyond the hearing of the poet of "The River." These
earlier poems leave a great deal to the imagination.

In 1929 Crane seizes an advantage similar to the one he took in 1927.
The three new poems follow guidelines set down by "The River." If the
1926 poems are open to the criticism that they center too exclusively on
an urban setting, then in "Indiana" we return from California (via Colo-

rado) to Indiana where a son (born in Kentucky) is pushing off for Rio de Janeiro; in "Cape Hatteras" we wander from Bombay to New York to South Carolina, back to Europe for some aerial warfare, then to the battlefields of Pennsylvania and the Ozark Mountains. (All three poems take for their titles a place-name outside of New York City.) The 1929 poems also attend to matters of history. When second-growth timber is chopped down in "Quaker Hill" to make way for new suburban tenants, Crane takes the opportunity to recall the rangers who once fought the Iroquois for this land. An abandoned hotel evokes memories of a vanished aristocracy, as "Powitzky" visits "Adams' auction." In "Indiana," the gold rush of 1859 is over, the frontier is closing, the immigrants return eastward; it is a thesis straight out of Frederick Turner, the notion that the long pioneer heritage of America is in jeopardy. But that heritage is recalled in "Cape Hatteras," a large segment of which addresses itself to the airplane, an invention the perversion of which leads Crane into the Great War and the Civil War. The poems of 1929 are responsible, even upright; they deal with admirable individuals: airplane pilots and the Wright brothers, rangers and Iroquois, and mothers of two races, and popular poets like Whitman and Dickinson instead of morbid ones like Poe. And the poems are topical: they take note of Prohibition, golf, suburbia, Hollywood, gin fizz, the stock exchange, periscopes, dogfights, and dirigibles.

All the minor flaws that harried "The River" come center stage in these three poems, each of which is charged with expanding the scope of the epic considerably, each of which is weighted down with elements that simply never occurred to the poet in 1926. With all this clutter, with all these trappings devised to rig the verse, what is remarkable is that Crane, having made his commitment to convention, continually refuses to play the game. He keeps turning against the very clutter he has introduced into his own poems: it is as though he had been forced into a corner by the advice and expectations of others, and his protest now takes the form of undermining the very poems that others had expected him to write. His "Quaker Hill" comparison of past with present is not calm and resigned but vexed and irritated. His homage to the maternal instinct in "Indiana" comes out as a fierce exposure of extreme possessiveness. And the airplane in "Cape Hatteras"—a favorite motif of Harry Crosby —flies only to crash.[8] If these poems are not up to the level of previous work, neither are they hack propaganda; Crane's torment and indecision, his irritation and revulsion, come through in the work time after time. The poems are distraught and twisted, a striking mixture of business-manlike craftsmanship undermined by flashes of integrity.

1

The last word on *The Bridge*, the last poem to be completed, "Quaker Hill" emphasizes the subterranean theme in all these last poems: the importance Crane attaches to getting out from under all that he has piled on himself. The poem itself piles up problems only to slip out from under them. The first six stanzas are a scornful dismissal of the multitudes who are characterized as no different than a herd of cows, disgustingly self-satisfied:

> These are but cows that see no other thing
> Than grass and snow, and their own inner being
> Through the rich halo that they do not trouble
> Even to cast upon the seasons fleeting
> Though they should thin and die on last year's stubble.

The multitudes look only to immediate gratification, as they relish feeling their "own inner being" through a "rich halo" of self-satisfaction. Indulgent, complacent, they merge into the "Czars / Of golf" or the inhabitants of roadhouses whose "gin fizz / Bubbles in time to Hollywood's new love-nest pageant." The Promised Land has lost its promise to the persuasions of the suburban land agent; pioneerhood has come down to moving into suburbia. Americans now dream of owning their own homes.

In contrast to the multitudes, who recognize no seasons changing (possibly because they cannot endure any form of death), there are those who stand in the midst of autumn, who "with pledge taste the bright annoy / Of friendship's acid wine." Friendship, if it is genuine, is neither bland nor docile but annoying, acid, with "Shifting reprisals" and the "jest" "too sharp to be kindly." Such a vision of a pugnacious community, however, may be as obsolete as "Old Mizzentop," an abandoned hotel whose multilevels simply pile up, neglected, like the history of the country ignored by the land agents and the czars of golf.

On the one hand, there is the ephemeral flash of the contemporary. On the other hand, there is the ponderous weight of history. And there is no significant way of relating the two. Crane's decision, then, is simply to turn away from both, to retire to an inner world of individual excellence that Emily Dickinson and Isadora Duncan knew—the fate, perhaps, of the artist in America. If the artist is thoroughly isolated, with no possible audience whatsoever, he can only retreat inward, expressing himself "as humbly as a guest who knows himself too late." This one line is almost a signature for these last poems, and a measure of his spirit in 1929: the form of the epic is not for him, but he "knows himself too late," and only in his last stanza is he able to transmit a personal expression of pain and despair that is not riddled with anger and scorn.

History, the multitudes, the machine are utterly forgotten at the close as he descends from "the hawk's far stemming view"—that aloof, condemnatory gaze of the self-assured predator—and discovers that his alternative is not, as he had feared, to become "as worm's eye" but rather to become that note of the whippoorwill, a humble creature that yields "That patience that is armour and that shields / Love from despair." In advising himself to "break off, / descend—/ descend—" he leaves behind his poetry of ambition, admitting he has failed in his effort at an epic, but asserting that what saves him is some inner sense of excellence, his intuitive knowledge that the love between persons is of utmost value. Isadora Duncan danced, oblivious to the catcalls of her disapproving audience; Emily Dickinson wrote, indifferent to whether anyone read or not. Crane accepts a similar fate for himself, as a lyric poet who wants to be an epic poet but whose ambitions are condemned by the vacuities of a hollow culture.

2

That Crane now feels he dwells in a vacuum, where the likelihood of a sensitive hearing verges on the impossible—both "Quaker Hill" and "Indiana" were completed in New York City, where Crane had returned after nearly a year in Europe—is conveyed with deepest bitterness in "Indiana." From one perspective, "Indiana" is simply a sentimental poem, a curiously awkward bit of narrative verse that offers a maudlin tale of sorrow. From another angle, however, it is an almost unbearably ugly exposure of the coercive efforts of a mother to make her son, striking off on his own, feel that he is betraying her. Duty and responsibility: Crane is especially sensitive to these in 1929, wanting to flee them, but at the same time feeling remorse at not fulfilling his proper role.

"Indiana" is, in one respect, closer to the 1926 poems than any of the other late work: like "Calgary Express" it has a double edge, it can be

read in two ways. It is unlike the 1926 poems, however, in that it withholds from the mother any awareness of the flaws in herself. She never
acknowledges her hideous possessiveness, she never wakens to hear the
sound of her own coercion, and she never turns to change. Her grip remains fast to the very end.

Crane may have set out to write this poem innocently enough. Simply
as a requirement to fill a gap, he needed a work that would transfer him
from the sacred world of the Indian in "The Dance" to the profane world
of the white man in "Cutty Sark." What better way to accomplish the
shift than through a transitional poem positioned in the nineteenth century, just as the white man's greedy search for gold had succeeded in
dispossessing the Indian? And what better way to present the situation
than through the eyes of a mother who looks back longingly to the simplicity of the lost Indian world and who looks ahead fearfully to the com-
mercialized, mercantile cityscape of the future? In dispossessing the Indian and those values of Indian culture, the white man eventually pays a
price. Furthermore, the mother resembles Columbus in that she too is a
prophet who denounces greed (and her display of affection toward her
children looks back to the bad mother in "Van Winkle" and ahead to the
good mother in "The Tunnel." In a defiant gesture, she signals her bond
with a deposed Indian squaw. Each mother holds up her child to the
other, as though to indicate that future generations must be instructed in
a drastically different mode of thinking. More precious than gold are the
bonds between persons:

> Oh, hold me in those eyes' engaging blue;
> There's where the stubborn years gleam and atone,—
> Where gold is true!

That her son, Larry, is now off to sea only continues, tragically, the pattern she had wanted to slip out from those many years ago, beginning
with her shared gesture to the Indian squaw. But the bonds between persons continue to be broken, generation after generation, as each group of
young men set out in their false pursuit of wealth, adventure, and freedom. Larry's fate is revealed in "Cutty Sark": having plundered the
West, Americans go even further afield and plunder the Orient. And now
there are no more frontiers.

"Indiana" seems innocent enough and it connects up so clearly with
so many significant strands in the final version of *The Bridge* that it
seems ready-made for extended exegesis. And yet from the moment of its

appearance, the poem has provoked the most violent reactions, almost all of them negative. The reason may be that this innocent poem conceals a viper: if Crane has bestowed upon his mother a group of outstanding attributes, he has also succeeded in portraying the coercive whine of self-sacrifice that makes her entire monologue an act of manipulation. Columbus could condemn the greed of Fernando without descending into self-righteousness because he was also recognizing that which he condemned as within himself and, having heard the sound of pride and greed in his own voice, was speaking to himself. But the mother of "Indiana" is given no comparable insight. She seems more intent on provoking guilt in her son, and she thrives on her own self-pity. She presents herself to him as the companion to a "bedraggled squaw," one who has been abandoned by her menfolk then as now. She pointedly reminds her son of the torments suffered by his difficult birth: "bison thunder rends my dream no more / As once my womb was torn, my boy, when you / Yielded your first cry at the prairie's door." She burdens her son with the ghostly presence of her lost husband, refusing to see that her son is an individual and even referring to him as though he were a surrogate husband: "You were the first," "all that's left to me of Jim," "the only one with eyes like him." In hoisting her child up for the Indian mother to see, as a symbol of a different, better future, she is tacitly confessing to using her son for her own stubborn purpose, however high-minded it may be. At the same time, her usage of him weighs him down with responsibilities that no one could reasonably fulfill. And there is the resentment which she still feels, years later, at the abandonment by her husband; she talks of his death not reverently but bitterly, as though he had been a failure, a hopeless fool:

> But we,—too late, too early, howsoever—
> Won nothing out of fifty-nine—those years—
> But gilded promise, yielded to us never,
> And barren tears . . .

She may be convinced that all gold is fools' gold, but her lingering resentment toward her husband makes us certain that she herself lacks the gold that is true.

On one level, "Indiana" is simply defining a moment in history, the crisis of the closing frontier when settlers had to accept the fact that the land was not teeming with riches—a moment of acute psychological importance for Americans, a time when they could have supplanted their belief in a frontier of riches with a belief in another idea of a frontier. They could have turned from aimless, endless wandering to pursue instead the task of founding relationships that endure. The poem, on this level, addresses itself with businesslike competence to important themes in *The Bridge*. But in writing his poem, Crane entered another level: he quite simply made his mother into a living personality, not simply a historical figure. She is not a mere caricature, though her personality is so lacking in character that she easily could have been. She resembles Fernando more than Columbus, and she demonstrates herself incapable of the magnanimous love of such importance to Crane. Entirely lacking in self-awareness, she is trapped in a dwindling universe: possessive, unresponsive to her son (who remains mute throughout, as if he hears all her words in a stony silence), self-pitying, manipulative, domineering. The surface of the poem is so innocent that the shock of discovering that this mother is a frightening personality is unnerving, and it may explain why this poem provokes such violent responses from even the most benign of commentators.

3

"Indiana" is close to being a complex poem. It argues for the importance of relationships instead of the possessive greed of wealth, at the same time as it dramatically reveals the distortions caused when no relationship exists between two persons. Though "Cape Hatteras" also focuses on the importance of relationships, there is no figure in it comparable in intensity to the mother of "Indiana." It is perhaps the simplest of all the poems in *The Bridge*.

The obligation Crane assumes in "Cape Hatteras" is to confront the problem of the machine, of which the airplane is made out to be the representative symbol. The airplane, Crane grants, has the potential to be an invention of wonder, but it has an even greater potential for misuse. In mulling over this problem, Crane recognizes that he cannot go it alone, and so he invokes the aid of a fellow poet who had himself sought to come to terms with a new technology. By cultivating a connection with Whitman, Crane affirms that this very association is itself the answer to the problem of the machine. For the airplane is disturbing not because of its capacity for destruction—which is, in any case, rare and limited to acts of warfare—but because of its ability to isolate individuals, leaving each one alone in "abysmal cupolas of space," soaring endlessly aloft, ever faster, in a self-enclosed orbit, all contact with others forsaken. The end of such soaring is inevitably a crash.

When Crane turns to Whitman, then, the point he is stressing is not necessarily that Whitman in his time was able to appreciate the machine in a manner that Crane envies and would emulate. No, the genuine point is that Crane reaches out to break from the isolation in which he had been immersed (and which the machine can only encourage) to take another by the hand. When Crane is in contact with Whitman, then he can imagine the smashed planes as resurrected and coursing outward on an open road.

That Crane is firmly committed to his relationship with Whitman, especially toward the end of "Cape Hatteras," accounts for the bizarre writing in this poem, some of the most awkward that Crane ever fashioned. It has been condemned as an elaborate, deliberate self-parody—an indication of his inability to believe in himself at this difficult time in his life; it has been defended as an impressive attempt to convey a simple enthusiasm that sophisticated readers are merely reluctant to acknowledge. It is almost certainly neither one of these, neither self-parody nor enthusiasm, but rather the result of his effort to demonstrate dramatically how far he is willing to go to move in relation with Whitman: to make his point against isolation, he is prepared to break open his own poem and to include Whitman's language with his own language.

Whitman and Crane must be coexistent, apparent within the same writing, and that is why Crane's language in the poem bends and yaws and crinkles to accommodate an alien presence. Crane retains his own preference for blank verse and rhyme, but welcomes Whitman's contribution of an expansive, casual, handmade diction and imagery:

> O early following thee, I searched the hill
> Blue-writ and odour-firm with violets, 'til
> With June the mountain laurel broke through green
> And filled the forest with what clustrous sheen!

This is identifiable as neither Whitman nor Crane but some deliberate amalgamation of the two. It is, admittedly, an unlikely combination, but such patently laborious writing can, in the context of "Cape Hatteras," win supporters because its awkwardness is preferable to the speed and purity and sleekness which the pilots represent. To carry so cumbersomely within the lines of your writing the presence of another may result in such teeth-jarring concoctions as

> Familiar, thou, as mendicants in public places;
> Evasive—too—as dayspring's spreading arc to trace is

—but the alternative afforded by the pilots, of speeding endlessly on, of never attending to anything outside of yourself, is unquestionably repugnant:

> Dream cancels dream in this new realm of fact
> From which we waken into the dream of act;
> Seeing himself an atom in a shroud—
> Man hears himself an engine in a cloud!

These lines clip along ever more rapidly in a hurtling anapestic gallop; the parallel syntax of "atom in a shroud" and "engine in a cloud" increase the momentum. By contrast, the excessive claims Crane makes for Whitman load down his lines with echoes of Whitman's phrasing and forestall any streamlined movement. Whitman is a "Meistersinger" who "set breath in steel" yet whose lines are "rife as the loam / Of prairies," a poet who has held "the heights" yet who is intimate with the wounds of "fraternal massacre." These extravagant oppositions are not persuasively held together, but in the context of "Cape Hatteras" they can be appealing just because they are so clumsy and ponderous. If the pilots are swiftly, summarily characterized, Whitman is an enigma, larger than life, an admixture of many oppositions.

Another way to apologize for Crane's approach to "Cape Hatteras" is to note that there are various ways to act foolishly as one writes. Crane runs through a gamut, discarding all but one. A poet can choose to describe "The nasal whine of power" until he finds his own control of language swept away, "giggling in the girth / Of steely gizzards" in an imitation of the rattle of machinery. That way leads to a kind of ecstatic, but maniacal, hysteria. Or a poet can choose to utilize a heavy irony, deflating airships by overdescribing them in pompous terminology, in a mock-heroic style:

> While Cetus-like, O thou Dirigible, enormous Lounger
> On pendulous auroral beaches—satellited wide
> By convoy planes, moonferrets that rejoin thee
> On fleeing balconies as thou dost glide,
> —Hast splintered space!

That way evokes some of the sheer vanity that attends upon the mastery of the air, the overblown ease of gliding through space and lounging in bloated satisfaction. But such exertion seems hardly worth the effort, rhetorical ranting bound for its own exhaustion. Or a poet can choose to imitate, through the actual arrangement of words on the page, the downward spiral of the plummeting airplane, writing in a "caligrammatic" style learned from contemporary French poets. That way provides a meaningless visual entertainment, destined to come to an abrupt halt as the novelty wears thin.

All these ways of adjusting one's language to expand its meaning eventually turn hollow except one: the strain of engaging wholly with another person, reproducing that other person's way of speaking in one's own. The strain of writing as Whitman-Crane is, then, somewhat prepared for by the experimental writing in the preceding parts of the poem. A certain ungainliness is offered as a virtue, in contrast to the obnoxiousness of the trim airships, in superiority to other ways of acting foolishly as one writes.

Still, the outrageousness of Crane's gesture, trying to write as Whitman-Crane, is a reminder that Crane's isolation always stands forth in these 1929 poems. "Cape Hatteras" affirms, it is true, the great theme of the 1926 poems, but with a curious mixture of boldness and reticence. Crane is bold to display so much affection for Whitman, a poet he admires for a host of personal reasons; but he is reticent in that he pursues a person who is not a genuine presence but a collection of phrases, a group of images, a slew of words. There is no real conflict between the two, no opposition to be overcome as there had been in "The Dance" between Maquokeeta and Pocahontas. The relationship is more brother to brother, with both sharing identical values. Whitman-Crane jogs along unabashedly, with the very real tensions that should exist between the two poets folded over into a poetic potpourri. The idea is right, but it fails to generate any life.

As Crane wrote to Winters in 1927, "I can never do anything worth while without the assent of my intuitions."[9] All three of the poems appended to *The Bridge* in 1929 reveal that he was willing to try to expand the scope of his poem but aware of how strained this effort was. The poems all display his attempt to unite the themes he now wishes to emphasize: the loss of the frontier, the illusory attractions of the machine, and the importance of abiding relationships. With these three poems in place, it is possible to guess at what he had hoped *The Bridge* to be in its final version. It is a poem in which the poet, starting out in the hope of loving America, finds that "America" is unlovable; but in the process he realizes what it is that he himself values. Columbus found a pristine land of sheer possibility, a land that Crane imaginatively recovers by going back to the dawn in "Powhatan's Daughter," only to lose again as he emerges into a bleak present. Whitman's phantom presence holds out a hope of allowing him to embrace America, in all its promise and splendor, by embracing Whitman. But that hope, too, is dashed in "Three Songs" and "Quaker Hill," in which the poet loses touch with his mentor. In "The Tunnel" he abandons all hope, to recover it momentarily in "Atlantis," suggesting by this recovery that the cycle of death and rebirth, loss and rediscovery is unavoidable.

The 1930 *Bridge* is blurred and vague in a way the 1926 *Bridge* was not. By arranging the poems as he did, Crane drastically alters their original meaning, then scurries to reorient his work through his later additions. The ideas are all in place but broadened out, conventionalized. The flashes of genius, the intuitive insights, and most of all the constant turning away from false to true aspirations, thinking his poems through in their very movement—all these are lost. What is left? A respectable poem, always straining against itself, throwing out general ideas (the virtue of the quest, the need for love, the treachery of the machine) which are acceptable enough but which are less than original. The poem was well received by the majority of reviewers, especially those who did not know Crane personally or were not familiar with his previous work. Only Crane's close friends, Tate and Winters, issued strong objections. They had been led to expect more.

14

The Late Poems (II): Letter-poems

What makes "The Broken Tower" stand out from Crane's other love poems is its concern with a love that is lasting. In "Faustus and Helen" Crane's Helen vanished at the coming of dawn; she existed for the duration of the night only. In *Voyages* the poet's lover drifted away, once the poet committed the error of trying to possess his love entirely. In the 1926 *Bridge* Crane found his hope revived at the close of his poem, though no one person had become his lover; he could only pledge to continue seeking despite his obstacles. But in "The Broken Tower" he emphasized that his new love was not only substantial and secure but carried the promise of a totally new life issuing out of it.

"The Broken Tower" could have effectively ended by its eighth stanza. Up to this point, Crane has been realizing that the source of his desperation is his willful effort to act alone, to remake the world by himself. When, however, he turns to another person, to mingle his blood with hers, he is able to see himself in a new light:

> or is it she
> Whose sweet mortality stirs latent power?—
>
> And through whose pulse I hear, counting the strokes
> My veins recall and add, revived and sure
> The angelus of wars my chest evokes:
> What I hold healed, original now, and pure . . .

If the poem concluded at this point, Crane would still have been asserting a familiar theme.

But the mingling of blood between a man and a woman is different than the blood brothers who join together in *Voyages*, and it is this differ-

233

ence which has struck Crane, permitting him to write his final two
stanzas:

> And builds, within, a tower that is not stone
> (Not stone can jacket heaven)—but slip
> Of pebbles,—visible wings of silence sown
> In azure circles, widening as they dip
>
> The matrix of the heart, lift down the eye
> That shrines the quiet lake and swells a tower . . .
> That commodius, tall decorum of that sky
> Unseals her earth, and lifts love in its shower.

To what extent Crane is consciously speaking of an act that conceives a
new, third life is impossible to determine. From one perspective, the images accommodate themselves, if in a blurry fashion, to the description
of a relationship which expands as the couple grow familiar with one another. From another perspective, though, it appears that this new relationship is creating out of itself a third life that lives beyond it. Out of the
"sweet mortality" in a woman, which stirs the "latent power" in a man,
issues a form of immortality, much as a child would continue to live beyond its parents, creating another generation. Mingling of blood, in this
case, creates more than simply calming the "angelus of wars" an individual bears within him. It builds "within" a "slip of pebbles," and this is
like sowing "visible wings of silence" that widen of their own accord "as
they dip // The matrix of the heart," and bring forth a new eye that
"shrines the quiet lake and swells a tower." This new eye worships the
mother and fills the father with pride. And if the sky is masculine and
the earth is feminine (as they had been in "The Dance"), then this third
being lends a "decorum" to the actions of the masculine sky and returns
a new fecundity to the earth.

Improbable as it first may seem, in his last two stanzas Crane is, on an
intuitive level at least, confronting an opportunity he had never had to
consider before. The responsibility implied here further promises a radically new future, a future of conventionality and stability and fidelity—a
series of surprisingly new possibilities (some of which, perhaps, were
made more meaningful by his father's sudden death in July 1931). But
there is some evidence that Crane had been longing for a radical and
permanent change in his life since 1928. The conventionalizing additions to *The Bridge* suggest a strong willingness to mitigate many of what
he may have felt to be his earlier excesses. Certainly in the few, fragmen-

tary, halfhearted verses he wrote from 1928 on, he reveals an increasing lack of interest in the grand rhetorical gesture, the extraordinarily intricate interplay of words. These late poems are modest almost to the point of self-effacement (and only a very few of them were submitted to journals).[1] Furthermore, in them he is searching for opportunities to speak, in an unexpectedly clear way, with persons on whom he can count. He is looking for that which does endure, the firm and lasting and stable.

1

Not surprisingly, the three most substantial of the late poems are addresses to the two women most important to him at the time (he had not yet met the woman to whom "The Broken Tower" is addressed): his mother and Sally Simpson, the elderly caretaker of the family cottage on the Isle of Pines. Of these three poems, only one, "A Name for All," appeared in print in his lifetime; it is very much a public poem, in contrast to the other two, "A Postscript" and "Eternity," both of which are so personal as to risk seeming negligible, at least to readers unfamiliar with details of Crane's private life. But "A Name for All" seems to have been conceived as a public poem, perhaps in accord with Crane's own break with his mother at this time. It takes a somber, formal tone, and it is as different from the other two poems as it can be—as different as Grace Hart was from Sally Simpson.

If "A Name for All" is a message to his mother, it is a plea for understanding fashioned in the form of a rebuke. It is most likely that all three of these late poems were written in the spring and summer of 1928, after Crane had confessed something of his personal life to his mother, then living temporarily in California and vaguely anticipating a call to a movie career. No direct account of the incident exists, but numerous allusions to it suggest that Grace Hart reacted awkwardly to her son's confession. "A Name for All" may be a retort to her lack of understanding.[2]

To name is to label, to label is to libel: names are clapped on the wind, and they confine it; or names crudely clutch the fragile moonmoth, and they maim it for life. Crane can only wish that this were not so:

> I dreamed that all men dropped their names and sang
> As only they can praise, who build their days
> With fin and hoof, with wing and sweetened fang
> Struck free and holy in one name always.

The poem is simply a plea for magnanimity from others, a plea for a living community of selfless understanding and forgiveness. But the poem is somber and regretful; it is saddened by the fact that so simple, so obvious, so appealing a notion need have to be expressed at all. It should be self-evident; that it is not, that qualities which should be bestowed openly and spontaneously now appear only as a dream, as a distant wish, is the source of Crane's abiding sorrow.

What Grace Hart lacked, Sally Simpson could provide. If one ponders the message of "A Name for All" it is not difficult to see why she had earned Crane's gratitude. She invited a tolerant, freewheeling, casual self-acceptance quite unlike anything his mother was prepared to provide. On the Isle of Pines, Crane shared anecdotes with her about his sailor friends; she took in the exoticism of his personality without blinking. As he enthusiastically reported in letters, she could react with equanimity even after he had arrived home "in a somewhat obvious condition."[3] And in a letter to his mother, he included this pointed reference: "Mrs. Simpson lets me completely alone when I'm busy; lets me drum on the piano interminably if I want to—says she likes it—and she has assumed a tremendous interest in my poem."[4]

He had already rewarded that interest once before; he went out of his way to mention her in one of the sunniest passages in "The River":

"—And when my Aunt Sally Simpson smiled," he drawled—
"It was almost Louisiana, long ago."

Just when he wrote the second of the three poems in which she figures is still a matter for conjecture. "Eternity" resembles that "description of the ruins" that he had promised as the final poem of his "Carib Suite" (and indeed the poem may have been written immediately after the October 1926 hurricane of which it speaks). The poem used in the "Carib Suite" was "The Hurricane," not "Eternity," surely because "Eternity" did not belong in the mordant atmosphere of the suite.

Like "A Name for All," "Eternity" is almost unrecognizable as a poem by Hart Crane: it is strikingly lucid, without dense or distorted imagery, written in a language that is playful but inherently colloquial. Though the poem strains noticeably at one point, when a mysterious white horse —the emblem of the hurricane—enters (which the poet dubs "Eternity!"), for the most part it is all delight and play—in the nature of a memento or a souvenir, a gift to Mrs. Simpson in memory of her affection. Together, in fact, the two of them underwent the hurricane he is recalling, and the poem provides her with an animated description of the ruins which she might not have been able to see because of her arthritic condition. Most notable, though, is Crane's pleasure in communicating easily and playfully, not intricately or evasively, with a person who simply listens with delight.

The buoyancy of this poem is its most engaging feature. If it is uncharacteristically prosaic, it is decidedly animated. The storm should have flattened out everything that fell before it, but Crane views the ruins with an invigorating eye:

> But was there a boat? By the wharf's old site you saw
> Two decks unsandwiched, split sixty feet apart
> And a funnel high and dry up near the park
> Where a frantic peacock rummaged amid heaped cans.

The peacock is just the right detail: vanity reduced to rummaging in the ruins. Its frantic scrabbling is like the chaos of the scene, a chaos the poet takes in with a gaiety and party-going air. There is a high good humor in the way he portrays even the most distressing aspects of the storm; he spins them out like tall tales:

> And somebody's mule steamed, right there by the pump,
> Good God! as though his stinking carcass there
> Were death predestined! You held your nose already
> Along the roads, begging for buzzards, vultures . . .

The world is topsy-turvy, a carcass by the pump, death alongside life, with vultures begged to provide relief. Even the appearance of a phantom white horse is a curiously apt symbol of the storm: it is a horse to be admired, appreciated for its vast mystery and power. Though wild, it is not forbidding. (And Crane may have found that Mrs. Simpson's tolerance of his antics made them less frightening to him.)

The poem hits its stride in its final lines:

> In due time
> The President sent down a battleship that baked
> Something like two thousand loaves on the way.
> Doctors shot from the deck in planes.
> The fever was checked. I stood a long time in Mack's talking
> New York with the gobs, Guantanamo, Norfolk,—
> Drinking Bacardi and talking U.S.A.

The great virtue upheld throughout the poem is to be able to take in the exotic and view it as unthreatening, to marvel at the bizarre innocently. Crane displays this attitude himself in his bemused report of "Two decks unsandwiched"; Mrs. Simpson acted in a similar way when confronted with him. Capable of taking the bad in confident stride, able to offer discreet encouragement when necessary, Mrs. Simpson is a bit like the president who, "In due time," sent down a battleship that, casually adapting to the exigencies of the situation, "baked / Something like two thousand loaves on the way." What an image of the maternal hearth! But what else to expect from Americans, with their accommodating doctors who "shot from the deck in planes." (Mrs. Simpson had nursed Crane in the summer of 1926 when he was dangerously ill.) "Talking U.S.A." is what the poem encourages: talking unpretentiously but ingeniously. As an upbeat example of the best way to respond to devastation, the poem moves to render the hurricane less devastating than it was. Indeed, the majesty, power, and dignity of the storm, as exemplified in the white horse, are left intact even as its destructive aspects are subdued. On the Isle of Pines, Crane could have fallen apart—especially after his creative frenzy had set in—but thanks to the flexibility and understanding of Sally Simpson, he was able to channel his energies in their most productive fashion.

Mrs. Simpson's third poem, "A Postscript," is not an effervescent homage as her two previous works had been, but a poignant lyric, almost a love poem. It can be dated, up to a point, by internal evidence: leaving California hastily in 1928, Crane journeyed by train to New York through New Orleans. In his poem, as he gropes for intimations of hope, he calls to himself:

> Remember the lavender lilies of that dawn,
> their ribbon miles, beside the railroad ties
> as one nears New Orleans, sweet trenches by the train
> after the western desert, and the later cattle country;
> and other gratuities, like porter's jokes, roses . . .

But these signs, precious as they appear, are ultimately derided for their insubstantiality: "Dawn's broken arc!" They are all too fleeting and fragile, like the seemingly "solid print" made by the "wren and thrush." What does endure? Wren and thrush vanish, and nothing seems more intangible than those lilies touched with "lavender" in the light of dawn.

Dawn's arc always breaks. Promises are never fulfilled. Only one person remains dependable:

> There were tickets and alarm clocks. There were counters
>   and schedules.
> and a paralytic woman on an island of the Indies,
> Antillean fingers counting my pulse, my love forever.

This love endures despite the gap separating the poet from the "paralytic woman." With her hands it is difficult for her to join with him, or even to reach out and take his pulse. That she does so, despite her difficulty, is proof of the depth of her affection. And in this sign of endurance there may be a promise of hope. Since she is so humble a presence, then the wrens and the thrush—the everyday birds of the earlier stanzas—may be regarded as her ensigns, agents of a "faith / toward something far, now farther than ever away." The poem plays with the idea that though someone (or, thinking of *The Bridge*, something) may be "farther than ever away," there is no cause to believe one has been abandoned from his or her thoughts.

These late poems may be modest simply because they are Crane's realization of how little he has. Or they may be a large step back from the burden of juggling the massive themes in *The Bridge*, still uncompleted in 1928 and with its themes growing even more massive with each passing day. Whatever their origin, almost all of Crane's other (mostly unpublished) verse of his late years falls under the category of an attempt to communicate with another individual. Crane's isolation is never more evident than in these desultory verses, some of which are, like "Cape Hatteras," encounters with the spirits of other poets ("To Emily Dickinson," "The Phantom Bark," "To Shakespeare"), and others of which are addresses to lovers ("—And Bees of Paradise," "Reply," "The Visible the Untrue"). It is a dismaying list because, aside from the poems to his mother and to Sally Simpson, he is speaking either to those who are dead or who are beyond his hearing in some other way, asleep or indifferent.

From the very start of this late verse, then, his attempt to speak with another is short-circuited; he is doomed to speak from isolation. The excitement with which he greeted "The Broken Tower" ("Here's a poem," he wrote Sam Loveman, "—about the first in two years")[5] is understandable in the light of his long creative paralysis. Not only is the poem an extensive work but in it Crane is actually speaking to another whom he feels can hear him and even respond to his words; no wonder she seems to hold out the promise of a lasting stability that had been absent from his life.

2

As Marius Bewley was first to suggest, "The Broken Tower" is a recapitulation (and to some extent a refutation) of Crane's career.[6] It should be read in the light of his July 13, 1930, remark to Allen Tate in which he accepts Tate's evaluation that *The Bridge* marks an end to the "tradition of romanticism." Crane goes on: "My vision of poetry *is* too personal to 'answer the call.' And if I ever write any more verse it will probably be at least as personal as the idiom of *White Buildings* whether anyone cares to look at it or not." "The Broken Tower" ratifies this decision: it is a public announcement of a break with public poetry.

The bells in the tower are a complex emblem of two things: of public poetry, first of all—poetry directed to others, for the joy and aid of others, but at the expense of the poet himself. After ringing the church bells in the predawn hours—bells that gather others to a satisfying sense of a divine order—the poet is not elated but exhausted. The bell rope "dispatches" him as though day were done, not dawning. Having served others so well, having wakened them to a glorious new day, he finds nothing left for himself.

Yet the bells as a public announcement of a divine order had been compelling to him for another reason; at one time, he heard them as sheer elation, in the same way those wakened by them still hear them. His public poetry, too, had meant to be uplifting and celebratory at the same time, and he was lured back to his task again and again, drawn by his conviction that a "corps / Of shadows" defined the tower. Yet nothing enduring came forth. The bells only grew into endless overtones of themselves, and they eventually turn agonizing:

> The bells, I say, the bells break down their tower;
> And swing I know not where. Their tongues engrave
> Membrane through marrow, my long-scattered score
> Of broken intervals . . . And I, their sexton slave!

If the tower is a mark of aspiring towards order, perhaps the sign of the desire of men to reach toward a God, then Crane, as bell ringer, sees himself as growing so absorbed in the sounds that he hears only their disruptive force. The public poet becomes the sensualist, absorbed in the sounds of his own words, absorbed in the sheer impression he strives to make. Thus his well-meant attempts to enter "the broken world" and "trace the visionary company of love" only lead to an awareness that his attempts were cries in the wind, echoing "each desperate choice." The fourth stanza of the poem indicates that the sound of bells has grown cacophonous, overwhelming; the bells are "heaping / The impasse high with choir," they are "Banked voices slain!," they are "terraced echoes prostrate on the plain."

A few stanzas later, Crane accedes to the conviction held by Tate and Winters that the lack of any common cultural matrix makes it impossible for the individual, isolated as he or she is, to conceive of a genuinely public poetry. "My word I poured," Crane says,

> But was it cognate,
> Scored of that tribunal monarch of the air
> Whose thigh embronzes earth . . . ?

Such a "cognate" word, in harmony with a God or the sun or some elemental force of undeniable power, is simply beyond one's reach:

> The steep encroachment of my blood left me
> No answer (could blood hold such a lofty tower
> As flings the question true?)

All that remains is the individual, with his lonely perceptions, which never ring with the authority he requires. The poet's outpouring never "strikes crystal word" but remains the endless, futile, overlapping overtone of the bells, with their "Banked voices slain."

If all this is Crane's conclusion, then the only solution is an inevitable one: the poet is to turn toward another individual, accepting the limits he has found, but discovering within those limits a world larger than he had expected. The image of a sun-god as a giant "Whose thigh embronzes earth" is set aside for the image of a human, a person of blood as this poet is of blood, another mortal with whom the poet can build "a tower that is not stone," a tower that is built of blood, a child, the center of a new life with another. In his other late poems, in his other letter-poems, he had used his verse not as he had earlier, not as a way of rousing a torpid audience, and not as he had in his most impressive writing, not as a means of questioning and exploring and ultimately realizing his own deepest conflicts, but as a simple effort to communicate with another person. In "The Broken Tower" he manages to hold together briefly (and with an air of distraught intensity), all these tendencies of his past. He recognizes his earliest idea of poetry and finds it limited. He explores a conflict within himself and resolves it by accepting that his vision of poetry "*is* too personal to answer the call." And he turns toward another person who this time is one who can hear him, who is neither asleep, nor elsewhere, nor deceased, and he expresses his satisfaction. Henceforward, he will write a personal verse only. This poem is a public disavowal of public poetry, a promise that there will be a new Crane, with surprisingly new beliefs.

3

Since "The Broken Tower" was to be Crane's last poem rather than the beginning of a new cycle of work, it holds out a tantalizing question. Would he have gone on to write a different kind of poetry, more intimate than his previous work, more modest, perhaps more in the line of his letter-poems? ("The Broken Tower," it should be noted, is more in the style of his 1926–27 writing than it is any breakthrough.) Or would he have ultimately resisted, seeking to return to his old idea of the poet as seer, inspired beyond himself? Crane's suicide may have had its origin in just such a dilemma, however unvoiced it was: he had failed in his role as public poet, the role he had set out to fill from his earliest days, and the alternative was to see himself as entirely changed, thoroughly reborn—a prospect to be met with mixed emotions.

From an early age, Crane had wanted to be recognized not just as a poet but as a cultural synthesizer, a spokesperson for the community, even a savior. He must have craved that approval for a number of reasons. His rootless, wandering existence, with its background of "illicit" love, could only encourage him to form a public self distinct from his personal one, a separation that would continually cause havoc in his writing. His gift for language led him, at first, into the merely celebratory, as the public poet capable of arousing others. But he had used his gift to enclose himself in a wall of words, to set a formidable barrier between himself and the world. As a barrier, this early poetry allowed him the convenience of hiding from the world which he could only address as a public figure. Creating a public poetry, ostensibly for the good of all, was simultaneously a way of denying himself; as an individual, he did not figure in the world he created, and the message of his work was that one should not attempt to exist as an individual, only as a small part of a larger whole.

This wall gave way in *Voyages* when it became crucially important to him to respond to another person in his work; hymns to the sea of love were inadequate for this revolutionary affair. And once *Voyages* expanded beyond its first poem, Crane inevitably had to expand his own language also; he had to include a range of events that implicated him— though how elaborately, how intricately! It must be difficult for us to appreciate how risky such an enterprise was for him: it left him open and vulnerable in ways that the sequence as a whole continually comments upon. But it also provided him (as the poems following *Voyages* indicate) with an urgent need to speak personally from within a language that still remained complex and true to him as a person: "The Wine Menagerie," with its poet lurking in the shadows yet remorselessly revealed, is the classic instance of his highly individualized integrity.

Yet the personal poems written after *Voyages* were not well received in their time. "The Wine Menagerie" was carved up into Marianne Moore's "Again." "At Melville's Tomb" could only be published after an extensive apology for its metaphors. Turning to *The Bridge* in 1925 and deciding again to take up the role of the seer was a natural enough relief from the tension of the preceding three years. This decision was, in fact, immediately rewarded: to throw energy into an impersonal panoramic view of American life and history (in which the poet's personality played no role except that of synthesizer) was supported by friends, lauded by critics, and even partially underwritten by a patron.

Yet he could not exclude himself from his writing, as the unexpected expansion of the 1926 *Bridge* so clearly reveals. Not only were these new poems among his best, but they were written with an unanticipated fluency and they touched upon matters more personal to him than any before. His impetus to write, in fact, came out of his decision, dramatized in the proem, to imitate the Bridge not as it soared up and out of the city but as it soared within it, in response to it. Everything about the 1926 *Bridge* indicates his sudden willingness to be more open, more receptive, more involved in the work before him: to accept his own weakness and to make that act of realizing limitations the central pivot of each poem.

Before he had accepted that, his epic was stalled. After accepting it, *The Bridge* unfolded as a personal poem, not dealing with heroes or heroines or historical figures but taking up the dilemmas faced by representative individuals in the modern city. Even the Indian couple is viewed as peculiarly "modern," faced as they are with nerve-racking anxieties. Furthermore, the poet is not only a character in his 1926 poems, but he insists that only through involvement with others can he realize what is the proper way to move. Intricate as it remains, even in its lucid 1926 version, *The Bridge* is a revolutionary breakthrough for Crane, not just as a poet but as an individual; it is, in fact, the great extended moment in which he acts as an individual and as a poet.

But *The Bridge* was not supposed to be a personal epic. And everyone was ready with an idea of what it should be instead. Allen Tate pressed him hard to write a historical poem; Waldo Frank looked forward to one more voice added to his dialogue with the machine and its problems; and Yvor Winters cautioned him, as he cautioned everyone, to marshal his thoughts in a more rigorous and logical manner. There were others who could not be disappointed: his parents, his patron, influential friends. The extraordinary breakthrough of 1926 was reassembled almost as it was still assembling itself, and what emerged at last offered a bit of something for everyone. The 1930 *Bridge* offered history to Tate, the machine to Frank, a stronger narrative line to Winters, even a passage on the airplane for his new friend and patron, Harry Crosby.

In the process, all these extras crowded Crane out of his own poem. There are a number of reasons why Crane had so much difficulty bringing his epic to a conclusion and so much difficulty writing at all after 1927, but first among them must be his own intuition that the poems as he was presently shaping them somehow excluded him. Only in the letter-poems, where he almost stubbornly insisted upon directly addressing those who mattered to him, did he thoroughly include himself; and in those works, he is as modest as he can be.

Would the cycle have come around again, had Crane continued to live? Would he have been able, under some extraordinary or unique condition, to risk again writing as intimate and personal and vulnerable as in the 1926 *Bridge?* Possibly not for some time. As his new relationship with a woman suggests, he was at this moment compelled to change his own life rather than to accept his life as it was; the relationship appears as a desperate swerve, an effort to lose who he is by believing he can become someone new and different. Out of such pressures, suicide seems to be a familiar alternative; so many preceding decisions are, in effect, miniature suicides themselves, decisions to die to one's self, to adopt a mask, to play a role.

But twice in his life he had let himself be more open than ever before—once in *Voyages*, again in 1926 with *The Bridge*. He carried within himself the seeds of understanding what it was that he needed; both of his extended poems, as well as some shorter works, were acts of self-understanding and achievements of self-therapy: confrontations of the problems that were crushing him. The problems were immensely complex, and made even more so by his own integrity. So complex were they that a third try might perhaps have been beyond his reach. Yet if he had lived longer, his own compulsion to write might have carried him through, or led him at least to another work in which, once again, he broke through to matters of deepest importance to him. It is impossible to imagine what kind of work could have accomplished all that; but what an extraordinary poem it would have been.

Appendix A
A New Background for
"Repose of Rivers"

"Repose of Rivers" (which Crane included in his 1926 volume *White Buildings*) has been widely considered to be one of three poems ("O Carib Isle!" and "The Mango Tree" are the other two) which Crane composed on the Isle of Pines in the early weeks of the summer of 1926. His first weeks in the Caribbean found him in a dark mood, in despair, thoroughly unproductive, and one accepted reading of "Repose of Rivers" is that it reflects this bleakness.[1] However, this dating of the poem, which establishes it as written in the Caribbean in June, or late May, or early July, is almost certainly an error. The poem must have been composed before Crane left New York, after he had decided to go to the Isle of Pines, in the last weeks of April 1926. Instead of being a product of deep despair, the poem presents an ebullient optimism.

How did this error of dating originate? In a June 19, 1926, letter to Waldo Frank, Crane acknowledged Frank's remarks on the last poem he had been sent, "The Mango Tree," and went on to promise new work: "I'm glad that the Mango poem meant something to you. I'm cooking up a couple of short poems to go with it ('Kidd's Cove' & 'The Tampa Schooner') under the common title of 'Grand Cayman.' Maybe I can sell them to Marianne M." (Marianne M. is Marianne Moore, editor of *The Dial*.)

These two titles, "Kidd's Cove" and "The Tampa Schooner," present a problem to Crane scholars, since no work was ever printed under either name, and references to them disappear from the published letters. In his pioneering study of 1948, Brom Weber believed that he had successfully identified both: "Crane returned from Grand Cayman the third week in June in more vigorous physical condition. . . . Inspired by the voyage and the scenes he had encountered, he completed two poems:

'Tampa Schooner' (published in *The Dial*, September 1926; later in *White Buildings* as 'Repose of Rivers') and 'Kidd's Cove' (published in *Poetry* and *transition* in 1927, and in *Collected Poems* as 'O Carib Isle!')."[2] Weber's study was sparsely footnoted, but he had access to many documents that were inconveniently scattered. There was no reason to question his identification of "Tampa Schooner" with "Repose of Rivers."

In retrospect, however, it would seem that to arrive at his identification he simply matched Crane's statement in his letter to Waldo Frank ("Maybe I can sell them to Marianne M.") with the appearance of "Repose of Rivers" in *The Dial* for September 1926. Weber's 1952 edition of Crane's letters, though, provides a part of the evidence that undermines his own identification. In a letter of May 22, 1926 (to an unidentified correspondent in Weber's edition), Crane wrote to Susan Jenkins Brown: "Yes, Marianne took the little specialty I wrote for her, and even proof has been corrected and sent back. This time she didn't even suggest running the last line backward. 'Again' is in the May issue; I s'pose you've seen the happy mixture."[3] The "little specialty" referred to here is "Repose of Rivers," which had been written, submitted to *The Dial*, accepted by *The Dial*, set in galleys, proofread by Crane, and returned to *The Dial* a full month before the letter to Frank announcing plans for a poem called "Tampa Schooner." (This is all a tribute to a most efficient U.S. mail service, then under the direction of the railroads.)

Though neither Weber in his edition of the letters nor Brown in her edition of selected letters identify "the little specialty" as "Repose of Rivers," there is ample evidence from other letters that this can only be the poem to which Crane refers. Three days after he and Waldo Frank arrived on the Isle of Pines, Crane wrote a letter to his mother on May 8, 1926, announcing the mail had arrived: "It will interest you to know that it contained a letter from The Dial (forwarded, of course) accepting a poem of mine which I sent them recently. There is another of mine in the current issue which I brought down with me."[4] Thomas S. W. Lewis, editor of the collection in which this letter was first published, tentatively identifies the poem just accepted as "probably 'To Brooklyn Bridge.'"[5] (The other poem, the one "in the current issue" of May 1926 is "Again," the poem referred to by name in the letter to Brown.) But Lewis's identification is incorrect, for three months later in a letter of August 13, 1926, Crane is reporting to his mother on the status of a poem that turns out to be "To Brooklyn Bridge": "Just had a fine letter from Kahn and sold another poem to *The Dial*. Watch for my work there from time to time. There should be one in the current issue."[6] In this letter, the poem that "should be . . . in the current issue" is "Repose of Rivers." As Crane pointed out in a later letter to his mother on January 23, 1927, in which is enclosed a copy of "To Brooklyn Bridge": "*The Dial* bought this part last summer but so far it hasn't appeared."[7] The poem sold to *The Dial* and mentioned in the August 13 letter can only have been "To Brooklyn Bridge," which means that the poem mentioned in the May 8 letter as accepted by *The Dial* must be "Repose of Rivers."

There is a less tortuous route that leads to a similar conclusion. In Kenneth Lohf's bibliography of Crane's manuscripts, he describes item A2 as a "Typescript of *White Buildings* in which the texts and sequences of the poems are identical to those of volume published in 1926."[8] Since "Repose of Rivers" appeared in *White Buildings*, it is a part of this group. Lohf speculates that item A2 was "probably manuscript referred to in letter from Crane to Waldo Frank, 19 June 1926." If Lohf is correct, then in the same letter to Frank in which he announced beginning "Tampa Schooner," he also referred to a typescript of *White Buildings* in which "Repose of Rivers" was included as a finished poem.

The time of the poem's composition can be even more specifically pinpointed. When Crane became convinced of his need to leave New York and move to the Isle of Pines (after his quarrel with the Tates with whom he had been living), he wrote to his mother for permission on April 18, 1926, and received her consent by April 24.[9] According to Thomas S. W. Lewis and John Unterecker, Crane left his Patterson, New York, quarters shortly after writing his April 18 letter, for a brief sojourn in New York City, and he returned to Patterson directly after receiving the April 24 letter.[10] Since his May 22 letter to Brown referred to the "little specialty" that Marianne Moore had accepted not by name but somewhat deprecatingly, and since Brown lived in the area near Crane's Patterson quarters, it could be assumed that his mention of the "little specialty" carried on a conversation they had shared about the poem. This would mean that Crane had composed a version of "Repose of Rivers" either just before returning to Patterson on April 24 or during that period before May 1, when he departed in the company of Waldo Frank for the Isle of Pines.

The evident chronology, then, is that sometime before his May 1 departure he mailed a copy of "Repose of Rivers" to Marianne Moore at *The Dial*. He learned of its acceptance on May 8, in a letter forwarded to him after he had arrived at the Isle of Pines. By May 22, he had read his

proof of the poem and was sharing his fortune in a letter to Brown. Instead of being a product of his early weeks of creative stasis on the Isle of
Pines, the poem is a product of his joyful days in New York, after his
mother had given permission to visit the family cottage in the Caribbean
(a permission asked for previously but always denied); the poem looks
ahead with optimism to a period of renewed vigor. Readings of the poem,
which often depend heavily on a biographical background, need to be
adjusted accordingly so that the work appears in a context proper to it. [11]

Appendix B
A Chronology for "O Carib Isle!"

Because no critic or scholar has ever acknowledged that the final version of "O Carib Isle!" is anything more than a minor variant on the original version, no one has ever investigated the chronology of the two versions. As it turns out, it is not difficult to establish the sequence of events surrounding the composition of the first version; but some speculation is involved in working out the composition of the final version. Complicating matters considerably is the fact that both versions of the poem exist in several individual complete manuscripts.

The first version almost certainly originates in June or July of 1926, just before Crane began extensive work on *The Bridge*. Item C1(c) in Kenneth Lohf's *Manuscripts* is a text of the final version (identifiable because of its thirty-five-line length in contrast to the thirty-one lines of the first version) which bears the following notation:

Grand Cayman
July '26
Transition (Paris)
April '27[1]

Though "April '27" might appear to be the date of the poem's revision, it cannot be accepted as such, primarily because the poem appeared in its first version in the April 1927 issue of *transition*. But the "July '26" date is almost certainly close to the origin of the first version, though in one copy of a manuscript Crane included a subtitle referring to "June 1926."[2]

By mid-October 1926, the first version was in complete enough form to begin its round of submissions to editors of journals. On October 6, 1926, Malcolm Cowley advised Crane that, as an intermediary for Eugene Jolas, he was soliciting poems for a French anthology.[3] Crane submitted three, and the first version of "O Carib Isle!" was published, translated rather crudely into a literal French, in Jolas's 1928 anthology.[4]

Shortly after his submission to Jolas, Crane must have sent a copy to *Poetry*, for in a letter to Yvor Winters on November 28, 1926, he reports that Harriet Monroe has just accepted the poem.[5] *Poetry* eventually published a variant of the first version in its October 1927 issue, along with "Cutty Sark."[6]

On January 7, 1927, Crane mailed off three contributions to the *Calendar of Modern Letters*, a British journal hospitable to previous submissions: "O Carib Isle!," "Cutty Sark," and "The Harbor Dawn."[7] Though all three were apparently accepted, none were to appear in print because the magazine would soon cease publication.

While Crane was busy submitting his first versions around the world, Jolas was busy expanding from an anthology-maker to a magazine editor. In a letter to Crane on February 24, 1927, he thanked him for his "prompt answer to our cable" and verified that "O Carib Isle!" would appear, in its original English, in issue number one of *transition*.[8] In a March 19, 1927, letter to his mother, Crane includes Jolas's note along with a copy of what is still the first version of the poem, the text as it would appear in *transition* no. 1 and (in French) in Jolas's *Anthologie de la Nouvelle Poesie Americaine*.[9]

With the exception of the submissions to the *Calendar*, all these submissions exist in various archives; all reflect minor variants in the poem, with no variant as extensive as the revisions of the final version. Is it safe to assume that the lost *Calendar* manuscript is a minor variant on the original? Crane implied that the *Calendar* submission was a variant on the original in the same degree as the *Poetry* submission was a variant of the *transition* / *Anthologie* submission: "I think *transition* is a good wedge to use—and I hope it appeals to you somewhat as it does to me. The version of Carib Isle which has appeared therein is slightly different than the version which appears in Poetry—which is again slightly different from the version as it will appear in the Calendar."[10] If the *Calendar* submission was only "slightly different" from the *Poetry* submission— slightly different in the way the *Poetry* submission was from the *transition* / *Anthologie* submission, then it was only a minor variant. In line 4 of the *Poetry* submission, the words "Stilting out of sight" replace the words "Flickering out of sight" in the *transition* / *Anthologie* submission, and in line 16 the words "Plaguing the hot groins" replace the words "Vining the hot groins." In short, the differences in these extant manuscripts are minor, the kind of touching up Crane frequently performed after submitting poems for publication, and there is no reason to assume

the *Calendar* submission would have differed markedly from the two previous submissions.[11]

The original version, then, has a fairly direct history. Written in June
or July of 1926, by the end of March 1927 it is scheduled to appear, with
minor variants, in four different publications. At what time, then, did
the original version become a final version?

That two distinct versions of the poem exist by February of 1929 seems
certain. Harry Crosby's journal for February 6, 1929, notes: "Hart Crane
came to tea and he gave us the MSS of his O Carib Isle (one of the five
best poems of our generation)."[12] The "MSS" referred to here, though, is
a copy of the final version, for at a later date, March 1, 1929, Crane
presented Crosby with a copy of another version. Acknowledging receipt
of this gift, Crosby mentions a phrase from it—"Clean enamel frames of
death"—which appears in the original, not the final, version.[13] The
later, March 1 gift appears to have been a transcription of the original
version, a follow-up to the enthusiastic reception accorded Crane's original gift, a transcription of the final version.

Can an earlier date be discovered for the existence of the final version? Lohf lists seven texts in his bibliography of Crane's manuscripts,
two of which are identifiable, by virtue of their thirty-five-line lengths, as
final versions. (In addition, he lists three copies of the poem found after
Crane's death in a folder labeled *Key West*; but his description of these is
inadequate for purposes of identification.) Of these seven manuscripts,
items C4, C5, C6, and C7 are original versions. C4 was "Enclosed in a
letter . . . to Grace Hart Crane, 19 March 1927,"[14] and is reproduced in
Family, ed. T. S. W. Lewis. C5 bears the inscription "for Harry and
Caresse Crosby"[15] and it is surely the March 1 follow-up gift. C6 is identified by Lohf as the "same text as item C5."[16] C7 is from the files of
Poetry, the original version as published in the October 1927 issue.[17]
C8 was a gift to Mr. John Mayfield, a holograph transcription of stanzas
1, 2, 3, 6, and 7, requested from Crane by Mr. Mayfield in a letter. (This
truncated copy was, therefore, an answer to a specific request, and,
though it is a copy of the original version, it need not rule out the possibility that another, final version exists in November 1927, when Mr.
Mayfield requested his copy.)[18]

C9 and C10 are the two copies of the final version. But C10 is a copy
made in 1932 by Samuel Loveman (and not, strictly speaking, a manuscript).[19] By elimination we arrive at C9, a final version which was located in the files of *Poetry*—except that *Poetry* printed not the final ver-

sion but the original version in its October 1927 issue. This manuscript is the focus for a number of questions.

According to his November 28, 1926, letter to Winters, Crane knew that *Poetry* had accepted the original version of the poem, and in addition, in a March 19, 1927, letter to his mother, Crane enclosed a copy of the original version and noted: "It is coming out soon in 'Poetry' in this country."[20] Why would Crane submit this final version to a magazine which had already accepted his original version?

This submission may have been prompted because of anxiety; his poem, in March of 1927, in its original version, was about to appear in a number of journals, and with only minor variants. One reason among many for revising the poem thoroughly was that Crane was about to be a victim of his own success. Originally, when Jolas had solicited the poem, it would appear in French in a French anthology; there was little reason not to submit the same poem in English to *Poetry*, as he did in the fall of 1926. And there was also little reason for conflict in submitting a slight variant of the same poem to the *Calendar*, a British journal of limited circulation. But when Jolas requested the same poem for inclusion in the first issue of *transition*, Crane may have begun to be nervous. Jolas inquired by way of a cable, which implies his need for a hasty reply; Crane's consent, perhaps given with haste, places him in a potential bind. For all he knew, his one poem was about to appear simultaneously in three separate journals. (News of the demise of the *Calendar* would not be reported by him until an August 3, 1927, letter to Winters.)[21] The crucial conflict, in his eyes, may have been that between *Poetry* and the new international journal *transition*. Since *Poetry* would not print the poem until its October 1927 issue, there was still time through the spring and even summer of 1927 to make the major changes from the original to the final version.

If this scenario narrows down the time of revision to the spring and summer of 1927, it is possible to be even more specific. The curator of the *Poetry* files confirms that the submission of the final version of the poem is printed on the same paper as two other poems in the files, "To Emily Dickinson" and "The Hurricane"; moreover, there is evidence that these three poems had been pinned together at one time. The assumption is that all three were submitted simultaneously.[22]

Poetry never published either "To Emily Dickinson" or "The Hurricane" (or, for that matter, the final version of "O Carib Isle!"). But *The Nation* published "To Emily Dickinson" in its June 29, 1927, issue.[23]

Since Crane would not have submitted his poem to *Poetry* after its acceptance by *The Nation*, he must have submitted it, and the final version of "O Carib Isle!," at a date previous to late June 1927.

It may be possible, still speculating, to narrow the time even further. Crane most likely started a revision no earlier than February 1927, after he had seen a copy of Jolas's French translation. (Though Crane did not acknowledge it, Jolas probably sent a copy in his letter to Crane of February 24, 1927.)[24] The translation is important because of an error in it which Crane may have carried over to his final version.

Jolas's translation is uninspiredly literal. Lines are rendered almost word for word:

> Que le pélerin ne se voie pas de nouveau
> lié comme la douzaine de tortues sur l'embarcadère
> chaque crépuscule,—encore vivantes, et de la saumure collée
>   à leurs yeux,
> énormes, retournées: un tel tonnerre dans leur effort!
> Et des becs serrés toussant pour retrouver la houle!

Because of Jolas's literalism, it is a noticeable mistranslation when he turns the last lines—"You have given me the shell, Satan—the ember / Carbolic, of the sun exploded in the sea"—into: "Tu m'as donné la coquille, Satan—la cendre / Carbonique du soleil explosé dans la mer." The error is in the translation of "Carbolic." The literal version would be "Phénique," not "Carbonique." "Carbonique" means "Carbonic," not "Carbolic."

But in Crane's final version, he substitutes "Carbonic" for "Carbolic." Is it possible the change was derived from pondering Jolas's translation? If so, and if Jolas had provided him with a copy in February, then his revision might have begun as early as March or April or May of 1927.

A final speculation: the original version appeared in *Poetry* with "Cutty Sark" in the October 1927 issue. According to Lohf, the "Cutty Sark" manuscript bears this notation: "Acd. Mar. 23, '27" and "Revision received Apr. 6 '27."[25] Evidently Crane had no sooner learned that *Poetry* had accepted "Cutty Sark" than he provided them with a revised version. Did he at the same time offer a revision of "O Carib Isle!" along with two new poems, "To Emily Dickinson" and "The Hurricane"— poems that were not accepted by the editor (and one of which was then accepted, a few weeks later, by *The Nation*)?

If so, that would mean that Crane's notation on Lohf's item C1(c)—

"Grand Cayman / July '26 / Transition (Paris) / April '27"—indicates not only the date of the original version (July '26) as well as the date the original appeared in *transition* (the April 1927 issue) but possibly even the date at which Crane undertook revising his original into its final form: April 1927.

Notes

Chapter 1. Modern Beauty

1. See, for example, Eda Lou Walton, "Hart Crane," *The Nation*, 136 (May 3, 1933), 508; Babette Deutsch, "Poetry Out of Chaos," *Virginia Quarterly Review*, IX (Oct. 1933), 62–63; and Lola Ridge, "A Modern Mystic," *Saturday Review of Literature*, Sept. 1, 1934, p. 82. Philip Horton, *Hart Crane: The Life of an American Poet* (1937; rpt., New York: Viking, 1957), defended what he considered to be the excess in Crane's life and works by appealing to a mystical tradition in American literature.

2. Gorham Munson, *Destinations: A Canvass of American Literature since 1900* (New York: Sears, 1928), p. 174.

3. Waldo Frank, "Introduction" to *The Bridge*, by Hart Crane (1932; rpt., New York: Liveright, 1970), p. xxiii. Munson, *Canvass*, p. 176.

4. R. W. B. Lewis, *The Poetry of Hart Crane: A Critical Study* (Princeton: Princeton Univ. Press, 1967), pp. ix-x, 50. One other reason Lewis's study often proves disappointing is that he restricts himself by searching out similarities among poems. Perhaps this strategy was dictated by the low reputation of Crane's work in the early 1960s; before Lewis's pioneering study, most critics would have been surprised to hear any element in Crane's work was coherent, much less that the entire body of writing revealed a certain discipline. Whatever its origin, the search for resemblances among the poems deflects Lewis from the individual poem, and it is in the individual poem that Crane's strength is revealed.

5. Though the poem did not appear in *White Buildings*, Crane seems to have considered it in his original manuscript collection, assembled in April 1925 when the owner of a private press offered to print an edition of his work at cost. Item A1 in Kenneth A. Lohf's *Literary Manuscripts of Hart Crane* (Columbus: Ohio State Univ. Press, 1967), pp. 3–5, is a collection of poems probably assembled in March or April of 1925. (It is not, as Lohf has it, circa "1917–1926," because the group excludes a number of poems written after the spring of 1925: "Passage," "The Wine Menagerie," "At Melville's Tomb," and "Voyages

V." Furthermore, "Lachrymae Christi" is represented only in a fragmentary form; the fragments were brought together, around March 1925, to form the final version (mailed to Waldo Frank on Mar. 3, 1925).) If Lohf's A1 is the manuscript Crane assembled for his private printer, then offered to various commercial publishers after the private press arrangement fell through, he did include "Porphyro in Akron" in his initial assemblage. But there are also half a dozen early poems in this manuscript collection that were dropped in the final arrangement of *White Buildings*. After the spring of 1925, Crane began several new poems, and he could afford to omit much of his earlier work from his manuscript.

6. In its own way, the subject of the immigrant was as daring as the subject of jazz dancing; hanging out in an immigrant speakeasy was eyebrow-raising in 1921. For a discussion of attitudes toward the immigrant at this time, see Richard Hofstadter, *The Age of Reform* (1955; rpt., New York: Vintage, n.d.), pp. 176–83.

7. Crane actually began section I first but could not proceed beyond an eight-line opening; see Brom Weber, *Hart Crane: A Biographical and Critical Study* (New York: Bodley Head, 1948), p. 175.

8. Consider these excerpts from a syndicated column by M. Addington Bruce, from the Rock Island Lines' employee monthly; published in the issue of Apr. 1922 (XVII, 63), the column is almost exactly contemporaneous with "The Springs of Guilty Song":

> The sooner we are rid of jazz the sooner shall we have a return of real national prosperity, dependent as that is on wholesome and vigorous thinking, earnest and sustained creative effort.
>
> . . . Jazz is demonstrably a cause of neurotic instability and impaired powers of reasoning. . . . Jazz has the misfortune of exciting emotions associated not with the higher but with the lower human trends.
>
> Thus it is atavistic in its effects. It makes a mockery of spiritual evolution and brings its devotees down to the carnalities of primitive man. One may even say of it with Dr. Percy Stickney Grant: "Jazz is retrogression. It rings the bell for full steam astern. It is going to the African jungle.
>
> "Its effect is to make you chatter, and, as Voltaire says, 'to go on all fours.'" To which I would add—"and swish your tail around a tree."
>
> . . . It may even insure soul wreckage. Last year, it has been established, 65,000 girls disappeared in the United States "leaving no trace." Jazz, you may be sure, had a hand in the disappearance of many.

For a further discussion of the scandal caused by flappers and ragtime dancing, see Gilman M. Ostrander, *American Civilization in the First Machine Age* (1970; rpt., New York: Harper Torchbooks, 1972), pp. 239–45, 249–53.

9. Two champions of the poem are R. W. B. Lewis, *Study*, pp. 80–119, and Herbert A. Leibowitz, *Hart Crane: An Introduction to the Poetry* (New York: Columbia Univ. Press, 1968), pp. 59–79.

10. Edmund Wilson, "The Muses Out of Work," in *The Shores of Light: A*

Literary Chronicle of the Twenties and Thirties (1952; rpt., New York: Vintage, 1961), p. 200.

11. Harriet Monroe, "A Discussion with Hart Crane," *Poetry*, 29 (Oct. 1926), 40.

Chapter 2. Alternatives to Eliot

1. Hart Crane, "General Aims & Theories," in *The Complete Poems and Selected Letters and Prose of Hart Crane*, ed. Brom Weber (New York: Liveright, 1966), p. 217.

2. Hart Crane to Gorham Munson, Jan. 14, 1923, *The Letters of Hart Crane, 1916–1932*, ed. Brom Weber (Berkeley: Univ. of California Press, 1952), p. 116. Hart Crane to Waldo Frank, Feb. 7, 1923, *Letters*, ed. Weber, p. 121.

3. There still remains some disagreement over just when "General Aims & Theories" was written. John Unterecker (*Voyager* [New York: Farrar, Straus & Giroux, 1969], p. 377) believes Crane may have begun work on them as early as spring 1924, when invited to contribute to the perennial symposium of modern poets. Though that may be possible, my belief is the piece was finished at the time he was revising his poems and assembling them into a book; the notes are part of his accumulating confidence in his work, following the spring of 1925. See the postscript in his letter to Gorham Munson, Mar. 17, 1926, *Letters*, ed. Weber, p. 240, in which he refers to the copy of the "Aims" he is sending to Munson as "notes for O'Neill."

4. Cited in Richard Allen Davison, "Hart Crane, Louis Untermeyer, and T. S. Eliot: A New Crane Letter," *American Literature*, 44 (Mar. 1972), 144.

5. Hart Crane to Louis Untermeyer, Jan. 19, 1923, in Davison, "New Crane Letter," p. 145.

6. Echoes of "Prufrock" in "Faustus and Helen III" are usually in opposition to Eliot's meaning, aimed at subverting his tone. Aside from the "eternal Footman" passage cited in Chap. 1, Crane's "Let us unbind our throats of fear and pity" stands in opposition to Eliot's "Let us go then, you and I . . ." with its evening as a patient etherized on a table. Crane's "in this street / That narrows darkly into motor dawn" stands in opposition to Eliot's "I have gone at dusk through narrow streets." Crane's "ominous lifted arm / That lowers down the arc of Helen's brow" is in contrast to Eliot's "And I have known the arms already, known them all," "Arms that lie along a table or wrap about a shawl." In addition, Crane displays a familiarity with *Poems 1920*, a volume rather different from *Prufrock and Other Observations* in that Eliot uses polysyllabic words, which sound exotic and elegant, in a wry context: "Polyphiloprogenitive / The sapient sutlers of the Lord." "Paint me the bold anfractuous rocks." "Branches of wistaria / Circumscribe a golden grin." When Crane wrote to Allen Tate (June 12, 1922, *Letters*, ed. Weber, p. 90) that he had discovered "a safe tangent to

strike which . . . goes *through* [Eliot] toward a *different goal*," he may have meant that he hoped now to transfer Eliot's rich, arcane vocabulary into a context that was not ironic. Before "Guilty Song," Crane's vocabulary was not particularly polysyllabic.

7. Though Eliot was still arriving in 1922, *The Waste Land* was given full treatment by *The Dial:* not only did it win the *Dial* award but accompanying the poem was an essay by "Edmund Wilson, Jr.," explicating it.

8. When "Faustus and Helen" (minus its second section) appeared in *Secession*, no. 6 (Sept. 1923), John Brooks Wheelwright (at Gorham Munson's urging) drew attention to a contrast with Eliot: "Hart Crane's three poems for the Marriage of Faustus and Helen are to be read with reference to T. S. Elliot[sic]. In Munson's opinion they are an affirmation that reveals the sub-stratum of the *Waste Land* to be a sentimentally[sic], namely, that depression is a mark of aristocracy" (p. 4). (*Secession* was printed in Italy.)

9. Hart Crane, "Lines Sent to Alfred Stieglitz, 4 July 1923," in Weber, *Critical Study*, p. 425. All versions of the poem are taken from Appendix C in Weber's volume, which traces the growth of the section of *The Bridge* that eventually became "Atlantis." Crane lacked a working title for these revisions, sometimes calling them "The Bridge," sometimes "Finale," sometimes leaving them as untitled fragments. For purposes of clarity, I have adopted "Finale" as a title to refer to Crane's writing for the last section of *The Bridge* prior to August 1926 when, in a full-scale revision, Crane composed "Atlantis."

10. Horton, *Life*, pp. 154–55, was first to draw attention to Crane's interest in Ouspensky. Weber, in *Critical Study*, especially laments Ouspensky's influence, p. 153ff. Of late, the tendency has been to discount Crane's involvement; Unterecker, *Voyager*, pp. 247–49, minimizes it, and R. W. B. Lewis, *Study*, pp. 94–99, argues that Ouspensky was redundant for a poet familiar with Blake. Sherman Paul, *Hart's Bridge* (Urbana: Univ. of Illinois Press, 1972), pp. 98, 116–17, is most useful, drawing connections between imagery by Crane and imagery by Ouspensky. It is proper to note, as Horton does (p. 54), that both Waldo Frank and Gorham Munson were Ouspensky enthusiasts.

11. For a concise summation of Frank's ideas and Munson's study of Frank's ideas, see Robert L. Perry, *The Shared Vision of Waldo Frank and Hart Crane* (Lincoln: Univ. of Nebraska Studies, no. 33, May 1966), pp. 11, 33–37. Paul's presentation of similar material (in *Bridge*, pp. 43–48) is, however, more suggestive. Perry expands a simple insight—that Frank and Crane shared a vision at one point—to encompass Crane's whole career, and the argument is strained. Paul concentrates on events in 1922–23 and presents the influence of Munson on Frank and Munson on Crane in proper perspective.

12. Perry, *Shared Vision*, p. 36.

13. Hart Crane to Gorham Munson, Jan. 5, 1923, *Letters*, ed. Weber, p. 115.

14. Half of the four-line opening eventually appeared in "Van Winkle." See

Hart Crane to Allen Tate, Feb. 12, 1923, *Letters*, ed. Weber, p. 123. For the relation of "Van Winkle" to the early versions of *The Bridge*, see Chap. 12, part 1.

15. Hart Crane to Charlotte Rychtarik, Sept. 23, 1923, *Letters*, ed. Weber, p. 148.

16. The original version as published (along with "Recitative") in the *Little Review* (Spring 1924) differs from the final version in two ways. First, it is more sexually traumatic: after the line "And stabbing medley that sways—" Crane originally added a line, "Rounding behind to press and grind." Second, the lines prior to the three-line conclusion emphasized the control one will gain after setting aside aggression; the original version leads to its conclusion in this way:

> Tossed on these horns, who bleeding dies
> Lacks all but piteous admissions to be spilt
> Upon the page whose blind sum turns
> Controllable to blended voices stripped
> Of rage, catastrophe and partial appetites.

17. The arrangement of the poems in Crane's 1925 assemblage for his first book (Lohf's item A1 in *Manuscripts*, p. 3) suggests that as late as spring 1925 Crane thought of both "Recitative" and "Possessions" as useful adjuncts to two of his long poems. The manuscript places "Recitative" as its opening poem (not "Legend," which forms a coda to *Voyages*), followed by "Faustus and Helen," then "Possessions," then an early version of *Voyages*. See Chap. 4 for the complete contents of this first collection.

18. L. S. Dembo's two-page note, "Hart Crane and Samuel Greenberg: What Is Plagiarism?" *American Literature*, 32 (Nov. 1960), 319–21, is a model of concision. He would disagree with my reading, however, in that he assigns the "chosen hero" of the final stanza to the wanderer, not the apostle. All literature on the Crane/Greenberg collaboration/plagiarism episode is exhautively discussed in Marc Simon's *Samuel Greenberg, Hart Crane and the Lost Manuscripts* (Atlantic Highlands, N.J.: Humanities Press, 1978). But see Dembo's dissenting review of Simon's conclusions in "Less than Kin," *Hart Crane Newsletter*, 2 (Spring 1979), 48–51.

Chapter 3. *Voyages*

1. M. D. Uroff, *Hart Crane: The Patterns of His Poetry* (Urbana: Univ. of Illinois Press, 1974), p. 59.

2. "Sonnet" is reprinted in Weber, *Critical Study*, p. 395; Weber dates it April 1924. Unterecker, *Voyager*, p. 354, establishes the time the love affair began; on p. 362 he quotes from the letter to Jean Toomer and refers to the en-

closure of an early version of "Voyages IV." There is some uncertainty as to whether *1924* ever published the poem. Thomas S. W. Lewis, in *Letters of Hart Crane and His Family* (ed. Thomas S. W. Lewis [New York: Columbia Univ. Press, 1974]), maintains the poem did not appear, but Marc Simon, *Lost Manuscripts*, p. 68, cites a New York University dissertation which has the poem appearing on p. 119. Lohf, *Manuscripts*, p. 16, describes item A23 as "Notes for / VOYAGES," beginning "That night off San Salvador" and dated "9/27/24." First mention of "Poster," under the title "The Bottom of the Sea Is Cruel," appears in a letter to Gorham Munson, Nov. 2, 1921, in *Letters*, ed. Weber, p. 69. "Belle Isle" is printed (and dated Jan.-Feb. 1923) in Weber, *Critical Study*, p. 391.

3. Paul, *Bridge*, p. 153.

4. R. W. B. Lewis, *Study*, p. 168

5. Hart Crane, "Sonnet," Weber, *Critical Study*, p. 395.

6. Reprinted in Simon, *Lost Manuscripts*, pp. 125, 126.

7. Leibowitz, *Introduction*, p. 86. My study of the manuscripts of "Voyages II" is based entirely on transcriptions of the manuscripts available from public sources. Leibowitz had access to the Crane archives at Columbia and his discussion draws generously upon Crane's worksheets; see pp. 86–88 especially. Simon cites fragments from the worksheets in *Lost Manuscripts*, pp. 61–66; and Lohf photographically reproduces a worksheet page in "Illustrations," *Manuscripts*, Fig. 1 (item A37), no pagination.

8. Lohf, *Manuscripts*, Fig. 1 (item A37). This is a typescript with holograph emendations which I have incorporated in my quotation. I have not quoted all of the typescript and want to draw attention to another passage which borrows a brief phrase from a Greenberg poem entitled "Love." Crane's typescript: "repeated ease, repeated awe / enclose me, aching with the night . . ." echoes Greenberg's "Its swell of perfect ease, repeated awe." Unaccountably, Simon neglects this borrowing; he in fact never cites "Love" as a Greenberg verse from which Crane borrowed.

9. Simon, *Lost Manuscripts*, p. 65.

10. Leibowitz, *Introduction*, p. 87.

11. A. Alvarez, *The Shaping Spirit* (1958; rpt., London: Grey Arrow, 1963), pp. 116–17. If ever there was an acknowledged classic commentary on "Voyages II," Alvarez's comments must qualify as the front-runner. Citations of it, all friendly, appear in Uroff, *Patterns*, p. 65; R. W. B. Lewis, *Study*, p. 156; Leibowitz, *Introduction*, p. 209; R. W. Butterfield, *The Broken Arc: A Study of Hart Crane* (Edinburgh: Oliver & Boyd, 1971), p. 97; Samuel Hazo, *Hart Crane: An Introduction and Interpretation* (New York: Barnes & Noble, 1963), p. 60; Evelyn J. Hinz, "Hart Crane's 'Voyages' Reconsidered," *Contemporary Literature*, 13 (Summer 1975), 324; and Richard Strier, "The Poetics of Surrender: An Exposition and Critique of New Critical Poetics," *Critical Inquiry*, 2 (1972), 187.

12. Hart Crane to Gorham Munson, Summer 1922?, *Letters*, ed. Weber, p. 99. The early version cited here is Lohf's item A31, entitled "The Bottom of the Sea Is Cruel," in the Gorham Munson Papers at the Ohio State University Library, Columbus, Ohio.

13. It is difficult to determine when "Voyages V" was written; no individual manuscript of it has surfaced, and it is represented in Lohf (*Manuscripts*, item A31, p. 15) only as one poem in a group of six. It was included in a group of four poems published in the *Little Review* of Spring-Summer 1926: "Voyages II, III, V, and VI." Why these four alone? Perhaps because "Voyages I" had already appeared in *Secession*, no. 4 (1923), and "Voyages IV" had already appeared in *1924* (Dec.).

Four poems from *Voyages* were at one time scheduled for printing in the *Guardian*, a Philadelphia journal; in an Aug. 2, 1925, letter to Allen Tate, Crane thanks him for arranging to print the poems along with an article by Tate. But something went wrong. By Oct. 21, 1925, Crane laments that the new *Guardian* has appeared, sans poems or essay, and with a flawed announcement: it urged its readers to look next issue for "'Voyages,' 4 remarkable poems by Allen Tate" (*Letters*, ed. Weber, p. 218). Which four poems were these?

The problem of identifying them is compounded by the fact that in early 1925 there are only four poems extant, "Voyages I, II, III, IV" (item A1 in Lohf's *Manuscripts*, p. 5). "Belle Isle" appears as a separate poem in this collection and "The Bottom of the Sea Is Cruel" (or "Poster") is excluded. By early 1925, then, "Voyages V" remained unwritten, but it was completed in time for publication in the Spring-Summer 1926 issue of the *Little Review*. This places "V" among the works of Crane's initial maturity: "The Wine Menagerie," "Passage," and "At Melville's Tomb."

Little attention has been paid to the sequence in which the poems were written and as a result scholars have been casual in properly identifying the individual poems. T. S. W. Lewis in *Family*, p. 371n, erroneously describes the sequence in the *Little Review* as "Voyages I-IV" instead of "Voyages II, III, V, and VI," and Lohf, in *Manuscripts*, p. 15 (item A31), gives an equally erroneous impression that all six poems were printed in the *Little Review*.

Unterecker drops a hint that even suggests "Voyages V" may be a relatively late composition. When the *Guardian* folded and proved unable to print either Tate's essay or Crane's poems, both essay and poems seem to have been submitted elsewhere. In an Apr. 5, 1926, letter, Crane reports that he had sent *Voyages* to the *New Masses* (just then beginning its publication) but: "Rorty [Richard Rorty, editor] was so swift in returning Allen's NOTE that I have been wondering if he had actually taken some interest in the 'Voyages'" (*Letters*, ed. Weber, p. 244). But did Crane send the same poems to the *New Masses* in spring 1926 that he had sent to the *Guardian* in fall 1925? Unterecker (*Voyager*, p. 428) states that in 1926 (when Crane and Tate were sharing quarters), "Allen Tate revised and again offered for publication his article on 'Voyages.'" If Tate revised his article in early 1926, was Crane then adding to his sequence at that late date; or had the sequence been filled out already with "Voyages V" in mid-1925?

Chapter 4. Inquiry and Analysis

1. The manuscript assembled in early 1925 is listed in Lohf's *Manuscripts* as item A1, pp. 3–5, misdated as circa 1917–26, since the collection omits all poems written after the spring of 1925.

2. See Lohf, *Manuscripts*, item A2, p. 5, for the final version of the *White Buildings* manuscript.

3. Lohf, *Manuscripts*, items A16, A17, A18, pp. 10–11, and D5, D6, pp. 84–85. Weber, *Critical Study*, pp. 226–27, reprints Lohf's A16 and A17.

4. Uroff, *Patterns*, p. 31, additional comments, pp. 198–99.

5. R. W. B. Lewis, *Study*, pp. 140–47. My reading is indebted to the questions raised by Richard Hutson in "Exile Guise: Irony in Hart Crane," *Mosaic*, 2 (Summer 1969), 71–86; rpt. in *Hart Crane, A Collection of Critical Essays*, ed. Alan Trachtenberg (Englewood Cliffs, N.J.: Prentice-Hall, 1982), pp. 131–49.

6. R. P. Blackmur, "New Thresholds, New Anatomies," *Form and Value in Modern Poetry* (Garden City, N.Y.: Anchor, 1957), p. 282.

7. R. W. B. Lewis, *Study*, p. 191, complains that "The ceremonial action of 'Passage'—its rhythm of gain, loss, and potential recovery—is badly cramped in execution." Uroff, *Patterns*, p. 33, states that at the end "The poet does not know what he has learned . . . but his memory has broken in the writing." Paul, *Bridge*, p. 121, is most helpful: "The poem does not relieve the poet of his responsibility: it is an enabling act, a *rite de passage*, of continued growth and maturity."

8. See R. W. B. Lewis, *Study*, pp. 191–200; Hazo, *Interpretation*, p. 64; Vincent Quinn, *Hart Crane* (New York: Twayne, 1963), pp. 52–54; Leibowitz, *Introduction*, pp. 211–13; Paul, *Bridge*, pp. 121–29; and Gregory R. Zeck, "Hart Crane's *The Wine Menagerie*: The Logic of Metaphor," *American Imago*, 36 (Fall 1979), 197–214. Uroff, curiously, omits this significant poem from her otherwise all-inclusive study.

9. Unterecker, *Voyager*, p. 405, reports Kenneth Burke as saying that Marianne Moore took all the wine out of the menagerie. Her drastic revision, entitled "Again," appeared in *The Dial* for May 1926, p. 570. It is reproduced, with brief commentary (including Crane's note acknowledging Moore's changes) in Thomas Parkinson, *Hart Crane and Yvor Winters, Their Literary Correspondence* (Berkeley: Univ. of California Press, 1978), pp. 9–11, 162. Queried about this alteration many years later in "The Art of Poetry IV: Marianne

Moore," *Paris Review*, no. 26 (1961), 59–60, she remained unrepentant of her ways, even though to revise a poem in order to print it was to disregard the usual rule of *The Dial*.

10. Susan Jenkins Brown, *Robbers Rocks: Letters and Memories of Hart Crane* (Middletown, Conn.: Wesleyan Univ. Press, 1968), p. 41.

11. Blackmur, *Value*, p. 277. See Chap. 5, sec. 2, for a continuing discussion of Blackmur's approach.

Chapter 5. Crane as Critic

1. A classic instance of this practice is available by comparing Max Eastman, "Poets Talking to Themselves," *Harper's*, 163 (Oct. 1931), 563–74, with F. Cudworth Flint, "Metaphor in Contemporary Poetry," *The Symposium*, 1 (1930), 310–22. Eastman insists that Crane's writing is gibberish; he matches Crane's work with Joyce's in *Finnegans Wake*, and concludes that both men are charlatans. Flint elaborately defends Crane's right to be experimental, and he demonstrates that Crane's poetics are useful in understanding not only other apparently obscure poets (he analyzes a new poem by Allen Tate) but also his own recent work, *The Bridge*. He virtually demolishes Stephen Rose Benet's fatuous parodies of Crane, and in the process indicates what is valuable in Crane's use of metaphor. Flint's essay is the first scholarly treatment of Crane as a poet, and it features an impressive extensive interpretation of *The Bridge*, a poem that had just been published. It has not been reprinted in any of the critical anthologies which feature instead the brief reviews of Winters and Tate, and it should be rescued from its neglect.

2. Crane's reply to Monroe appears in *Complete Poems*, ed. Weber, pp. 234–40. The entire interchange appeared in *Poetry*, 29 (Oct. 1926) 35–41 (buried in the back of the magazine along with newsy notes about poetry groups meeting in Boston). The following critics draw directly upon Crane's comments to elucidate "At Melville's Tomb": Leibowitz, *Introduction*, pp. 129–34; Uroff, *Patterns*, pp. 199–203; Butterfield, *Arc*, pp. 112–15; Hazo, *Interpretation*, pp. 32–34; R. W. B. Lewis, *Study*, pp. 200–210; Strier, "Exposition," pp. 182–86; Alfred Hanley, *Hart Crane's Holy Vision: "White Buildings"* (Pittsburgh: Duquesne Univ. Press, 1981), pp. 155–57; and Gregory R. Zeck, "The Logic of Metaphor: 'At Melville's Tomb,'" *Texas Studies in Literature and Language*, 17 (1974), 673–86. With the exception of Strier, who questions Crane's adequacy as a critic (but never extends his questioning to address the poem), the commentators all agree on the aptness of Crane's interpretation.

3. There is some uncertainty as to when Crane's reply was written. Unterecker, *Voyager*, p. 463, implies that the reply was written on the Isle of Pines in the summer of 1926, obliquely citing a letter from Sally Simpson, caretaker of the family cottage on the Isle of Pines, which begins: "I remember your corre-

spondence with Harriet Monroe." But Susan Jenkins Brown, in *Rocks*, p. 74, states that Crane shared with her an early draft of the reply; Brown was Crane's neighbor in the spring of 1926.

4. This remark to Frank lends credence to Unterecker's belief that the reply was written on the Isle of Pines; Crane seems to be suggesting that, by June 19, no American journal had accepted the Melville poem.

5. Blackmur, *Value*, p. 277.

6. A good example of a critic deciding that he must supply the missing clue to "Repose of Rivers" is represented in Yvor Winters's belief that the poem is a monologue spoken by a river. This answers the questions raised by certain portions of the poem, but in the process makes the whole work pointless. Francis Fike cites Winters as a precedent for his own reading in "Symbolic Strategy in 'Repose of Rivers,'" *Hart Crane Newsletter*, 1 (Winter 1977), 18–28.

7. The outline appears in Hart Crane to Otto H. Kahn, Mar. 18, 1926, *Letters*, ed. Weber, p. 261. See Chap. 7 for a longer discussion of it.

8. Paul, *Bridge*, pp. 133–39.

9. Hazo, *Interpretation*, p. 34.

10. No two critics, it would appear, can quickly agree on the prosody underlying any poem, largely because there are still a variety of ways to notate even so basic and common a thing as a line of blank verse. Harvey Gross's notations in *Sound and Form in Modern Poetry* (Ann Arbor: Univ. of Michigan Press, 1964) seem to be the most reasonable for Crane. Gross dispenses with the elaborate descriptive machinery of some prosodists by focusing on the individual line as a patterned unit. He admits that the strength of the beat placed on any syllable may vary within the unit of the line, but he insists that it is less important to note that than to note the variations in emphasis that shifts in the rhythm bring to the overall movement within a line or passage. He would scan "An embassy. Their numbers as he watched," as five iambic feet with a caesura enforced by the syntactical break of the period after the second foot: a standard blank-verse line. It is clear in this instance that the foot "he watched" is more heavily accented than the foot "-ers as." But such a detail is of minor importance; the point to note is that both feet together create an iambic pattern, and the deviations from that pattern are the sources of interest. Linguists would find Gross's method crude, but Gross would find linguists' notations uselessly overdescriptive and fussy. The advantage of Gross's "simple" approach is that it recognizes that prosody is one of the aspects of a poem, along with imagery and syntax and diction; prosody is not carrying the burden of an all-inclusive meaning, so it can be noted with some lightness and it need not take into account each nuance of tone. His misreading of Crane (*Sound*, pp. 215–25) is surprising, given the tools for understanding provided by his own approach.

11. R. W. B. Lewis, *Study*, pp. 200–215, is the most eloquent defense of

Crane's reply and its bearing on the poem; Paul's counterargument appears in *Bridge*, pp. 137–38.

Chapter 6. The Two Versions of "O Carib Isle!"

1. "Lachrymae Christi" first published in *The Fugitive*, 4 (Dec. 1925), 102–3; "The Harbor Dawn" in *transition*, no. 7 (June 1927), 120; and "The Tunnel" in *The Criterion*, 6 (Nov. 1927), 398–402.

2. Eugene Jolas, *Anthologie de la Nouvelle Poesie Americaine* (Paris: Simon Kra, 1928), pp. 46–47.

3. *Poetry*, 31 (Oct. 1927), 30–31.

4. Hart Crane to Yvor Winters, Mar. 27, 1927, Parkinson, *Correspondence*, p. 74.

5. The changes are all minor. Line 4 in the *Poetry* variant reads "Stilting" where the *transition* variant has "Flickering"; line 18 in the *Poetry* variant reads "Plaguing" where the *transition* variant has "vining." I use the *Poetry* variant for my text of the original version.

6. See Appendix B for an explanation of why March or April 1927 is the likely time of the revision.

7. Hart Crane to William Wright, July 16, 1926, *Letters*, ed. Weber, p. 267.

8. I. A. Richards, "A Background for Contemporary Poetry," *The Criterion*, 3 (July 1925), 511–28. Though Weber (*Critical Study*, p. 271) identifies this essay as that mentioned to Monroe, the only critic to have investigated it, R. W. Butterfield, deflects interest away from it by mistakenly describing it as a "precis of his *Principles of Literary Criticism*" (*Arc*, p. 114n, p. 50n). In fact, only a small portion of the essay, a part rehearsing the idea of the "pseudo-statement," resembles Richards's *Principles*. The essay was included, virtually unchanged, as chapters 5, 6, and 7 in Richards's brief volume *Science and Poetry*, published in 1926.

9. Hart Crane to Waldo Frank, Oct. 26, 1925, *Letters*, ed. Weber, p. 218.

10. Arthur Rimbaud, *A Season in Hell*, trans. T. Sturge Moore, Appendix in Edgell Rickword, *Rimbaud: The Boy and the Poet* (New York: Knopf, 1924), p. 230. With only a vague knowledge of French, Crane would have known "Eternity" from the Moore translation rather than from an earlier translation by "H. C. Blum," in *The Dial*, 49 (July 1920), 1–26, because Blum translated only the prose sections and left the poetry (such as "Eternity") in French. Weber states: "Waldo Frank relates that on the trip which he took with Crane to the Isle of Pines in May 1926, and during the course of his stay on the island, Crane and he spent much of their time in reading and discussing Rimbaud's poetry" (*Critical Study*, p. 248).

Chapter 7. The Bridge in *The Bridge*

1. See Appendix A for the chronology of "Repose of Rivers."

2. Hart Crane to————, May 22, 1926, *Letters*, ed. Weber, p. 255; also Crane to Susan Jenkins Brown, *Rocks*, p. 59.

3. Unterecker, *Voyager*, p. 446.

4. Horton, *Life*, chap. 8, esp. pp. 203–8. The most amusing and concise account is in Susan Jenkins Brown, *Rocks*, pp. 63–64. When Crane arrived on the Isle of Pines, a letter from O'Neill soon followed (cited in *Letters*, ed. Weber, p. 254). O'Neill reported Liveright was not waiting for a preface from O'Neill but waiting because of a talk he had had with Otto Kahn; Crane's assumption— that Liveright had learned of *The Bridge* and was delaying publication till it was ready for inclusion—placed more pressure on Crane to finish his epic.

5. Horton, *Life*, p. 208; Unterecker, *Voyager*, pp. 447–48.

6. R. W. B. Lewis, *Study*, p. 230.

7. R. W. B. Lewis, *Study*, p. 231.

8. Hart Crane to Waldo Frank, June 20, 1926, *Letters*, ed. Weber, p. 261.

9. Allen Tate, "Introduction" to *White Buildings* by Hart Crane (1926; rpt., New York: Liveright, 1972), p. xi.

10. Tate, "Introduction," p. xiii.

11. Allen Tate, "Hart Crane," in *The Man of Letters in the Modern World* (Cleveland: Meridian, 1955), p. 287. It is interesting to compare Tate's harsh evaluation of *The Bridge* with his temperate evaluation of Archibald MacLeish's *Conquistador* (*Man of Letters*, pp. 299–305). Tate uses the same language to praise MacLeish as he uses to damn Crane: "The poem is one of the examples of our modern sensibility at its best; it has the defect of its qualities." For a perspective on Tate's position as an early New Critic, see Paul, *Bridge*, pp. 287–89.

12. The "Ode" is dated "New York, 1926 / Charlottesville, 1930" on p. 52 of *Poems: 1928–1932* (New York: Scribner's, 1932). Crane responds to an early version of the "Ode" in a letter to Tate of "ca. January 7" 1927 in *Letters*, ed. Weber, pp. 282–83. The complex relationship between Tate and Crane would make an ideal subject for a small volume. Unterecker agrees that the "Ode" was Tate's response to Crane's epic in an interview in the *Hart Crane Newsletter*, 2 (Summer 1978), 29–30. A more intriguing connection, however, lies between the "Ode" and "O Carib Isle!" It seems plausible that Crane was familiar with portions of the "Ode" before he left for the Isle of Pines. The overall situations of the two poems are strikingly similar: an isolated man meditates in a deserted graveyard—a graveyard that, as it turns out, has larger implications for the culture as a whole. Tate's poet is paralyzed; Crane's poet strives to act, but without success. There are similar images in each work: blind crabs, a wind blowing overhead, the serpent (in Tate, in a mulberry; in Crane, in the wind itself), and

(in an earlier version of Tate's poem) a turnstile. In brief, if Tate's "Ode" was his version of *The Bridge*, Crane's "O Carib Isle!" is his version of the "Ode."

13. Allen Tate, "Narcissus as Narcissus," (1938), rpt. in *Man of Letters*, pp. 332–45.

14. Cited in "Narcissus," *Man of Letters*, p. 337. Weber's transcription of this letter (which he dates "ca. January 7 (1927)") is slightly different; it shows Crane underscoring his point by stressing the quote: "'which *should* be yours tomorrow'" (*Letters*, ed. Weber, p. 282).

15. Thomas A. Vogler, "A New View of Hart Crane's *The Bridge*," *Southern Review*, 73 (1965), 382–83.

16. The word may have originated in poem I of "&: Seven Poems," sec. 2, "N," of *&* (1925) in E. E. Cummings, *Complete Poems: 1913–1962* (New York: Harcourt Brace Jovanovitch, 1972), p. 122.

Chapter 8. *The Bridge* in 1926 (I)

1. Lohf's item B8 (*Manuscripts*, p. 8) is taken from a letter of Mar. 20, 1926, to Waldo Frank and described as an "Early typescript draft of stanzas 1 and 2, 16 lines." The lines would have been written shortly after reading Frank's *Virgin Spain*.

2. Helge Nilsen, "Crane and Frank: Images of America," *Hart Crane Newsletter*, 1 (Winter 1977), 39.

3. Waldo Frank, *Virgin Spain* (New York: Liveright, 1926), p. 298.

4. Hart Crane to Otto H. Kahn, Mar. 18, 1926, *Letters*, ed. Weber, p. 241.

5. In a Nov. 21, 1926, letter to Waldo Frank (*Letters*, ed. Weber, pp. 277–78), Crane refers to *In the American Grain* and maintains: "I put off reading it until I felt my own way cleared beyond chance of confusions incident to reading a book so intimate to my theme." The extended convulsion of this sentence is most uncharacteristic of Crane's epistolary style, even when writing to Waldo Frank (with whom he was careful to be particularly sober). Crane was almost certainly aware of portions of Williams's book. "The Discovery of the Indies," for example (the earlier version of Williams's Columbus myth), appeared in the *Broom* issue following the issue printing Crane's "The Springs of Guilty Song" in 1923.

6. William Carlos Williams, *In the American Grain* (1925; rpt., New York: New Directions, 1956), p. 26.

7. In the letter introducing this poem to Peggy and Malcolm Cowley, Crane offered the cryptic explanation: "In the middle of *The Bridge* the old man of the sea (page Herr Freud) suddenly comes up" (July 29, 1926, *Letters*, ed. Weber, p. 268). Though commentators usually think of "Cutty Sark" with reference to Melville, it seems more connected to Eugene O'Neill's derelict sailors, like

Paddy in "The Hairy Ape" (1922), who live out their dereliction by clinging fiercely to impossible dreams. The "Herr Freud" reference recalls O'Neill's interest in the unconscious mind. Crane had seen O'Neill's "mask plays" and he had sent a mask from an O'Neill production to friends in Cleveland. He mentions "The Hairy Ape" in a Nov. 16, 1924, letter to his mother, in *Family*, ed. T. S. W. Lewis, p. 372.

8. "Southern Cross" recalls Tate's "Ode." It may not be fanciful to suggest that each of the "Three Songs" were dedicated to certain friends. If "Southern Cross" is dedicated to Tate, the man who would rather turn to stone than give up the purity of the ideal before him ("the nameless Woman of the South"), then the second song is surely dedicated to Slater Brown and E. E. Cummings, who frequented the Houston St. Burlesque. The third song would be dedicated to Susan Jenkins Brown, who worked in an office editing a pulp magazine of romance tales (see Susan Jenkins Brown, *Rocks*, pp. 40–41). All the unexpected additions to *The Bridge* in 1926 utilize personal experiences: "Cutty Sark" details a rendezvous in a bar of a kind with which Crane must have been familiar (the old South Street harbor was by the Brooklyn Bridge and lay athwart Crane's regular path home); "The Harbor Dawn" unfolds in the Brooklyn Heights room where he had first met the lover of *Voyages;* and "Van Winkle" is notable for its references to his mother and father.

9. John R. Willingham, "'Three Songs' of Hart Crane's *The Bridge:* A Reconsideration," *American Literature*, 27 (Mar. 1955), 66.

10. See Susan Jenkins Brown, *Rocks*, pp. 110–11, for lyrics to the tune and confirmation that Crane had intended to echo it.

Chapter 9. *The Bridge* in 1926 (II)

1. Hart Crane to Waldo Frank, Aug. 12, 1926, *Letters*, ed. Weber, p. 272.

2. Crane's letters often seem to require interpretations as subtle as those demanded by his poems; this makes the problem of constructing a chronology very tricky. Did he stress that he was still involved in Pocahontas, John Brown, and the subway (all mentioned in the Aug. 12 letter to Frank) in order to allay Frank's possible fear that, in his new poems, he had completely abandoned the framework he had set out for himself? As both Susan Jenkins Brown (*Rocks*, p. 60) and Paul (*Bridge*, p. 171n) note, Crane often took pains to present his best side to Frank. Interestingly enough, it appears that Crane sent a copy of "Cutty Sark" to Peggy and Malcolm Cowley before sending it to Frank (July 29, 1926, *Letters*, ed. Weber, p. 268), though he mentions the poem in a later letter to Frank. Frank might not have approved of so autobiographical a poem as "Cutty Sark," so curious a contribution to an epic that was, as Crane often maintained, largely built on Frank's support. Cowley, however, could have enjoyed

the poem (see letters of Mar. 20 and Mar. 28, 1926, in *Letters*, ed. Weber, p. 242, in which Crane's letter to Frank speaks of a "hideous experience in New York" and Crane's letter to Cowley boasts of a "one night spree").

3. Hart Crane to Waldo Frank, Aug. 23, 1926, *Letters*, ed. Weber, pp. 274–75.

4. Crane may have finished a version of "The Dance" as early as Aug. 19, 1926. It is possible that it was the poem enclosed in a letter of that date to Frank, a letter which begins: "Here, too, is that bird with a note that Rimbaud speaks of as 'making you blush'" (*Letters*, p. 272), and which continues with praises for the storms on the island. Since the storm scene is central to "The Dance" it is likely that Crane was moved to comment on the storms because of his new enclosed poem, and the reference to *Les Illuminations* is to a primitive forest (where the clocks have no hands) which also suggests the primitivism of "The Dance." On the other hand, a follow-up letter to Frank on Aug. 23 characterizes the previously sent poem as a photograph, which suggests it could as easily have been "Virginia," the last of the "Three Songs" which had not been previously sent.

5. Hart Crane to Yvor Winters, Parkinson, *Correspondence*, p. 68.

6. Yvor Winters, *In Defense of Reason* (Denver: Alan Swallow, n.d.), p. 593.

7. See Paul, *Bridge*, pp. 216–22, for a defense of the traditional reading; also, Vogler, "View," pp. 388–89.

8. R. W. B. Lewis, *Study*, p. 313.

9. James McMichael, "Hart Crane," *Southern Review*, n.s. 8 (1972), 303.

10. Winters interpreted these lines as Crane's inadvertent confession of "the inadequacy of his belief," and Crane reacted by insisting that all he had intended "amounts in substance to this; 'Mimic the scene of yesterday; I want to see how it looked.'" Especially when confronted by adverse criticism, Crane almost always reacted defensively, asserting that his lines were in actuality quite lucid. He should be approached cautiously as a critic of his own work. The interchange with Winters appears in Vivian H. Pemberton, "Hart Crane and Yvor Winters, Rebuttal and Review: A New Crane Letter," *American Literature* 50 (May 1978) 276–81. (This letter completes the Crane side of the Crane-Winters correspondence; it is the missing document noted in Parkinson's volume.)

11. Alan Trachtenberg, *Brooklyn Bridge: Fact and Symbol* (New York: Oxford, 1965), p. 148n; rpt. in *Hart Crane*, ed. Trachtenberg, pp. 115–16n.

12. This smile episode has usually been considered as straight autobiography; perhaps it was, but consider the second half of Eliot's "Morning at the Window," a poem with bearing on both "The Harbor Dawn" and "Van Winkle":

> The brown waves of fog toss up to me
> Twisted faces from the bottom of the street.
> And tear from a passer-by with muddy skirts

An aimless smile that hovers in the air
And vanishes along the level of the roofs.

It is a commonplace to say that *The Bridge* was a retort to *The Waste Land*, but it is more accurate to say that "The Tunnel" was a retort to *The Waste Land* while other poems in *The Bridge* (of 1926) picked up or echoed or negated lines from earlier poems by Eliot, largely those in *Prufrock and Other Observations* (1920). From "Portrait of a Lady," "Inside my brain a dull tom-tom begins" (itself Eliot's little joke), is echoed in "National Winter Garden"'s "tom-tom scrimmage." The "street-piano, mechanical and tired" that "Reiterates some worn-out common song," appears, rejuvenated, in "Van Winkle" as the hurdy-gurdy and grind-organ. The lilacs and the smell of hyacinths also appear in "Van Winkle." In "The Tunnel"" the last four lines of "Preludes: III" are recalled. "La Figlia Che Piange"'s "Weave, weave the sunlight in your hair" is picked up in "Cutty Sark"'s "Heave, weave / Those bright designs the trade winds drive"; and in fact all of "Cutty Sark" may be regarded as the monologue from "Gerontion"—"an old man driven by the Trades / to a sleepy corner"—rewritten from a point of view that underscores the vitality of the derelict.

Chapter 10. *The Bridge* in 1926 (III)

1. R. W. B. Lewis, *Study*, p. 362; Paul, *Bridge*, pp. 270–71.

2. Winters's reading is in *Primitivism and Decadence* (1937); rpt. in *Reason*, p. 20.

3. See Paul, *Bridge*, pp. 266–68, for the connections that exist between the overheard fragments and the major themes in the poem; also, Vogler, "View," p. 402.

4. L. S. Dembo, "The Unfractioned Idiom of Hart Crane's Bridge," *American Literature*, 27 (May 1955), 222–23. Dembo's original insight has been sanctioned by the majority of critics following him: Quinn, *Hart*, pp. 99–100; Hazo, *Interpretation*, pp. 112–13; R. W. B. Lewis, *Study*, p. 364; Butterfield, *Arc*, p. 204; Paul, *Bridge*, p. 271; Uroff, *Patterns*, p. 144; and Richard Combs, *Vision of the Voyage* (Memphis: Memphis State Univ. Press, 1978), p. 166. Vogler, "View," pp. 404–5, sees the moment as crucially ambiguous.

5. R. W. B. Lewis, *Study*, p. 372. He notes that Trachtenberg stated (*Fact*, p. 61) that for travelers in Columbus's day, "Cathay" and "Atlantis" were frequently interchangeable.

Chapter 11. From "Calgary Express" to "The River"

1. Parkinson, *Correspondence*, p. 66, notes "early 1927" as a possible date for this outline, but in a Nov. 15, 1926, letter (pp. 20–21) Crane speaks of "The

Dance" as part four of "Powhatan's Daughter," section two of his long poem. This implies his scheme may have been fixed earlier.

2. Parkinson, *Correspondence*, pp. 66–67, rightly quarrels with the statement in Joseph Schwartz and Robert C. Shweik, *Hart Crane: A Descriptive Bibliography* (Pittsburgh: Univ. of Pittsburgh Press, 1972), p. 16, that "The Calgary Express" was "probably never started." Though Unterecker never treats the issue and Weber is ambiguous on the point (*Critical Study*, p. 370), it seems clear that "Calgary Express" was begun. On June 18, 1927, before beginning work on "The River," Crane sent his mother a copy of the last seven quatrains of what would become "The River" (*Family*, ed. T. S. W. Lewis, pp. 584–85). These quatrains must be the fragment of "Calgary Express"; they were published as a separate poem in the *New American Caravan* for 1928.

3. Hart Crane to Yvor Winters, Mar. 19, 1927, Parkinson, *Correspondence*, pp. 68–69.

4. It is possible, too, that the opening "jazz" introduction to "The River" may have also been composed in 1926; it fits neatly into the theme of the black Pullman porter, it allows for the planned modulation into the spiritual, and it is playful in a way typical of other poems of 1926.

5. Weber, *Critical Study*, p. 261 (an expanded version of the outline sent to Otto Kahn, Mar. 18, 1926, *Letters*, ed. Weber, p. 241). Weber does not identify whether this quotation came from a letter or Crane's papers.

6. Hart Crane to Yvor Winters, Jan. 19, 1927, Parkinson, *Correspondence*, p. 31. Horton also reports this in *Life*, p. 130.

7. "The chapter on DeSoto was used by Hart Crane in 'The Bridge,'" from William Carlos Williams's *I Wanted to Write a Poem* (Boston: Beacon Press, 1958), p. 43, cited in Paul, *Bridge*, p. 215n.

8. Work on the poem was first noted in Hart Crane to Waldo Frank, Aug. 12, 1926, *Letters*, ed. Weber, p. 271.

9. See Hart Crane to Otto Kahn, Sept. 12, 1927, *Letters*, ed. Weber, p. 307, for Crane's assertion that "The Dance" contains racial conflict.

10. Hart Crane to Grace Hart Crane, (May 13, 1924?) and July 4, 1924, *Family*, ed. T. S. W. Lewis, pp. 315, 327.

11. Winters, *Reason*, p. 593, and esp. p. 92n., where he quarrels with Tate's assessment. Earlier, in a review, Winters thought that "The River" fell into "three distinct and unsynthesized parts," the jazz introduction, the long middle, and the concluding quatrains (*Hart Crane*, ed. Trachtenberg, p. 26).

12. Tate, *Man of Letters*, p. 290.

13. The strength that emerges when two opposites are joined is quite different from the powerful energies that accumulate once one's feelings are repressed. This difference is one of the major distinctions in the 1926 *Bridge*. Up to "The Dance," power is associated with repression, in "Cutty Sark" and "Three Songs." After "The Dance," strength is involved in actively seeking out another.

The basic form of the 1926 *Bridge* is that the poet learns of the strength he has, but has wasted because it is all repressed, all without a direction; then he understands that he must bring that strength to bear by seeking out a direction. Judging from internal evidence, then, "Calgary Express" precedes "The Dance."

14. Crane noticed the names on Pullman cars; see Unterecker, *Voyager*, p. 268, for an example. Crane rode the New York Central (which operated the 20th Century Limited) back and forth from New York to Cleveland, but it did not name its cars after Indian tribes. However, the Milwaukee Road, which Crane may have taken on his westward journey with his mother in 1915, did have that practice. (The New York Central did call its 4–8–2 steam engine types "Mohawks," but these would have been reserved primarily for freight service.)

15. Gross, *Sound*, p. 223, calls this "Perhaps Crane's greatest sustained passage . . . exactly suited here to Crane's feelings of relentless movement and religious awe."

16. Joseph E. Brogunier, "The Two Cranes and 'Blind Baggage,'" *Hart Crane Newsletter*, 2 (Summer 1978), 33–35.

Chapter 12. The Late Poems (I): The "Carib Suite"

1. Uroff, *Patterns*, p. 153–80.

2. Hart Crane to Yvor Winters, July 18, 1927, Parkinson, *Correspondence*, p. 99. Marc Simon, who has inspected the originals, has reported that Parkinson mistranscribed the July 18 letter; it is paraphrased here according to Simon's corrections. (*Hart Crane Newsletter*, 2 (Spring 1979), 54.)

3. Hart Crane to Yvor Winters. July 26, 1927, Parkinson, *Correspondence*, p. 24–25.

4. Hart Crane to Yvor Winters, July 26, 1927, Parkinson, *Correspondence*, p. 99.

5. This is Crane's paraphrase of Winters's remark, in a return letter from Hart Crane to Yvor Winters, Aug. 3, 1927, Parkinson, *Correspondence*, p. 101.

6. In an Aug. 1926 postcard to the sculptor Gaston Lachaise, Crane associated a nearby quarry with Lachaise's work. *Letters*, ed. Weber, p. 271.

7. Uroff, *Patterns*, pp. 173–74.

8. Hart Crane to Waldo Frank, Feb. 1, 1928, *Letters*, ed. Weber, p. 315.

9. In his notes for the *Complete Poems*, p. 288, Weber suggests the poem may be unfinished. Lohf, *Manuscripts*, reproduces two early versions, but not the semicomplete one to which Weber tantalizingly refers (figs. 5 and 6, items C1x and C1y).

10. Uroff, *Patterns*, p. 177.

11. Of all the poems in "East of Yucatan," "El Idiota" (as it was titled in *transition*) has been most revised. The changes all move toward emphasizing the humanity of the idiot boy as well as indicating his isolated position. In *transition*

his eyes were "dead lanterns"; revised, they are "squint lanterns." Previously, "the children laughed // And screamed so in a circle"; now, "those children laughed // In such infernal circles." (In the first, the innocence of the children is preserved; in the second, the infernal torment of their jeering is emphasized.) Previously, Crane saw the boy "across the arroyo's wall of green"; now he views him "through those hot barricades of green." This change underscores Crane's new awareness of the distance between himself and his subject.

Chapter 13. Later Additions to *The Bridge*

1. Winters: "*Indiana*, probably one of the worst poems in modern literature" (*Primitivism*, rpt. in *Reason*, p. 22). Tate: "one of the most astonishing failures made by a poet of Crane's genius" (*Man of Letters*, p. 290).

2. Paul, *Bridge*, pp. 231–42, offers the strongest defense of the poem. R. W. B. Lewis, *Study*, pp. 323–40, wants to be sympathetic but keeps intruding on his own presentations with comments defining the poem as "poetic rant" (p. 324) with unfathomable lines (p. 327n) and "oddly limp and passive . . . lines" (p. 336).

3. The quotations are from Hart Crane to Otto H. Kahn, Sept. 12, 1927, *Letters*, ed. Weber, p. 305ff.

4. Hart Crane to Eda Lou Walton, Apr. 23, 1930, *Letters*, ed. Weber, p. 351.

5. Hart Crane, "Two Letters on *The Bridge*," *Hound & Horn*, July-Sept. 1934. Blackmur quotes from the Sept. 1927 letter in *Value*, pp. 272–74.

6. Paul is the critic who senses most acutely the falseness in "The River." See *Bridge*, pp. 210–14.

7. Clarence Arthur Crane to Hart Crane, July 12, 1927, *Family*, ed. T. S. W. Lewis, p. 595.

8. Though Crane had written of aerial warfare in "Faustus and Helen III," the source for this portion of "Cape Hatteras" may have been Harry Crosby, who was infatuated with airplanes and who had agreed to publish *The Bridge* in a special limited edition. See Geoffrey Wolff's *Black Sun: The Brief Transit and Violent Eclipse of Harry Crosby* (New York: Random House, 1976), pp. 253–58.

9. Hart Crane to Yvor Winters, Mar. 19, 1927, Parkinson, *Correspondence*, p. 69.

Chapter 14. The Late Poems (II): Letter-poems

1. Out of the thirteen poems listed in a table of contents in a folder entitled *Key West* and found among Crane's papers after his death, all but "Imperator Victus" had been published in journals. Of five other poems found in the same folder (according to Weber's arrangement in *Complete Poems*, pp. 170–74; Lohf, *Manuscripts*, pp. 57–61, lists a sixth poem), only two were submitted to

journals. The poems submitted by Crane are nearly always Caribbean work (circa 1926–27); the poems not submitted are usually letter-poems or poems of Mexico (circa 1927–31).

2. For the events surrounding his last encounter with his mother, see Unterecker, *Voyager*, pp. 529–41.

3. Hart Crane to————, May 22, 1926, *Letters*, ed. Weber, p. 255; complete text in Hart Crane to Susan Jenkins Brown, *Rocks*, p. 59.

4. Hart Crane to Grace Hart Crane, July 30, 1926, *Letters*, ed. Weber, p. 269; complete text in *Family*, ed. T. S. W. Lewis, p. 507. Also see Unterecker, *Voyager*, p. 440, for more information on Sally Simpson, and the July 8, 1926, letter from Crane to Grace Hart Crane, *Family*, ed. T. S. W. Lewis, p. 503.

5. Hart Crane to Sam Loveman, Easter 1932, *Letters*, ed. Weber, p. 406.

6. Marius Bewley, "Hart Crane's Last Poem," *Accent*, 19 (Spring 1959), 75–85; rpt. in *Hart Crane*, ed. Trachtenberg, pp. 150–62.

Appendix A: A New Background for "Repose of Rivers"

1. For readings which interpret the poem as a product of Crane's despair and indecision, see R. W. B. Lewis, *Study*, p. 211; Uroff, *Patterns*, pp. 44, 162; and Paul, *Bridge*, p. 171.

2. Weber, *Critical Study*, p. 279. Unaccountably, R. W. B. Lewis's version of the same episode smoothes out the ambiguity in Weber's version: "In June he had a trip to the nearby island called the Grand Cayman. When he came back to the Isle of Pines, he felt physically fit ('rather toughened and well') but imaginatively drained. Nonetheless, he brought with him two poems, one of them at first, mysteriously, called 'The Tampa Schooner,' later 'Repose of Rivers'" (*Study*, pp. 395–96).

3. Hart Crane to Susan Jenkins Brown, *Rocks*, p. 59.

4. Hart Crane to Grace Hart Crane, May 8, 1926, *Family*, ed. T. S. W. Lewis, p. 489.

5. *Ibid.*, p. 489n.

6. Hart Crane to Grace Hart Crane, Aug. 13, 1926, *Family*, ed. T. S. W. Lewis, p. 508.

7. Hart Crane to Grace Hart Crane, Jan. 23, 1927, *Letters*, ed. T. S. W. Lewis, p. 523.

8. Lohf, *Manuscripts*, p. 5.

9. Hart Crane to Grace Hart Crane, Apr. 18, 1926, and her reply, Apr. 24, 1926, *Family*, ed. T. S. W. Lewis, pp. 478, 484 (also *Letters*, ed. Weber, p. 245).

10. *Family*, ed. T. S. W. Lewis, p. 484; Unterecker, *Voyager*, p. 434.

11. The unanswered question is what happened to the poem known as "The

Tampa Schooner"? Did it, as Unterecker implies, metamorphosize into "The Air Plant"? (*Voyager*, p. 444: "There was a Grand Cayman poem ('The Air Plant') as a direct consequence of the trip, and others that derived incidental imagery from it.") But Unterecker may only mean to say that "The Air Plant" describes Grand Cayman vegetation. My nomination for "Schooner" is "Bacardi Spreads the Eagle's Wings," a poem which underwent several changes in title, once printed as "Overheard" (in the "East of Yucatan" sequence in *transition*, no. 9 [Dec. 1927], 132–36) and which once may have been entitled "Uncle Zeff in Cuba" (Lohf, *Manuscripts*, p. 59, item p). This poem makes reference to the "Cayman schooner." It is intent on exposing the callousness of tourists to the natives, and since Crane had a bad reaction to the natives on his ship to and from Grand Cayman, he may be dramatizing his own failure to appreciate native ways. For his violent reaction to the natives on the Cayman schooner, see *Letters*, ed. Weber, pp. 258–60, 264–66, and Parkinson, *Correspondence*, p. 32.

Appendix B: A Chronology for "O Carib Isle!"

1. Lohf, *Manuscripts*, p. 57.

2. "*Grand Cayman, West Indies*," appears after the last lines in the *transition* printing (no. 1, [Apr. 1927], 102); in a copy sent to Grace Hart Crane, Mar. 19, 1926, *Family*, ed. T. S. W. Lewis, p. 537, "Grand Cayman, June '26" appears as a subtitle.

3. Malcolm Cowley to Hart Crane, Oct. 8, 1926, Susan Jenkins Brown, *Rocks*, pp. 65–66. Jolas had read a sequence of poems by Cowley in the Spring-Summer 1926 issue of the *Little Review*. Entitled "Anthology," each poem in the sequence was dedicated to a writer or a critic (including the fictitious Walter S. Hankel); evidently Jolas had thought this group of original poems by Cowley was indeed an anthology, and a ripe source of new poets for his own anthology of new American poetry. Though the mistake seems to discredit Jolas's credentials, a glance at any issue of the *Little Review* shows that it had a haphazard way of identifying its authors; for example, it never deigned to list a table of contents for each issue.

4. Jolas, *Nouvelle Poesie Americaine*, pp. 46–47.

5. Hart Crane to Yvor Winters, Nov. 28, 1926, Parkinson, *Correspondence*, pp. 24–25.

6. Crane, "O Carib Isle!" and "Cutty Sark," *Poetry*, 31 (Oct. 1927), 30–36.

7. Hart Crane to Edgell Rickword, Jan. 7, 1927, *Letters*, ed. Weber, p. 283.

8. Eugene Jolas to Hart Crane, *Family*, ed. T. S. W. Lewis, p. 536.

9. Hart Crane to Grace Hart Crane, Mar. 19, 1927, *Family*, ed. T. S. W. Lewis, p. 537.

10. Hart Crane to Yvor Winters, Mar. 27, 1927, Parkinson, *Correspondence*, p. 74.

11. See Chap. 6, introduction, for examples of similar changes.

12. Unterecker, *Voyager*, p. 581.

13. *Ibid.*, p. 586.

14. Lohf, *Manuscripts*, p. 62.

15. *Ibid.*, p. 63.

16. *Ibid.*

17. *Ibid.*, p. 64.

18. Explained in an Aug. 6, 1973, letter from John S. Mayfield to me.

19. Lohf, *Manuscripts*, p. 64.

20. Hart Crane to Grace Hart Crane, Mar. 19, 1927, *Family*, ed. T. S. W. Lewis, p. 536.

21. Hart Crane to Yvor Winters, Aug. 3, 1927, Parkinson, *Correspondence*, p. 102.

22. Letter of Aug. 29, 1973, from Margaret McFadden, Assistant Curator for Manuscripts and Archives, Special Collections, Joseph Regenstein Library, University of Chicago, to me.

23. Hart Crane, "To Emily Dickinson," *The Nation*, 124 (June 29, 1927), 718.

24. Eugene Jolas to Hart Cra.ie, Feb. 24, 1927, *Family*, ed. T. S. W. Lewis, p. 536.

25. Lohf, *Manuscripts*, p. 41.

Index